THE DARK SIDE

Other books by Clive Small and Tom Gilling

Smack Express: How organised crime got hooked on drugs

Blood Money: Bikies, terrorists and Middle Eastern gangs

Betrayed: The shocking story of two undercover cops

Milat: Inside Australia's biggest manhunt—a detective's story

Evil Life: The true story of the Calabrian Mafia in Australia

THE EXPLOSIVE STORY OF CORRUPTION, GREED AND MURDER IN THE AUSTRALIAN DRUG TRADE

THE DARK SIDE

CLIVE SMALL &
TOM GILLING

ALLEN&UNWIN
SYDNEY • MELBOURNE • AUCKLAND • LONDON

First published in 2017

Allen & Unwin
83 Alexander Street
Crows Nest NSW 2065
Australia
Phone: (61 2) 8425 0100
Email: info@allenandunwin.com
Web: www.allenandunwin.com

Cataloguing-in-Publication details are available from the National Library of Australia
www.trove.nla.gov.au

ISBN 978 1 74331 152 3

Index by Puddingburn
Set in 11.5/15.5 pt Sabon by Midland Typesetters, Australia
Printed and bound in Australia by Griffin Press

10 9 8 7 6 5 4 3

MIX
Paper from responsible sources
FSC
www.fsc.org
FSC® C009448

The paper in this book is FSC® certified. FSC® promotes environmentally responsible, socially beneficial and economically viable management of the world's forests.

1985

*'"We are dangerously close to . . . ruination point . . . the hour is late." The title of this book [*A Quarter to Midnight*] carries my message.'*

Athol Moffitt, *A Quarter to Midnight*

2001

'In the years that have followed 1985, an appraisal of what is contained in this Commentary merits the conclusion that A Quarter to Midnight on Justice Moffitt's clock in 1985 has now become 23:55 on our computer or other digital screen.'

National Crime Authority, *Organised Crime in Australia*

2010

'Organised crime poses a threat to Australia's national security.'

Australian Crime Commission,
Organised Crime in Australia (2010)

2016

'According to the United Nations Office on Drugs and Crime, organised crime has "gone global" with illicit goods being sourced from one continent, trafficked across another and marketed in a third . . . Transnational crimes currently posing the greatest threat to Australia are people smuggling, human trafficking especially for the sex industry, illicit drug trafficking and high tech crime.'

Australian Institute of Criminology,
www.aic.gov.au/crime_types/transnational/other.html

Contents

Preface

This book is a sequel to *Smack Express: How organised crime got hooked on drugs* and *Blood Money: Bikies, terrorists and Middle Eastern gangs*. While organised crime groups engage in a wide variety of criminal activity, including fraud, identity crime, high-tech crime, human slavery, tax evasion and money laundering, we have once again focused on their primary source of income: the drug trade. According to the Australian Crime Commission's report *Organised Crime in Australia 2011*, Australians are 'among the world's highest per capita consumers of illicit stimulants, and drug prices in Australia far exceed prices overseas, making domestic drug production and importation highly profitable.' At a conservative estimate organised crime in Australia is worth $15 billion every year, half of which comes from illicit drugs. Indirect costs associated with drug addiction, family relations and community violence add more than $8 billion annually to this estimate. Each year at least $10 billion is laundered in and through Australia. Much of this money is derived from illicit drugs.

Acknowledgements

Our sincere thanks to those on both sides of the law—many of whom must remain nameless—who helped directly or indirectly in the writing of this book. Thanks also to the journalists who over the decades have reported fearlessly on the growth and influence of organised crime.

Special gratitude to ABC TV—*Four Corners*, Bob Bottom, Peter Butt, John Cushion, Michael Kennedy, Lorna Knowles, Michael McGann, Jayson McLeod, Neil Mercer, Charles Miranda, Brian Murphy, Michael Purchas, Lloyd Saxon, Adam Shand, Bob Small, John Sylvester, Ray Tinker, Dylan Welch, Kate McClymont and Marian Wilkinson for their support and advice.

About the authors

In 2008 Clive Small and Tom Gilling published the bestselling book *Smack Express: How organised crime got hooked on drugs*, which exposed the growth and transformation of organised crime in Australia since the late 1960s. They followed this with *Blood Money: Bikies, terrorists and Middle Eastern gangs*, *Betrayed: The shocking story of two undercover cops*, *Milat: Inside Australia's biggest manhunt—a detective's story*, and in 2016, *Evil Life: The true story of the Calabrian Mafia in Australia*.

CLIVE SMALL is a 38-year New South Wales police veteran. Much of his time was spent in criminal investigation. He was awarded several commendations. From 1977–80 he worked as an investigator with the Woodward Royal Commission into Drug Trafficking. During 1987–88 he was an investigator on Strike Force Omega, which reinvestigated the 1984 shooting of Detective Michael Drury. In the early 1990s Small led the backpacker murder investigation that resulted in the conviction of Ivan Robert Milat for the murder of seven backpackers in the Belanglo State Forest, south of Sydney, between 1989 and 1992. In 2001, as head of the Greater Hume Police Region, he helped dismantle the Vietnamese street gangs that had made Cabramatta Australia's heroin capital. After retiring from the police force he joined the New South Wales Independent Commission Against Corruption as the executive director of operations. Since March 2007 he has been writing full-time.

TOM GILLING's first two novels, the *The Sooterkin* (1999) and *Miles McGinty* (2001), were both shortlisted for major awards and chosen as notable books of the year by the *New York Times*. They have been translated into several languages. His third novel, *Dreamland*, has been published in Australia, Britain and the United States. As a journalist he has worked for numerous publications including the *Sydney Morning Herald*, *Rolling Stone*, the *Guardian* (UK) and the *New York Times*. Before *Smack Express* he co-wrote two non-fiction books, *Trial and Error* (1991), about the Israeli nuclear whistleblower Mordechai Vanunu, and *Bagman: The final confessions of Jack Herbert* (2005), about the events that led to the Fitzgerald Inquiry into police corruption in Queensland.

THE DARK SIDE

Introduction

Mark Standen spent 33 years in federal and state law enforcement before he was arrested in 2008, at the age of 51, and charged with conspiring to import pseudoephedrine, a precursor for the manufacture of methamphetamine. Three years later he was convicted and jailed for 22 years.

Standen had risen to become the third most powerful figure in the secretive New South Wales Crime Commission. His ignominious fall left a stain on the Crime Commission and on the people who worked there, and raised serious questions about the capacity—and even the commitment—of both the New South Wales Police and the New South Wales Police Integrity Commission to prevent corruption. But the evidence given by the prosecution during his five-month trial told only part of the extraordinary story of Mark Standen's career, which carried him almost to the top of Australian law enforcement despite irrefutable evidence of his dishonesty.

Mark Standen was not a good cop who went bad, but a reckless and greedy law enforcement officer whose duplicity had been evident almost from the start of his career. Standen was a punter who could never keep up with his losses, an investigator who saw no problem socialising with criminals. The corrupt relationship between Standen and the English drug trafficker James Kinch lasted five years and saw several drug importations take place and more planned. Standen was neither innocent, as he would claim at his trial, or a dupe: in his sentencing remarks the judge noted that Kinch and Standen communicated as equals.

Kinch was sitting in a Thai prison cell when the first draft of this book was written. Since then, the authors have uncovered new information about Mark Standen and the Dutch drug syndicate whose Australian operations were masterminded by Kinch; about an earlier drug syndicate run by Ian Saxon, a major trafficker whom Standen first arrested and then befriended; and about Standen's disturbing relationship with the safe breaker, drug trafficker and suspected rapist and murderer Neville Tween. In *The Dark Side* we piece these stories together for the first time to create a detailed picture of a compulsive gambler who bet everything and lost.

CHAPTER ONE

Ian Saxon syndicate

The Ian Saxon drug syndicate, led by one-time pop singer Ian Hall Saxon, came to public attention in 1990 when several of its members, including its leader, were arrested in Sydney by the National Crime Authority (NCA) and charged with importing 10 tonnes of cannabis worth $77 million. By then the international drug network had been operating for nearly two decades, importing hundreds of tonnes of cannabis into the UK, Canada, the United States and Australia.

Ian Saxon was born in 1943 in Auckland, New Zealand. By his twenties he was well known as a cabaret compere in Auckland and was already dealing in cannabis. In 1967 he moved to Sydney and became involved in pop bands and music management. At one stage he was leader of Ian Saxon and the Sound, a band that included the future Queen of Pop, Colleen Hewett. For a time Saxon also worked at the infamous Latin Quarter in Kings Cross. He lived in a

Darlinghurst apartment and was a frequent visitor to the bars and nightclubs of Kings Cross and Paddington. Drugs were plentiful and Saxon dealt in them—mostly cannabis and cocaine. By the early 1970s Saxon was himself a heavy user of both.

In 1976 Saxon left Australia and went to California, where he dabbled in the entertainment industry and continued to buy and sell drugs. A year later, in August 1977, he was arrested and convicted of possessing around an ounce of concentrated cannabis. He was fined US$500 and placed on probation for three years, but the conviction didn't deter him. In fact, he set about expanding his business. In 1978 Saxon travelled to Europe and Pakistan, where he met several Australian traffickers, including a lifelong importer, trafficker and drug user who was organising his own importations to Australia. This person was later given the court-ordered pseudonym 'Mr Andrews'. In Europe, possibly on the same trip, Saxon met the 36-year-old Dutch national Tamas 'Tom' Lazlo Schneiders, a man already well known in the international drug trade. It was through Schneiders that Saxon met another up-and-coming international trafficker, 24-year-old David Kulik, a naturalised US citizen born in Canada.

During this time Saxon gained his practical education in the international drug trade, and particularly the cannabis trade. He learnt about the 'middlemen'—such as Schneiders and Kulik—who linked buyers and suppliers, and guaranteed delivery and payment for major importations. The hash was from around the Hindu Kush, not far from the Khyber Pass and near the Pakistan–Afghanistan border, and was transshipped through Pakistan to the coast, where it was loaded onto a mother ship lying offshore. Picking up multiple consignments, the mother ships would drop individual loads at ocean rendezvous 100 nautical miles or more off the coasts of countries including the United Kingdom and Australia before dropping much larger consignments—said to be up to 40 tonnes at a time—off the west coasts of Canada and the United States.

From his base in the US, Saxon organised several successful importations of cocaine to Sydney, assisted by Garry Morton, his close friend and partner in the drug trade since the mid-1970s. In 1980 Saxon and Morton were arrested in Tahiti and convicted of importing 2 kilograms of cocaine, and of importing other goods without declaring them. Saxon had bought the cocaine in California: it would sell for about five times its US value in Australia. Saxon was jailed for four years for importing the cocaine. On the second charge he was given a fine of around $800,000 or two years' imprisonment. Morton was also jailed.

Saxon's brother, Lloyd, visited him twice while he was in jail in Tahiti. Explaining how they had been arrested, Saxon told his brother, 'I got through Customs okay, but Garry was nervous and attracted attention. Once they got him they got me because we were travelling together.' They were both carrying similar suitcases that had been specially manufactured in South America to carry cocaine concealed in the lining. On their release from jail the two men were deported. By early 1984 both were back in Sydney.

In the late 1970s Tom Schneiders arrived in Australia and settled in Sydney's Bondi Beach, where he quickly established himself in the local drug trade and began importing cannabis supplied by Kulik. He became known in the Kings Cross underworld and developed a network within the entertainment industry. One person who knew Schneiders described him as being 'a skinny little runt and all-round nasty bastard,' before adding, 'but he knew what he was doing and always had a supply of good dope.'

Schneiders became a regular at the newly opened and trendy Benny's Bar and Restaurant on Challis Avenue, Potts Point. Martyn 'Marty' Clapp, from Mangaroa Valley, New Zealand, was the doorman at Benny's, a place he described as 'a late night hide-out for rock 'n' rollers, road crew, management, music executives, film and television and advertising gurus.' It was especially popular among New Zealanders. So many drug users frequented the place that the toilets were said to hold more people than the bar itself.

During the early 1980s 60-year-old William Sommerville was introduced to Schneiders as someone who could move cash overseas. Thereafter, Sommerville transferred Schneiders' cash, no questions asked, for a commission of between 0.5 and 2.5 per cent. Sommerville was born in New Zealand and worked in accounting and industrial relations. After moving to Australia in 1972 he opened a management consultancy business and a finance brokerage. The businesses failed and by 1981 or 1982 Somerville was moving funds offshore. His money-laundering business continued to expand for the next decade. He later told enforcement authorities, 'In all explanations given to me there was no doubt that this money was tax avoidance funds [not drug money].'

Returning to Sydney in the mid-1980s after his stint in a Tahitian jail, Saxon became a regular at Benny's. It was good for his business interests in both the entertainment industry and the drug trade. Over the next few years Saxon built a successful career as a rock promoter and part-time tour manager for the Frontier Touring Company. Frontier's co-founder was industry veteran Michael Chugg. He and Saxon had first met in Tasmania in the 1960s. According to Chugg's book, *Hey, You in the Black T-shirt: The real story of touring the world's biggest acts,* Saxon's official title at Frontier was 'Musicians' Liaison', but really 'he did whatever had to be done'. It was clear to his colleagues at Frontier that Saxon was more than just an occasional tour manager. 'He always had money,' wrote Chugg. '[H]e owned property in Sydney and elsewhere and he had a boat, *Rolling Thunder* . . . We had an idea of what he was up to, but had no concept of its scale.' In fact, some of Saxon's colleagues had more than an idea of what he was up to—they were his customers. 'We knew Ian sold hash,' Chugg recalled. 'We used to get it from him, wrapped in a beautiful gold seal.'

By 1989 Saxon had won the lucrative job of tour manager for Frank Sinatra, Liza Minnelli and Sammy Davis Jnr on their first joint appearances in Australia. He would also become the tour manager for other international acts such as Bon Jovi, John Mellencamp and Billy Joel.

The money Saxon made in the entertainment industry paled beside the profits from his drug business. Once again, the drug trade brought him into contact—and, for a time, competition—with Schneiders. But they were, above all, businessmen, and soon pooled their resources and activities. Their operation expanded rapidly. Before long Schneiders was asking whether Sommerville could move larger amounts of cash—'in the order of seven figures'—overseas. This time Sommerville would be paid a much higher commission of 5.5 per cent. According to Sommerville, Schneiders explained that the cash belonged to a man who 'was involved with performing artists, rock concerts and the general entertainment industry'.

Schneiders and Saxon were partners in Saxon's first importation after returning to Australia in the mid-1980s. The overseas organisers were David Kulik—whom Saxon had met years earlier through Schneiders—and 32-year-old Gary Matsuzaki, a US citizen. Saxon's 5-tonne hash consignment was one of several Kulik and Matsuzaki had organised to be loaded onto a vessel waiting off Pakistan. There would be several drop-off points and, once again, the largest importations were destined for Canada and the US.

Saxon's importation went off without a hitch. It was quality stuff; most was sold in Sydney, while some reached the streets of Queensland, Victoria and Western Australia. About fifteen months later Saxon and Schneiders made a second importation of 7 tonnes of hash. The arrangements were the same and again it was successful.

In May 1987 Saxon went to Perth to consolidate and expand his distribution network and to sell some of the cannabis he was holding. There he saw 'Mr Andrews'—their common interests and overlapping networks meant the pair had kept in touch since meeting in Pakistan nine years earlier—and gave him some hash, saying, 'Here is something you will recognise from the old days.' He showed Andrews a cardboard box containing 20 kilograms of the drug and told him he had 'plenty'.

A week later Andrews flew to Sydney where Saxon gave him 20 kilograms on credit. Andrews took his package back to Perth by train and sold it for $190,000. A few weeks later he returned to Sydney, paid Saxon $160,000 and picked up another 20 kilograms.

In October Andrews again returned to Sydney, but this time he only had $140,000—he was $20,000 short. Saxon was not happy and refused to give Andrews any more credit until the debt was paid, but did put a proposition to him. Another importation was being arranged: did Andrews want to be part of it? Andrews did not hesitate.

Over lunch the next day Saxon introduced Andrews to Garry Morton. After lunch Saxon said, 'There is an offshore pick-up . . . I think it will be sometime next year.' Asked how big the shipment would be, Saxon replied, 'Between 5 and 20 tonnes.'

Over the next couple of days Morton took Andrews to Pittwater, 45 minutes north of Sydney, and showed him the launch, *Rolling Thunder*, that would be used to bring the cargo ashore. Andrews returned to Perth a member of the team.

As the importation was being organised, Australian law enforcement agencies were targeting a group of drug importers and traffickers known to be part of the East Coast Milieu, a loose-knit group of organised crime figures and syndicates centred in Sydney's eastern suburbs. Surveillance picked up a meeting attended by several drug bosses, some of whom appeared to suspect that they were being watched. This aroused suspicion within the enforcement agencies: had they slipped up or was there a leak? The question was never properly answered, but several of those at the meeting had a history of avoiding arrest. Well known for their corrupt contacts, they had been tipped off before, and would be again.

One of those at the meeting was Saxon but, ominously, investigating authorities failed to spot his involvement. Saxon was not only selling cannabis to the group, he was also buying from the group's head honcho, Michael Nicholas 'Mikel' Hurley, as well as from importers Richard 'Snapper' Cornwell, Victor Spink and Raymond Dumbrell.

During 1988 Saxon and Andrews remained in touch, but it was not until 3 January 1989 that Andrews was contacted by Saxon and told the importation was imminent. After arriving in Sydney, Andrews was driven by Saxon to the coastal city of Coffs Harbour, about 500 kilometres north of Sydney, where the *Rolling Thunder* was moored. Morton was there, together with Lloyd Saxon and an American who introduced himself as 'Sep'.

In fact 'Sep' was Kulik. He had arrived in Australia several days earlier to meet his money couriers, the Williams sisters from Mexico. Dressed like a surfer, Kulik had bought a Kombi van, from which he would keep in touch with the mother ship and track both its movements and those of the *Rolling Thunder*. As before, Kulik's job was to ensure the importation went as planned and that money due on delivery was paid. Andrews was to be the navigator; he was shown a photo of the mother ship and given details of where the rendezvous was to occur.

The next day the *Rolling Thunder* left Coffs Harbour with Morton, Andrews and Lloyd Saxon on board and sailed south for about 140 nautical miles to Crowdy Head, where it anchored overnight. The next morning the launch sailed to a point about a 100 nautical miles off the coast to rendezvous with the mother ship.

Under cover of darkness, 500 canvas bags containing 10 tonnes of cannabis resin were transferred to the *Rolling Thunder* by 'twelve to fifteen Oriental seamen' from the mother ship. With the transfer complete, one of the seamen asked Andrews whether he had the money. When he explained that he did not, the seaman produced a 'receipt', which Morton signed.

With its cargo on board, the *Rolling Thunder* motored to

Broken Bay, about 50 kilometres north of Sydney, the main estuary of the Hawkesbury River, where it was met by Ian Saxon. In Smiths Creek, a tributary of the Hawkesbury, the cargo was transferred to a houseboat hired by Saxon.

Their jobs done, Lloyd Saxon and Andrews were each given 25 kilograms of resin. Morton was later paid $1 million in cash. Two million dollars cash was given to Oleta Williams who, with her sister, returned to Mexico.

Andrews returned to Perth and quickly sold his 25 kilograms. Within days he was back in Sydney and over the following week he helped offload the resin from the houseboat. Safely landed, it was taken and stored by Saxon somewhere on Sydney's north shore. In return for his help, Andrews' debt of $20,000 to Saxon was waived. He also bought 25 kilograms of resin to sell in Perth, and three months later bought a further 60 kilograms.

Another member of Saxon's team who helped unload and store the resin was 45-year-old Peter William Hamill, who lived on the Central Coast, an hour's drive north of Sydney. Hamill had been convicted of a 1985 importation and sentenced to jail, but won an appeal and was on bail awaiting a retrial (see Chapter 3). He was given 25 kilograms of resin for his efforts.

Over the next ten months Saxon arranged the sale of the remainder—nearly 10 tonnes. More than 1 tonne was sold by Hamill for almost $8 million. In July Hamill pleaded guilty to the 1985 importation and was jailed for six years.

On 30 November 1989, as Schneiders, Saxon and their crew were celebrating another successful year, their old friend Marty Clapp from Benny's was arrested while trying to buy 5 kilograms of cocaine, on behalf of a number of 'investors', from two US Drug Enforcement Administration (DEA) undercover agents working with the Australian Federal Police (AFP). Benny's had closed and Clapp was now the manager of a new Kings Cross nightclub called Springfields. When he realised that his suppliers were undercover cops, Clapp dropped a rubbish bag containing $450,000 cash and attempted to flee. Six years later Clapp pleaded guilty and was sentenced to three years and six months' jail.

On 26 January 1990, as Saxon and his mates rued the arrest of their mate Clapp, the NCA, federal and state police executed a search warrant on Saxon's Darlinghurst apartment and found 2 kilograms of resin, $192,000 in cash and diamonds valued at $72,000. When arrested, Saxon had 27 grams of cocaine in his briefcase. He was to manage a concert that night for the US singer–songwriter Tracy Chapman. The concert went ahead, but without Saxon.

Three days after his arrest a search warrant was executed on a garage at 8/9 Carr Street, Coogee, rented in the name of Lloyd Saxon's company, Nowsan Pty Ltd. Another 4 kilograms of hash was found, as well as $5.53 million in cash, 40 gold Krugerrand coins and three gold bars.

Ian Saxon was charged with offences including supplying cannabis resin, possessing the proceeds of crime (cash), money laundering and tax conspiracy. Bail was refused.

Lloyd Saxon was arrested a few weeks later when he returned to Sydney from New Zealand and faced similar charges to his brother.

Morton and Schneiders were arrested and charged with drug and money-laundering offences. Hamill was taken from jail and charged, like them, with drug and money-laundering offences.

Two others, 45-year-old publican Robert James See of Bronte and 54-year-old Brian John Buckett of Elanora Heights, were charged with money laundering.

William Sommerville—one of the principal money launderers—rolled in return for indemnity against prosecution. In later court proceedings he was given the pseudonyms 'Mr X' and 'John Gray' and placed on the witness protection program.

Ian Saxon remained locked up in Long Bay Correctional Centre at Malabar on the southern tip of Sydney's eastern suburbs, but was determined not to stay there. During 1990 and 1991 jail authorities foiled three escape attempts. In one plot a small helicopter was to land in the sports field of the jail's remand centre, pick up Saxon and another prisoner, and fly out to sea, where it would be hard to track. Saxon had made a down payment of around $100,000 for this to happen.

Finally, on 2 March 1993, Saxon escaped. With the help of two inmates, he hid in a laundry trolley and was wheeled out to the waiting laundry van. After scrambling into the van he hid in the laundry. Saxon jumped from the van when the driver, following his usual routine, stopped to buy a cup of coffee. However, two other accomplices, the brothers 24-year-old Ralph Reynold Quinlan and 30-year-old Charles Frederick Quinlan, both of whom had lengthy criminal records for stealing, robbery, violence and firearms offences, did not turn up and Saxon had to make his own way to the safe house.

Saxon spent several days at the safe house, a vacant property in Newtown, before being driven to Queensland by another associate. On the way they were stopped by police for a driving offence and the driver (not Saxon) was given a speeding ticket before being allowed to continue.

In Queensland, Saxon obtained the personal details of a local man who had never been in trouble with the police, never travelled overseas and was never going to leave Australia. Using his own photograph, Saxon applied for a passport in the other man's name. Weeks later he left Australia. His brother, Lloyd, recalls:

> Ian told me that when he left Australia he went to South Africa. He was doing it pretty tough because he didn't have much cash. Despite all the stories about him having millions of dollars stashed away when he was arrested, there wasn't anything left. He did some small-time drug dealing and made his way to Europe where he was helped out and was able to make some cash and live comfortably. He said that he spent time in the Netherlands and Belgium before making his way to the US. He looked up some old friends in California and got back into the drug trade, but at a pretty low level. He was worried about being caught by police and went down to Mexico where he lived in Loreto or Cabo San Lucas [Loreto is a tourist resort on the coast of the Gulf of California; Cabo San Lucas is one of Mexico's top tourist destinations at the tip of the Baja California peninsula]. He told me there was less chance of being caught in Mexico. When he got enough cash together he went back to Carlsbad, a Californian seaside resort town in San Diego County.

Having fled Australia, Saxon burnt his false Australian passport—it was too risky to keep using it—and travelled on fake British and Belgian passports and various other false identification documents, including a US driver's licence, organised by associates in the drug trade.

A week before Saxon's escape, Schneiders, who was on bail awaiting trial, made his scheduled report to police before absconding on a false passport to Europe, where he continued in the drug trade with Kulik and Matsuzaki.

As the search for Saxon and Schneiders continued, the fates of several of their colleagues were being determined by the courts in Sydney.

Andrews, the *Rolling Thunder*'s navigator, a lifelong drug trafficker and self-confessed 'hopeless junkie', was offered a deal. In return for cooperating with authorities he would be charged with money laundering but not with the importation. Andrews jumped at the offer. He pleaded guilty to money laundering and was placed in the witness protection program. As he later told a court, the offer was like 'swinging a carrot in front of a donkey's nose'.

Saxon's brother, Lloyd, was jailed for thirteen years. In 1999 Lloyd was released from jail after serving eight years of his sentence. He moved to the New Zealand island of Waiheke, where he now works as a carpenter.

Garry Morton was jailed for fifteen years.

In the mid-1990s, after serving his sentence for the 1985 importation, Hamill pleaded guilty to the Saxon importation and was jailed for seven and a half years.

Robert See and Brian Buckett were convicted of money laundering. See was sentenced to twelve months' periodic detention and fined a total of $4000, while Bucket was ordered to perform 300 hours' community service.

In return for his evidence against the syndicate, Sommerville was indemnified against prosecution. He and his wife spent seven years in the witness protection program. In 1997 the NCA withdrew their protection, deciding they were no longer in danger. William Sommerville received a tax bill of $127,000 based on the payments and benefits he had received whilst being a protected witness. Three years later, at the age of 77, he died of cancer. His wife sued the NCA, arguing that she should not be financially disadvantaged for having been in the program—a commitment allegedly made to both of them by the NCA. The resulting legal action was settled in the mid-2000s, with Mrs Sommerville winning a partial victory.

■ ■ ■

According to Lloyd Saxon, the police stumbled upon Ian Saxon in California largely by chance.

> Ian was a close friend of [a person we will call Mr X] who was a big-time cocaine importer and they did a lot of business with one another. Mr X lived south of Wollongong [he was in fact living in the Southern Highlands, 110 kilometres south-west of Sydney]. They kept in touch after Ian was arrested [in 1990] and then after Ian escaped from jail [in 1993] and was living in California. Ian was careful not to identify himself when he rang Mr X, but Mr X knew who he was. He was lucky because the police were listening to Mr X's telephone and could hear these conversations but they didn't know who he was talking to. Mr X was still dealing in lots of cocaine and that's what the police were after. I don't know if they even knew that Mr X and Ian were close. Then one day Mr X's girlfriend got on the phone and started saying to Ian, 'There's a big article on you in *Penthouse*, they're still looking for you,' and stuff like that, and that's how they got onto Ian.

The article to which Lloyd was referring was in the April 1995 edition of *Australian Penthouse* and was titled 'Mr Big: How Ian Hall Saxon, Australia's most wanted man, took the money and ran'. Mr X continues in the drug trade to this day.

■ ■ ■

At the time of his arrest Saxon had been with an unidentified Englishman, who was held by US authorities while they made inquiries. The Englishman was 30-year-old Joseph 'Joey' Sansom, whom Saxon had first met in Sydney in the 1980s. Sansom was a seasoned criminal from a well-known British crime family whose involvement in international drug trafficking dated back at least to the 1970s. Sansom had been living in Sydney for several years and was a close associate of crime boss Michael Hurley and his network of criminals known as the Coogee Mob. Sansom had been a linchpin between the East Coast Milieu and crime families, including his own, in the UK and Europe.

During his visits to Australia Sansom had been the target of at least fifteen federal law enforcement operations and several state operations. In 1991 he had been arrested and charged by the drug squad after 5000 ecstasy tablets were found in his Seaforth home on Sydney's north shore. Police had become suspicious when Sansom paid three months' rent in advance in cash for the waterfront home while apparently having no job. While on bail Sansom was the driver of a car that hit and killed a pedestrian in North Sydney. It was after this that Sansom fled Australia on a false passport provided by one of Hurley's gang; the same supplier who a year earlier had arranged false passports for Saxon and Schneiders.

Extradited to Australia, Sansom beat his drug charges and was later acquitted of the culpable driving charge. Fearing that more charges were looming, he left Australia and wound up in Spain, a popular haunt for British criminals on the run. He was arrested entering Malaysia on a false passport and deported to England.

Saxon pleaded guilty to the 1989 drug and money-laundering charges. Six months later he was sentenced to 24 years' jail; it would be another two years before he faced charges of escaping from jail.

In 1997, while in Lithgow jail, Saxon was stabbed. According to Lloyd, 'two inmates were trying to stand over Ian on behalf of a third inmate, a jail kingpin. They demanded that [he] hand over his hidden millions and transfer them to a bank account for the "boss".' Saxon told them to 'fuck off'. After a third or fourth unsuccessful attempt to get Saxon to hand over the money they stabbed him in the back about six times. 'It was pretty stupid,' Lloyd said, 'because there was no cash. All Ian's money went when he was arrested [in 1990]. I don't know why Ian didn't just tell them he didn't have anything. I guess he just wanted all the inmates to keep thinking that he was a big-time crook and had a lot of money.'

In mid-1998 Saxon was in Bathurst jail, where he met Ivan Milat. They discussed their cases over several weeks and Saxon became convinced that Milat was innocent and had been framed by the police. It was, perhaps, no surprise that Saxon began proclaiming Milat's innocence, since he was similarly deluded about his own escape from jail. At a private hearing conducted by the New South Wales Independent Commission Against Corruption, Saxon gave evidence that after falling asleep in his cell at Malabar he was woken by two figures dressed in uniforms and black boots 'like those worn by members of the Malabar Emergency Unit'. Saxon claimed to have been sedated by the men and to have woken up sometime later alone in a house in Newtown. He escaped from his abductors, he said, by climbing out of a window onto the roof of an outbuilding and fleeing down an alley that ran along the rear of the property. Saxon repeated these claims under oath at his trial for escaping from lawful custody in 1993. The jury was unable to reach a unanimous verdict. In November 1998, before the retrial, Saxon changed his plea to guilty: there had been no mysterious men in black and he had not been abducted. He was sentenced to two years' jail. The sentence added one year and four months to the 24-year sentence he was already serving.

When Saxon's escape was investigated by the NSW Independent Commission Against Corruption, the commission noted that Saxon's escape 'reflects a remarkable degree of good fortune' if corrupt assistance had not been involved. Although it remained 'sceptical and suspicious' about some aspects of the evidence, it found that 'the evidence does not support a finding of corrupt conduct on the part of any public official'.

Saxon kept meticulous records of the proceeds from the 1989 importation. The sales from this shipment alone totalled $77.5 million, of which around $8 million in profit was laundered by Sommerville through Hong Kong, Singapore, Europe and the Middle East. Kulik was paid $53 million to cover his costs and profits. Christopher John Hopwood—a millionaire living in Middle Harbour on Sydney's north shore—was recorded as having sold around half the shipment. At the time of Saxon's arrest in 1990 the NCA raided Hopwood's home, but a 'lack of evidence' allowed Hopwood and others to escape arrest. For six years the police took no further action on Saxon's notebook.

■ ■ ■

Although this was not known to police, NSW Crime Commission chief investigator Mark Standen had maintained both a close professional and personal relationship with Ian Saxon since his arrest in Carlsbad in 1995 (see Chapter 11).

As a member of the AFP, Standen had played a minor role in the 1989–90 federal law enforcement investigation into the drug activities of Saxon and his syndicate. When Saxon escaped from jail in 1993 Standen was involved in the search—this time as a member of the NCA. Two years later, as a senior officer in the NCA, he was in charge of assembling a team to track down Saxon. Liaising with the US Federal Bureau of Investigation, Standen and others travelled to the US while the Bureau kept up surveillance. Standen was there when Saxon was arrested by officers of the Bureau and the DEA at Carlsbad, California, on 21 April 1995 and helped escort Saxon back to Australia.

He received information from Saxon that led to some significant arrests and drug seizures and the confiscation of valuable assets. In return, he fought for leniency in Saxon's treatment before the courts and in jail, and for his early release. As Lloyd commented, 'There was no money involved. They were both trying to play one another. Mark was playing Ian and Ian was playing Mark. Ian thought he was the winner and I agree with him.'

In July 2005, while on holidays in Fiji with his family, Standen wrote to Saxon, who was then in Cooma Correctional

Centre. Beginning 'Bula [Hello], Ian', Standen wrote: 'I am in Fiji testing how far a credit card or two can be stretched. The prices are so scary and my family is spending so much that you may have to reserve a spot for me in Cooma when Visa catches up to me.' Turning to his efforts to secure Saxon's release from jail, Standen described his lack of success as 'frustrating', but emphasised that he had not 'given up'. He wrote: 'When I return from Fiji, [I will] give it one big, last try. If nothing else works I will put stacks of Kava in his [New South Wales Corrective Services boss Ron Woodham's] coffee and then ask him to speak up on his objections or not for approval.'

Standen reminded Saxon that jail classifications were 'only the small battle . . . your release . . . is the main objective'. Accordingly,

> I intend to write a new personal letter to Canberra giving my opinion on your situation. I did this once before but as you know the election timing did not assist . . . If I had known this matter would have turned out the way it has, I would not have been so keen to get my arse over to Carlsbad and yours back to Oz. I think the price has been too high and it has taken some of the fun out of playing cops and robbers.

Standen ended his letter by warning Saxon to 'take care' and offering 'Warm Regards'.

There are clear similarities between Standen's relationship with Saxon and the relationship he was cultivating at the same time with the British drug trafficker James Kinch, although his involvement with Kinch would go much deeper.

■ ■ ■

In May 2008, after thirteen years in jail, 65-year-old Ian Saxon was paroled six months early and deported to New Zealand. The *Daily Telegraph* reported that the Minister for Home Affairs, Bob Debus, signed the early release after being told Saxon had 'provided substantial assistance to authorities'. The advice supporting Saxon's release came from Standen who, at that time, was an assistant director of investigations at the NSW Crime Commission.

Saxon returned to New Zealand, working briefly for his brother before moving to Thailand, where, for a time, he teamed up with one of Australia's biggest cannabis traffickers, Lawrie McLean (see Chapter 6). He now lives in New Zealand, where he works in tour management, artist liaison and marketing.

Speaking of his client in 1994 to the *Sun-Herald*, barrister Patrick Costello described Saxon as being 'a very personable man, a very engaging person, a person who had a thorough grip on the rock industry. He was highly respected by people like Frank Sinatra and Whitney Houston . . . very competent, capable at his job.'

Several of Saxon's old mates agree with this description of him. Saxon's boss at the Frontier Touring Company, Michael Chugg, says that he 'never thought of Ian as a criminal . . . He was and still is a good friend', although Chugg points out, 'He's not allowed to enter Australia.' An old colleague explained, 'Saxon does not see himself as a criminal, but as a businessman supplying a product to meet popular demand.'

CHAPTER TWO

Benny's Bar

The Ian Saxon story did not end with his jailing. His distribution network in Australia remained in business and his international contacts—the Dutch national Tamas 'Tom' Lazlo Schneiders and the Canadian-born US citizen David Kulik—found replacement buyers for the drugs they were sending to Australia.

After having played a significant role in the 1995 arrest of Saxon in California, Standen was eager for a big case that would bolster his reputation as a crime buster. He remembered Saxon's notebook and its detailed account of the 1989 importation. Saxon recorded that 9974 kilograms of hash was sold through seven wholesale distributors. Among them were 'CHOP' (a codename for C[hristopher] HOP[wood]), who had sold around half the shipment; the Perth-based seller known as 'Mr Andrews'; Lloyd Saxon; Peter Hamill; Tom Schneiders; and two others who cannot be named for legal reasons.

In 1996 Standen moved to the NSW Crime Commission, which took possession of Saxon's notebook. The information it contained led to the formation of Operation Skippy. With personnel drawn from the Crime Commission, state and federal police and the NCA, it aimed to investigate the cultivation and distribution of cannabis throughout New South Wales, Victoria, South Australia and Western Australia, and the international money laundering of drug profits. Hopwood was Skippy's first and biggest target.

Electronic and physical surveillance quickly confirmed that Hopwood was still active in the drug trade. He was filmed with a friend packing cannabis at a rented north shore garage. The friend was an ageing mid-level drug distributor from the Saxon days. This time the cannabis was not imported but grown in the Riverina region.

Surveillance teams followed Hopwood to hotels around Sydney and the north shore and watched him supplying at least fifteen dealers. His profits were estimated to be around $70,000 a month.

Hopwood's supplier was a 40-year-old Melbourne-based millionaire named Wayne Groves. Like Hopwood, Groves had been a member of the original Saxon distribution network. Groves was the owner of a car hire business, Rentabomb, and a silent partner in Melbourne's first tabletop club, the Sante Fe Gold in Russell Street. In March 1997 his business partner told the *Sunday Age* journalist Mark Forbes that the club was 'no different to any bar or pool hall, you've just got sexually explicit entertainment as a backdrop'.

But at the time of his arrest Groves—a lifelong cocaine, ecstasy and cannabis user—was desperately short of cash. The Sante Fe Gold was losing money and Rentabomb was in financial trouble. To make things worse, Groves' ex-girlfriend had just sent their son to live with him. She had left Groves for big-time drug importer Richard 'Snapper' Cornwell, but after breaking up with him could no longer afford to support the child.

Cornwell had a long history in Sydney's drug trade. During the early 1970s he had been a heavy gambler at the racetrack and in the gambling dens that dotted Sydney. He was also a successful cannabis importer. For a time in the mid-1970s Cornwell and former New South Wales police officer Murray Stewart Riley were members of the Michael Moylan cannabis syndicate. Later Cornwell partnered Riley in cannabis and heroin importations before setting up his own operations in the late 1970s, importing cannabis and cocaine. For a time, one of their biggest customers was Michael Hurley.

Cornwell later served several jail terms for importing and trafficking in drugs. During one of his court hearings, Stephen Angelini, a Californian member of Cornwell's syndicate, described Cornwell as reminding him of 'some guy who had watched too many gangster movies'. At the time of his arrest in the mid-1980s Cornwell's assets were estimated to be worth around $23 million. The courts seized $6.9 million. Cornwell was sentenced to 24 years' jail for importing 120 kilograms of cocaine.

Police watched Hopwood and his friend travel to Melbourne and hand Groves a shopping bag stuffed with $100,000 cash. In a little over a year Hopwood paid Groves a total of $1.4 million for cannabis he had sold in Sydney.

In turn, Groves took his 'commission' and gave the rest of the money to his supplier, the Toorak carwash millionaire Anthony 'Tony' Ryan. It was Ryan who had originally invited Groves to sell cannabis for him. Groves made the arrangements through his Perth friend, Andrews.

In later court proceedings Ryan claimed that he 'might have' paid a friend of his, the Melbourne millionaire Robert Meares, up to $200,000 for blocks of marijuana. In early 1998 a farmhand found a cannabis crop on Meares' 2400-hectare Murray River property, Bultara. He videotaped the crop and told his foreman. Police later alleged that six cannabis crops had been grown on the property between 1992 and 1998.

Operation Skippy lasted eighteen months and resulted in 35 people being arrested and charged with 106 drug trafficking and related offences. Among those charged were Groves, Ryan, Andrews, Meares, Hopwood and fifteen of his Sydney distributors. Property, cash, jewellery and other assets totalling $6 million were seized in Australia, New Zealand, Europe and the Philippines.

Hopwood pleaded guilty to drug supply charges and on 12 March 1999 was sentenced to five years and six months' jail. Described as an 'easygoing hippie type', Hopwood is believed to have surrendered to authorities around $3 million, which was held in a Swiss bank account at the time of his arrest.

The same month, Groves pleaded guilty to one drug conspiracy charge. Finding 'special circumstances', the judge sentenced him to four years' jail.

Tony Ryan was sentenced to three years' jail.

In 1999 a jury acquitted Meares of five charges of having cultivated cannabis crops and failed to reach a verdict on the sixth charge. Meares claimed that his farmhands must have been doing things behind his back, and that when he heard about the crop he destroyed it. Meares was also acquitted of laundering $3 million in cash over a period of eight years. Meares explained that his practice of visiting up to five different bank branches on the same day to make cash deposits was the result of a bank manager's complaint about the lengthy paperwork caused by customers who deposited more than $10,000 in cash. The cash was mostly from hay and grain sales, he said.

The drug charges against Andrews were dropped when he became a protected and indemnified witness for the prosecution.

■ ■ ■

Ronald Jeffrey Montgomery lived in Peru and had spent time in a Bolivian jail for cocaine trafficking. A US citizen, Montgomery used false passports and identification to enter Australia, having previously been declared a 'prohibited non-citizen' (that is, someone with no legal right to be in Australia) by the Department of Immigration. When in Sydney organising the distribution of one of his regular cocaine importations, Montgomery was a frequent visitor to Benny's Bar and Restaurant, the nightclub in Challis Avenue, Potts Point, that had brought Ian Saxon and Tom Schneiders together. Well connected with US drug importing and trafficking networks, Montgomery knew Schneiders and knew of Saxon, but had not met him. In Sydney, Montgomery's main contact and distributor was Robert Bruce Stalder, a Kings Cross thug whom Montgomery had met during the mid-1980s.

In 1968 the seventeen-year-old Stalder and two other teenagers broke into a Kings Cross flat and savagely raped, bashed and robbed two women—one the mother of three children—and bashed a male friend who went to their assistance. According to a 1969 *Sunday Mirror* report, doctors who treated the male victim 'could not find one patch of skin from his head to his feet that was not badly bruised and discoloured'. The man spent three weeks in hospital as a result of his injuries. Stalder was sentenced to fifteen years' jail for these and other offences, including stealing a motor vehicle, and breaking, entering and stealing. His two accomplices in the rapes and robberies received similar jail sentences.

Released in the mid-1970s, Stalder was soon back in Sydney's eastern suburbs drug trade, as both a dealer and heroin addict. During the late 1970s he was convicted of drug offences and stealing, and did short stints in jail. Sentenced in 1981 to six years' jail for armed robbery, he was released after just a couple of years. In 1984 he was again arrested for drug-related offences and spent a short time in jail.

From the mid-1980s Stalder dealt with Billy Bayeh and his network, selling them cocaine (mostly obtained from Montgomery) and other drugs and buying heroin from them. Bayeh had entered the Kings Cross drug trade in the late 1970s before teaming up with Detective Trevor Haken in an attempt to take over. (Haken later became the Royal Commission's most infamous police rollover, admitting to taking bribes on an almost daily basis and to being part of a widespread network of corrupt police, drug traffickers and other criminals.) In 1999 Bayeh was convicted of supplying drugs and sentenced to eighteen years' jail, backdated to 1996. He was released in June 2011, having served fifteen years.

In January 1986 Charlie Staunton, an eight-year uniformed constable in the New South Wales Police, was transferred to Darlinghurst Police Station. Kings Cross in those days was a free-for-all and Staunton was eager to grab his share of the bribe money, which would help him cover the costs of his own gambling addiction. A former colleague described Staunton as being a punter who 'couldn't let a race go by without having a bet on it'. On one occasion Staunton and other police were carrying out a drug search of a flat when 'Charlie stopped and turned the radio on and listened to a race, calling for the horse he had bet on to "come on",' he recalled. 'Even the bloke whose flat we were searching couldn't believe it. Charlie's horse ran second or third and he said something like, "Oh well, it was an each way bet. I haven't lost money," and went back to searching the flat as though nothing had happened.'

It was not long before Staunton became involved with Bayeh. As one of Bayeh's 'right-hand men', Staunton sold and used cocaine. This brought him into contact with Stalder. Staunton also dealt with other Kings Cross criminals and corrupt police, usually doing Bayeh's bidding. But Staunton's zeal soon made him the target of a police corruption investigation. Eighteen months after arriving at Darlinghurst he resigned from the police.

Out of the police and now a private investigator working around the Cross, Staunton kept his corrupt police contacts and underworld connections, including Stalder. He remained on Bayeh's payroll and, with Haken, supported Bayeh's attempt to take over the Kings Cross drug trade.

Sooner or later Staunton was bound to run into Montgomery. By now, Benny's Bar and Restaurant had closed. Many loyal patrons had moved to Springfield's, a new Kings Cross nightspot owned by former Benny's doorman Marty Clapp. Here, the spirit of Benny's—and its intricate links to Sydney's drug trade—lived on. It was at Springfield's that Staunton and Montgomery met and quickly discovered a common interest in cocaine. The pair had only a year to cement their friendship. On 11 December 1989 the AFP raided an apartment in Tamarama, in Sydney's eastern suburbs, where Montgomery was staying with one of his drug distributors. Montgomery was inside the apartment with the last half kilogram from his most recent importation. He also had a small quantity of cannabis, $10,000 in cash and a loaded .357 magnum revolver—the serial number had been filed off—as well as equipment for weighing and using drugs.

As the police searched the apartment there was a knock on the door. They answered it to find Stalder standing there. Realising they were police, Stalder threw the plastic shopping bag he was carrying at them and tried to escape, falling down two flights of stairs. In the fall and ensuing fight with police Stalder suffered fractured ribs, a punctured lung and a fractured heel and right wrist. The bag he had been carrying contained 50 grams of cocaine, hashish and small quantities of other drugs, and more than $6000 in cash.

Stalder was taken to St Vincent's Hospital where he was admitted and treated for his injuries. Under guard in a bedside court he was charged with supplying and possessing cocaine, possessing heroin and other drugs, goods in custody, assaulting police and resisting arrest. He was transferred to the hospital at Long Bay jail. Three days later he was dead from a heroin overdose administered while in the jail hospital.

Montgomery was charged with supplying and possessing cocaine, and related drug and firearms offences. He was refused bail. (A short time later Saxon and several members of his syndicate were arrested.)

Staunton did a lot of work for Montgomery, well beyond helping him with his defence. Staunton carried messages to Montgomery's girlfriend and to other friends outside the jail. He also spent tens of thousands of dollars of his own money on behalf of Montgomery, who in return promised to buy Staunton a 'home unit for his troubles' once his problems were sorted out.

Staunton knew Montgomery could afford to make such a promise; the problem was that Montgomery could not touch his cash while he was stuck in jail. Meanwhile, Montgomery had another reason for keeping Staunton on side. He wanted to continue with his drug importations and saw Staunton as someone who could play a useful role.

In September 1992 Montgomery was convicted of possessing cocaine and related drug offences. He was sentenced to eight years' jail, backdated to December 1989. In jail Montgomery met and became friends with Ian Saxon. As a former associate said, 'They had similar backgrounds and both were likeable blokes. They were good mates from the time they met.'

Staunton continued to visit Montgomery and used his connections to ensure Montgomery was comfortable and had no problems from other prisoners. He also continued to do 'jobs' for Montgomery. At the same time Staunton started visiting Saxon. As he was doing for Montgomery, Staunton became a conduit between Saxon and his friends on the outside. The favours he did included 'picking up cash and delivering it to girlfriends and others on the outside'.

The Wood Royal Commission into the NSW Police Service began in 1994, the year Montgomery was released from jail and deported. At the time Staunton was in Lebanon with Kings Cross identity John Ibrahim. Ibrahim, who has extensive business interests in the Cross and elsewhere, has been charged with murder but the charge was dismissed by a judge before it got to trial. He was in business with the sons of the late crime boss George Freeman. Staunton was not happy when he heard the news of Montgomery's deportation. He had spent a lot of money on Montgomery's behalf but none of it had been repaid. Now Montgomery was beyond reach and Staunton did not know how to contact him. He guessed that once back in the US, Montgomery would assume a false identity and head for South America to resume his cocaine-smuggling operations.

But Staunton had more urgent problems than trying to recover his money from Montgomery. For several months the Wood Royal Commission had kept Billy Bayeh in its sights. Now it summoned Staunton to give evidence. Appearing before the commission in mid-1995, Staunton refused to answer questions. He was charged with contempt and jailed. Four months later he was again brought before the commission and again refused to answer questions. This time Staunton was sentenced to eleven months' jail for contempt. His refusal to roll over impressed many in the underworld. More than a few 'tough guys' had already rolled or were in the process of rolling. Gangsters, drug dealers, corrupt police, lawyers and others would have had plenty to fear from Staunton's evidence.

Released from jail in April 1996, Staunton flew to Bali for a holiday—the Royal Commission was closing down and he was no longer a focus of its attention. Meanwhile, Montgomery had not forgotten his debt and was grateful to Staunton for having kept his mouth shut.

Using Sydney contacts who had kept him informed of the commission's activities, Montgomery tracked down

Staunton in Bali and arranged for him to be given an immediate payment of $20,000 cash. He also arranged for Staunton to fly to Amsterdam for a meeting. There, Montgomery told Staunton, 'There's someone I think you should know. He has a proposition for you.' That 'someone' was the Dutchman Tom Schneiders.

Staunton was taken aback but listened with growing enthusiasm as Schneiders outlined his own role in an international cannabis operation. Then came the proposition: Schneiders wanted Staunton to become a money collector for the syndicate. Staunton was offered so much money he could not refuse. Before long Staunton was introduced to two more members of the organisation—David Kulik and Gary Matsuzaki—the same people who, during the 1980s, had supplied the hashish for Ian Saxon's multi-tonne importations.

Some months earlier, Kulik and Schneiders had successfully imported 50 tonnes of cannabis into Canada for distribution to both the Canadian and US markets. Staunton's first job was to collect money owing on that importation. Within months Staunton had collected one payment of US$20 million and a second of US$10 million.

In late 1996 Matsuzaki and Staunton flew to Cork, Ireland, to liaise with John Noonan, described as one of Ireland's biggest drug traffickers, over the imminent importation into Britain of 25 tonnes of cannabis worth an estimated £250 million. Their confidence was misplaced. In December the US DEA intercepted a ship in the south Pacific, seizing the 25 tonnes of cannabis and arresting eighteen members of the gang. Noonan was later arrested in possession of almost 2000 ecstasy tablets and sentenced to eight years' jail.

The 1996 seizure followed one made two years earlier, when a 13-tonne shipment worth around £130 million had been intercepted and several people arrested, including Noonan. On that occasion Noonan had been released without charge. The cargo had been monitored as it was offloaded from the mother ship onto a trawler for landing in west Cork. When the surveillance operation leaked, enforcement authorities were forced to act. The US DEA had been targeting Kulik and Matsuzaki ever since.

By now Staunton was part of the syndicate's inner circle, assigned to play a significant role in drug shipments planned for Australia, Canada and the US.

In June 1996 Kulik, Schneiders and others were in Geneva talking to cashed-up drug gangs from all three countries who placed orders and agreed to broad delivery timetables and arrangements. With orders placed and deposits paid, things moved quickly. Two months later a ship left Pakistan with 25 tonnes of hashish on board. Staunton made several trips overseas, visiting Europe and North America, conveying messages and checking on progress. During October–November he delivered almost A$500,000 to syndicate heads in Canada for transport fees and warehouse rental. The next month he visited Bangkok and met the various parties to the importation to confirm last-minute distribution arrangements.

On 5 December 1996, the day after Staunton's Bangkok meeting, the mother ship met its Australian connection, the sloop *Highlander*, north of the Solomon Islands. Over several hours, 8.4 tonnes of hashish was transferred to the yacht. Eight days later the *Highlander* arrived off Tin Can Bay, north of Noosa Heads. Closer to shore, the cargo was offloaded from the *Highlander* onto five flat-bottomed boats that made their way to shore through the mangrove swamp to a waiting truck.

The shipment was to be driven to Sydney, but before it could leave, the federal and Queensland police pounced. The drugs were seized and over the next few days eighteen people were arrested, several properties were searched and nearly 3000 cannabis plants were found.

The arrests and seizures were kept from the media. The federal police had been tipped off about the importation by their US counterparts, who had been pursuing Kulik and his network for years. No announcement would be made about the Australian arrests until the Canadian and US authorities moved. It was a tense time.

Following the Australian drop-off, the mother ship sailed towards the US. On 12 December the vessel was intercepted off Hawaii and the remaining cargo of 17 tonnes of hash was transferred to a barge crewed by undercover agents with the US DEA. In a high-risk operation, the drugs were transported to Los Angeles. US agents made three controlled deliveries of more than 4 tonnes each to Los Angeles, Montreal and upstate New York. Over several days nine people were arrested. They included US, Dutch, Canadian and Australian citizens. Among them were Kulik in Mexico (he had been attempting to provide an alibi for himself to cover the time the shipments were being delivered) and Staunton, who was detained as he left a meeting in a Montreal restaurant where plans had been made to distribute 4 tonnes of hash in Canada. All were charged with what US authorities described as a 'massive conspiracy dedicated to the distribution of drugs worldwide'.

Despite being charged with conspiring over almost two decades to import drugs into Canada and the US, Kulik beat the most serious charges and was given just four years' jail. Several of his US and Canadian colleagues were sentenced to much longer jail terms.

Staunton pleaded guilty and was sentenced to ten years' jail, but served only nineteen months in a Canadian jail before being released. After returning to London, he applied in 2001 for entry to Australia, but the Department of Immigration refused his application. Staunton is a British citizen and although he had come to Australia at the age of seven and served nine years in the NSW Police, he had never taken Australian citizenship. At the time of writing Staunton's wife and family still live in Sydney. Despite being barred from Australia, it is understood that since 2001 Staunton has 'discreetly' visited Sydney several times.

During the two years that followed the Australian importation, most of the eighteen conspirators arrested in Queensland were sentenced to jail terms of around ten years. Andrew Robert Hyde, the skipper of the *Highlander* and an alleged major player in the importation, was granted bail of $250,000 with strict reporting conditions, but this failed to stop him fleeing Australia within a year. Hyde lay low for the next eight years. On 14 September 2005 he was arrested by immigration officials at the Alajuela Airport in Costa Rica attempting to enter the country from Guatemala. Almost two years later Hyde was returned to Australia. On 24 July 2007 he appeared before the Brisbane Magistrates Court and was, once again, granted bail. Eighteen months later, following a seven-day trial, Hyde was acquitted of all charges.

The Sydney financiers of the importation escaped arrest.

CHAPTER THREE

Bateman and Bateman

Among the gangs in the East Coast Milieu was a group of dealers and importers in Sydney's Bondi Beach, led by Russell Douglas Bateman and Maximiliano Diez, eager to resurrect their careers as drug kingpins.

No gang was more daring and reckless in its efforts to reach the top of the pile than Bateman's. Born in the United Kingdom, Bateman was in his late twenties when he moved to Australia around 1981. After entering the local drug trade, he was soon making a handsome living dealing in cocaine, LSD, cannabis and amphetamines.

Among Bateman's close associates was 25-year-old Thomas McCaffrey. A British citizen, McCaffrey was a drug user and small-time dealer in cannabis, LSD and ecstasy. From time to time McCaffrey acted as Bateman's debt collector. They became friends and went into the scaffolding business together. Eventually, McCaffrey became the godfather of Bateman's child.

In 1987 Bateman was convicted of cultivating and supplying cannabis and placed on a two-year good behaviour bond. The following year McCaffrey was convicted of a minor drug offence and fined. The convictions didn't stop them. In 1992 Bateman was sentenced to five and a half years' jail for cultivating cannabis. McCaffrey beat the more serious charge and was convicted only of a minor drug offence, for which he was fined.

In jail Bateman met Diez and another prisoner, Sir Thomas Graham Fry. Both would play key roles in Bateman's drug operations.

Born in Medellin, Colombia, one of the world's cocaine capitals, Diez arrived in Australia in 1978 at the age of 25. A cocaine user, Diez soon made a name for himself in Sydney's eastern suburbs drug trade. In January 1994 he was convicted of importing 6 kilograms of cocaine and sentenced to two years and nine months' jail—a sentence many considered too light. Released after fifteen months, Diez resumed both his drug use and dealing.

Diez was connected with Colombian cocaine suppliers through his nephew, Louis Salazar, known as El Flaco, who lived in Colombia. In court, Diez was later described as 'a principal member of an international organised crime syndicate with strong links to South America'. He was also involved in international money laundering.

Fry was a 44-year-old New Zealander. His life as a fraudster arguably began when he was given the name Sir Thomas Graham Fry. Although it was a name, not a title, Fry did not hesitate to use the word 'Sir' to curry favours and gain advantage throughout his adult life. After one of his arrests the

British media even described him as a 'New Zealand knight'. Fry's criminal record dated back several decades. He moved to Australia in 1979 and two years later, at the age of 29, stole a yacht in Sydney. After sailing it to New Zealand to visit his son he was arrested, extradited to Australia and sentenced to three years' jail. On his release from jail, Fry began dealing drugs. In the early 1990s he was jailed three times for drug offences. In 1994 he was convicted of manufacturing a prohibited drug and sentenced to five years and four months' jail.

While in jail, Bateman, Diez and Fry began discussing ways of importing large amounts of cocaine into Australia. In June 1994 Bateman decided that he had spent enough time in jail. On his next outing from the minimum security Silverwater Correctional Centre to play soccer at Panania in Sydney's south-west, he escaped. As one corrective service officer quipped, 'He got the ball and started running towards the goal. Everyone cheered, but he just kept running.'

Living openly in Bondi, Bateman teamed up again with McCaffrey. For the planned cocaine importation, McCaffrey would act as Bateman's deputy and debt collector—of both cash and drugs—and his paymaster, handing out funds as required.

After Diez was released, he and Bateman set about accumulating the capital they would need for their importation.

Fry was released a year later, in December 1996. Before he had any chance to join the conspirators, he was placed in immigration detention and deported to New Zealand, but his deportation made little difference to the plan. Through his Colombian connections, Diez would organise the cocaine. As an experienced sailor, Fry would organise a yacht and be its captain. Bateman would distribute the cocaine. To reduce his risk of detection, Bateman would relocate to Melbourne and use his networks in that city to distribute ecstasy. McCaffrey would manage the money.

Another central figure in the conspiracy was 48-year-old Robert Angelo Roberti, whom Bateman had known for almost a decade. Roberti had a long criminal record, but for relatively minor matters. A solitary drug conviction in 1997 had seen him sentenced to 184 hours' community service.

After escaping from jail in 1994, Bateman obtained and used a false Australian passport in Roberti's name. Later, when Roberti needed to travel overseas, Bateman obtained false passports for him in the names of Brian Russell and James Simmons. They travelled to Hawaii, Argentina and New Zealand together, both on false passports—Bateman on a passport in the name of his travelling companion, Roberti, and Roberti on a passport in the name of either Russell or Simmons. Roberti's role in the importation was that of a messenger. Several others played lesser roles.

While on the run and preparing for the importation, Bateman met 47-year-old Jeffrey Allan Martin, a US citizen. Bateman and Martin had several things in common. Both were wanted by the police, Bateman for escaping from jail and Martin for absconding while on bail for sex charges in California. Both were determined to keep their freedom and both were active in the drug trade.

Martin had come to Australia on a three-month tourist visa and settled in Bondi. Aware that if found he would be deported, Martin asked Bateman for help in establishing a new identity. Bateman was happy to oblige, agreeing to sell Martin his own passport and other identification documents. Martin was now Russell Bateman.

Things went well for the two Batemans until April 1999 when police arrested Martin for a sexual assault on Sydney's north shore. Producing Bateman's identification, Martin was charged with Bateman's 1994 escape. Unperturbed, Martin pleaded guilty to Bateman's escape and was sentenced to nine months' jail for the assault and an extra six months' jail for the escape. In addition, he would have to serve out the last years of Bateman's 1992 conviction for drugs. Martin knew enough about the conditions inside US jails to realise his life would be easier as a prisoner in New South Wales.

Martin's deception lasted almost a year. During this time Roberti visited Martin in jail, giving him several thousand dollars for his continued silence and promising further financial rewards and fake identification documents when he was released. Martin did not know how critical his continued silence was to Bateman and his team: their cocaine importation was already on its way.

Fry, meanwhile, had settled in Gisborne on New Zealand's North Island after his 1997 deportation. There, he bought a dilapidated yacht called the *Lone Bird* and spent more than $200,000 of the group's money making it seaworthy and fitting it out for use in the importation.

In late August 1999, using a variety of passports, Diez flew from Sydney to Bogota, Colombia, and later to Panama, where he booked into the InterContinental Miramar hotel to finalise the deal. The Colombians would supply 500 kilograms of cocaine on credit, but Bateman and his gang had to provide A$1 million upfront for transport costs and to cover the Australian end of the operation. The credit was worth around A$2.5 million, but three to four times that amount would be needed to repay the 'interest' due after the cocaine was landed and sold. The suppliers were neither benevolent nor trusting: they had security in the form of Diez's family, who lived in Colombia. Their safety depended on the debt being honoured. Despite the high interest, it was still a very profitable arrangement—in Australia the cocaine was worth around $60 million on the streets.

Fry, using a false passport in the name of Graham Streetley, flew from New Zealand to Panama, where he met Diez and was introduced to the South American suppliers, Raul Ospina and a person known only by the names Escobar and Angel. The Colombians wanted to meet and assess the man who would have control of the cocaine shipment during the last part of its delivery to Australia. Details of the shipment were finalised. The cocaine would be off-loaded from the mother ship to a yacht, skippered by Fry, off the coast of New Zealand. Fry would be responsible for landing the consignment in Australia.

On 17 October 1999 the yacht *Bora Bora II* sailed out of the Port of Cristóbal on the Panama Canal. With its three-man Colombian crew, the boat sailed to an agreed location on the South American coast, picked up its cargo and began its journey to the rendezvous point.

In late November several of the Sydney-based conspirators flew to New Zealand, some travelling on false passports. But there was a serious problem: the *Lone Bird* would not be ready in time. Another yacht had to be found. Diez began to worry for his family and reminded the syndicate, 'You cross these people . . . you get killed easy.' Like Diez, the rest of the gang were worried, but unlike Diez their concern was for the money they had invested and the loss of the potentially huge profits they stood to make.

The 13-metre ketch *Ngaire Wha* was bought in Auckland for $157,000 and quickly fitted out with parts stripped off the *Lone Bird*. To hone his sailing skills Fry entered and sailed the yacht in New Zealand's Bay of Islands Tall Ships Race on 6 January 2000.

In Sydney, Diez kept in touch with the crew of the *Bora Bora II* as it made its way from South America. On 9 January Bateman received the message he had been waiting for—the delivery was close—and relayed the news to Fry. Four days later the *Ngaire Wha*, with Fry, Roberti and Hamish Edmond Thompson on board, sailed out of the Bay of Islands for its rendezvous with the mother ship off Spirits Bay on the northern tip of New Zealand's North Island.

After transferring 21 bales of cocaine totalling around 500 kilograms to the *Ngaire Wha*, the Colombians sailed to Opua on New Zealand's North Island to celebrate before setting off on their next delivery run. In Sydney Diez was visited by two representatives of the Colombian drug syndicate. They accompanied Diez to Melbourne to meet 'the boss' (Bateman) and arrange for a few thousand dollars of 'spending money' to be sent to the crew in New Zealand. Assured that everything was going to plan, the two Colombians returned to South America.

Meanwhile, Fry sailed towards the small township of Patonga on the shores of the Hawkesbury River, about 70 kilometres north of Sydney, not far from where Ian Saxon had landed his 10-tonne hash shipment a decade earlier. The shipment was only days away and members of the syndicate were about to become instant multimillionaires. Then trouble struck.

On 20 January 2000 the *Daily Telegraph* reported the seizure of 50 kilograms of ecstasy imported through Melbourne and bound for Sydney. Four men had been arrested. One was 47-year-old Michael 'Popeye' David Hughes, an eastern suburbs drug dealer and former member of the Mr Asia heroin syndicate who had escaped arrest when the syndicate began to collapse in the late 1970s. At one stage,

Hughes was to have been one of Bateman's major distributors for the cocaine. On learning of the arrest, Bateman and McCaffrey were heard discussing Hughes' bad luck.

Bateman said, 'I tell you what, it's a good job we fuckin' . . . we stopped talking to that lad.'

'I fuckin' reckon,' McCaffrey agreed.

The Melbourne importation was the work of an international syndicate based in the Netherlands. Dutchman Jan de Groot van Embden, 42, was in charge of the Australian operation. The group had dealt with other former members of the Mr Asia syndicate in New Zealand and these had recommended Hughes, who became van Embden's contact in Australia. Hughes recruited two other former Mr Asia members, 51-year-old Hans 'Bumbles' Johannes Czajkowski, who had completed an eight-year sentence during the 1980s, and 50-year-old James 'Diamond Jim' William Shepherd, who had been out of jail for only thirteen months after serving fourteen years of a 25-year sentence for importing and trafficking heroin.

After being arrested with Hughes, van Embden rolled and was taken to the Netherlands, where he gave evidence in the Rotterdam Court against the European members of the syndicate. Eleven members were eventually jailed for up to ten years. In July 2002 van Embden pleaded guilty in the Sydney District Court and was given a reduced sentence of twelve years' jail, which took into account his cooperation with the police in both Australia and the Netherlands. Later he was secretly returned to the Netherlands where he disappeared into witness protection along with his wife and four children. He still lives in fear for his life and the lives of his family. In February 2002 Shepherd and Czajkowski were convicted and sentenced to jail. They successfully appealed their convictions but pleaded guilty as their retrial was about to begin. Shepherd was sentenced to nine years and six months' jail and Czajlkowski to nine years. Rather than go to jail, Hughes committed suicide by gassing himself.

While Bateman and McCaffrey commiserated over Hughes' arrest, another police telephone intercept picked up a conversation about a false passport used by Roberti. 'Vinnie', who had supplied the passports, was heard complaining to McCaffrey about Roberti's use of the Brian Russell passport on 30 November 1999 for a trip to New Zealand. An agitated Vinnie said he had been assured that the passport had been 'shredded' after an earlier use, but that Roberti had now used it a second time. The real Brian Russell had had his 'collar felt' by the authorities and did not have a story prepared. 'Mate,' Vinnie complained, 'about six months ago I do him [Bateman] a favour [and] I've had people sticking guns in me since doing him a favour. I've had to go and bash fucking people . . . I've had people sticking guns in me fuckin threatening to bash me, bash me partner, get me barred out the fuckin pub, I mean fuck me dead this is . . . unreal.'

The implications of the conversation were clear enough. Vinnie was hinting—none too subtly—that he hadn't been paid enough for his troubles. He had picked up a sniff that something big was about to happen.

Meanwhile, law enforcement authorities monitoring the cocaine shipment had a problem of their own: how could there be two Batemans? One was under surveillance and another was in jail. However, if the police revealed their knowledge of the false Bateman, they risked blowing their investigation into the 500 kilograms. They decided to leave things as they were; after all, the false Bateman was not only serving jail time for crimes he had not committed, he was also in jail for a sex crime he had committed.

Delivery of the cocaine was now imminent. Diez was heard reassuring his Colombian connections by telephone: 'We'll be ready for the ball in a couple of days.' In another conversation he told them, 'We would be able to have the party probably this weekend.' On the night the *Ngaire Wha* was due to land, Diez told the Colombian connection, 'We'll be dancing the tango tomorrow.'

Everything seemed to be going well as the yacht sailed up the Hawkesbury River, but as it docked at Patonga on 1 February 2000 the AFP swooped, seizing the yacht and its cargo and arresting eight men. Bateman was arrested driving away from Brooklyn, near Patonga, on his way to Sydney. The syndicate had been under police surveillance for eighteen months.

McCaffrey avoided being arrested with the others and for most of the next nine months lived in Bondi under the name William Connor. Finally arrested on 15 September 2000 at the popular Swiss-Grand Hotel, McCaffrey claimed police had arrested the wrong man and produced Queensland identification in the name of Connor.

After the real Bateman's arrest, rumours spread that he had rolled. Jail inmates incorrectly believed that the 'dog' was the false Bateman (Martin). Would he also give up the inmates for their lurks and perks? His life was at risk. Living in a squalid US jail suddenly looked like a better prospect than dying in a comfortable Australian jail. Martin told authorities the full story of his deception. As a result he was charged with perverting the course of justice by assuming Bateman's identity and serving his jail sentence for him. Sentenced to two years' jail, Martin was deported in late 2000. On arrival in Los Angeles he was arrested and charged with his outstanding crimes in the US and served more jail time.

As a lawyer involved in the case said, 'I don't know how this stuff-up could have occurred. Bateman is 190 cm tall,

70 kilos, blue-eyed and a Welshman with a Welsh accent. Martin is a 180 cm, 95 kilos, brown-eyed, and an American with an American accent.'

In custody and facing a long jail sentence, the real Bateman cut a deal. He rolled and pleaded guilty. In September 2000 he was sentenced to thirteen years' jail. The other conspirators pleaded not guilty. As they faced their committal proceedings, Bateman spent his time taking pottery classes at Sydney's Long Bay Jail. Giving evidence against his co-conspirators, Bateman was taken from his cell to the court by prison officers. One day a keen-eyed officer noticed how tightly Bateman was clutching his folder of papers. He resisted the officer's attempt to look at the papers, but the officer persisted. Hidden among the papers was a small replica handgun made of pottery and painted black—it looked like the real thing. Once again Bateman thought he had spent enough time in jail, but this time his escape was foiled.

There were no more pottery classes for Bateman and he was not called to give evidence at the trial of his former colleagues. Claiming to be mentally ill, he was housed in the psychiatric ward of the Long Bay Corretional Complex. He rejected food and claimed that he was on a hunger strike, although not eating didn't seem to be doing him much harm. Suspicious wardens discovered that Bateman had been surreptitiously eating food that he had hidden in his cell. It was Bateman's last scam: after that he became a model prisoner.

At the trial all the blame was directed at Bateman. McCaffrey admitted to being a drug trafficker, but denied he was an importer.

Roberti portrayed himself as an 'untrustworthy drunk', a 'boofhead . . . a simpleton and the butt of jokes' who only became aware of the cocaine importation after he and the others had taken possession of the load from the mother ship off New Zealand. Roberti followed Bateman's lead and had himself admitted for psychiatric treatment, but was told that he did not have any mental problems.

Fry admitted being involved in the importation, but claimed to have played only a minor role. Two months before the cocaine was due to arrive he had decided to withdraw from the operation, he told the court, but was visited in Gisborne, New Zealand, by unidentified 'dudes' who threatened him with a gun and a knife and told him to 'do it or die'. From then on, Fry said, he had participated only because he feared for his life. Not only that, he was confused about what it was that they were importing. He thought it was 5 tonnes of 'pot', not cocaine. Later, Fry described how he 'met a girl [and] fell madly in love' and wanted no further part in the importation.

At the end of a seven-month trial, the Crown prosecutor, Mr Michael King, addressed the jury:

> The defence cases all focus on Mr Bateman essentially being the greatest criminal known in history since the day that Sherlock Holmes first set off in pursuit of Moriarty . . . [According to the defence Bateman was] the combined reincarnation of Svengali, Rasputin, Machiavelli and let's not leave out Nostradamus . . . The one person in history that Mr Bateman was clearly not the reincarnation of was, of course, Houdini.

When the time came to instruct the jury, Justice Dodd quoted from a Humphrey Bogart movie:

> You will all know the film *Casablanca* which starred Humphrey Bogart and Ingrid Bergman, or at least you will

> know some famous lines from it. Claude Rains played the corrupt police chief, Louis. One of his lines is now part of our general language. A man had been shot. He waved his arm at his subordinate and told him, 'Round up the usual suspects'.

The problem for the conspirators was that they were the 'usual suspects' and they had committed the crime. In October 2001, following a seven-month trial, all were found guilty and were subsequently sentenced to long periods in jail: Maximiliano Diez with a 25-year non-parole period; Garry William Bartle, 48, and Robert Angelo Roberti, 52, were convicted and sentenced to sixteen years' jail; Thomas McCaffrey, 44, was convicted, appealed, and the sentence was increased from sixteen years to twenty years' jail; Peter Darryl Fox, 34, was convicted and sentenced to sixteen years in jail, appealed, and the sentence was increased to 21 years; and Hamish Edmond Thompson, 49, was convicted, appealed, and the sentence was increased to twenty years and six months in jail. Russell Douglas Bateman, 48, pleaded guilty in a separate hearing and was sentenced to sixteen years. He had rolled over, assisted police with their inquiries and given evidence against his drug-trafficking colleagues.

Bateman, however, served only a few years in Australia before being deported to the United Kingdom to serve out the rest of his sentence. At the time of his arrest, he owned two homes in the Melbourne inner-city suburb of St Kilda and had bought his parents an expensive home in Wales. According to some, it was Welsh gossip about the new-found wealth of Bateman's parents that had sparked the interest of local police. This led to information being passed to Australian law enforcement agencies. It was a case of Bateman being too nice to his mum and dad.

CHAPTER FOUR

The big league

As the Bateman crew waited for their 500-kilogram shipment of Colombian cocaine to arrive at Patonga, police sprung the trap on another of Sydney's big-time drug traffickers. In November 1999, 39-year-old Ricky Montgomery, a prominent member of the East Coast Milieu, was arrested and charged with supplying 750 kilograms of cannabis resin valued at around $7.5 million. It was part of a larger importation carried out by crime bosses Michael Hurley and Malcolm Field—Montgomery was one of their major distributors. In February 2001 Montgomery pleaded guilty to supplying about 10 kilograms of cannabis (the more serious charge was dropped) and was sentenced to three years' jail.

Between 1983 and 1985 Montgomery played more than 50 professional rugby league games for the South Sydney Rabbitohs—three in first grade—but his earnings were not enough to give him the lifestyle he desired. After hanging up his boots Montgomery planned to become a career shoplifter, but quickly saw the greater and easier profits to be made from drugs.

Common friends guided Montgomery into Hurley's drug distribution network. He took to the business easily, selling around 2 tonnes of the 12 tonnes of cannabis imported in 1993–94 by Hurley and Field, and making $15 to $20 million for the gang. Along the way Montgomery acquired an extensive criminal record that included convictions for possessing a prohibited weapon, stealing, carrying cutting weapons, assault and robbery, and supplying drugs.

Released from jail in mid-2001 after serving eighteen months of a three-year sentence, Montgomery found Hurley and Field locked in battle with the NSW Crime Commission and the courts over assets confiscation proceedings and their attempt to get George Costi of De Costi Seafoods to lie to the commission about a money-laundering scheme. A few years earlier Hurley and Field had identified De Costi's seafood business as a good investment opportunity and an ideal vehicle for money laundering. By the time De Costi realised what was going on it was too late. He knew of Hurley's reputation and had seen Field's violent outbursts. In desperation, he went to the Crime Commission. Their fight with the commission disrupted Hurley's and Field's drug activities, cutting into their cash flows. The pair was almost certainly headed for a stint in jail.

Montgomery, as usual, needed money to fund his extravagant lifestyle and compulsive gambling. He couldn't wait for Hurley and Field. Within days of his release he found an alternative supplier, 32-year-old Anthony 'Tony' Gerard Hines, a standover man with a reputation for violence.

A heavy cocaine and ecstasy user, Hines was a member of Maroubra's notorious Bra Boys. He narrowly escaped arrest in June 2001 when the AFP seized more than 16 kilograms of cocaine from a rented garage in the southern Sydney suburb of Rockdale, near Botany Bay. A vehicle leased by 31-year-old Clovelly surfer Hayden Rogers had been used to transport the cocaine to Rockdale. It was not the first time a vehicle owned or leased by Rogers had been used to move drugs, and it wouldn't be the last.

Over the following months Montgomery dabbled in the sale of heroin. This caused a rift with Hurley, who had been warned off the heroin trade by Stan 'The Man' Smith in the late 1980s. Smith hated the heroin trade—one of his sons had died as a result of a heroin overdose—and Hurley was well aware that there would be no further warning. The next message would be delivered with violence. After falling out with Hurley, Montgomery turned to an old friend, 41-year-old Steven Robert James.

Montgomery and James had known each other since the late 1970s and had cooperated in various drug ventures. James was known by the nicknames 'Gekko' and 'Gordon' after the unprincipled stockbroker Gordon Gekko in the movie *Wall Street*. In 1984 James started work as a flight attendant with Qantas, a job that enabled him to smuggle cocaine into the US. In January 1992 he was arrested in Hermosa Beach, California, after police searched a hire car he had parked in a no-parking zone and found 2 kilograms of cocaine. James later admitted that he had carried out earlier importations of cocaine into the US and Australia.

While serving his three-year sentence in a Californian jail, James met 33-year-old John Donald Morrison, who was doing six years for drug offences. Morrison was born in Scotland and moved to the US during the 1980s. Having long outstayed his visitor's visa, he used false names—Craig Alan Schultz and, from time to time, Alan Broom—to avoid detection and deportation. Morrison later claimed that almost from the moment he and James met, they had talked 'a lot' about cocaine and about the 'market opportunities for the sale of cocaine in Australia'. James admitted that he 'had been selling cocaine in Australia for a while' but Morrison insisted that the idea of 'importing cocaine into Australia' arose from their conversations in jail.

In November 1993, after being released from jail and deported, James returned to Sydney's eastern suburbs. Although he was still on the Qantas payroll, his conviction for cocaine trafficking made his employment as an airline steward untenable. According to James, 'in 1994 I took a redundancy package'.

By late 1995 Morrison had been released from jail and the two men were busy plotting to import cocaine into Australia. The plan was to send 'cocaine to Steven [James] in Australia every couple of weeks,' according to Morrison.

In mid-1996 James and Morrison attempted their first importation. They would share the costs and profits equally. Once in Australia, the cocaine would be distributed by Montgomery, whose network included Tony Hines.

A Qantas steward friend of James couriered US$22,000 cash to Morrison in the US to buy a kilogram of cocaine, but the importation failed when the US courier recruited by Morrison was arrested. The courier, who had worn the cocaine strapped to his body, made it safely through Australian Customs, but was later arrested at his Sydney hotel.

Montgomery and James lay low, not knowing whether the police were looking for them or not. A few weeks later, satisfied that they had escaped the net, Montgomery, James and Morrison began to plan their next importation, hoping it would be more successful than their first. According to Morrison, around October 1996 'Steven and I talked about him sending over his old lady to give me some cash for some more cocaine.' James' 'old lady' duly arrived and gave Morrison US$22,000 for another kilogram. Morrison described the importation:

> I went to a computer store within a shopping mall and I bought several boxes of computer software . . . I bought a kilo of good quality cocaine . . . from a Mexican guy whose nickname was 'Chicken' . . . I then wrapped this block of cocaine up in tape and packaging material. This block fitted really neatly between two ends of some polystyrene packaging from one of the computer software boxes. I placed plastic wrap back around the computer software box with the cocaine inside, to make it look like the seal hadn't been broken and the box was intact . . . Later on I took this box and the other boxes of computer software I bought to an overnight freight company [and mailed it to an address James had given me in Sydney].

A few days later James telephoned Morrison with bad news: the package had been found. James told him: 'a contact of mine told me that the cops were trying to deliver it to the address.' Despite this second failure, Morrison and James again escaped arrest.

By now James and Montgomery were desperate for money. The next importation had to succeed. In early 1997 'Jim', an Australian drug courier also known as 'The Bushman', arrived in Redondo Beach, California, with around US$50,000 in cash. Morrison bought 2 kilograms of cocaine and helped Jim strap it to his body. It was a case of third time lucky; Jim was an old hand and the importation went off without a hitch. Hines distributed the cocaine in Sydney, and James and Montgomery were able to cover their earlier losses and make some cash.

Despite the success, contact between James and Morrison cooled for the next three years although, according to Morrison, James' importations did not stop. 'It was my impression that Steven was working with someone else over here in the States to obtain cocaine,' Morrison explained. James told Morrison that during the late 1990s he worked 'with another guy that he trusted'. Morrison went on:

> Steven may have met this guy . . . when Steven was serving time in the California jail . . . He was a Colombian guy who had a Mexican passport . . . the Colombian guy went down to Australia and stayed at Steve's mother's place . . . [Eventually] this guy ripped him off for about $100,000 and . . . he [Steve] was pretty pissed at him.

Montgomery's falling-out with Hurley over heroin was the spur for him to renew his partnership with James. Again, the Bushman was involved. Around New Year 2002 the Bushman met Morrison in a Redondo Beach sushi bar and handed him US$70,000 for 4 kilograms of cocaine. According to Morrison, '[I] helped Jim [the Bushman] strap it [the cocaine] to his body with the Velcro straps like he used last time he was here.'

The importation was a success—their biggest so far. Once again, Hines was the main distributor. According to evidence he gave later, James made 'probably half a million dollars' from this and earlier successful importations. Montgomery made about the same.

It didn't take long for James and Montgomery to gamble away most of the cash. One morning in January 2002, as they walked along Sydney's Clovelly Beach, Montgomery volunteered, 'I have people who can get things off boats.' James replied, 'I might know a bloke who can put things on to boats.'

Confident that they had learnt from their mistakes, both agreed that bigger importations were the answer to their financial problems. But while bigger importations brought bigger profits, they also meant bigger upfront costs, more people on the payroll and more complex arrangements. For the next importation they decided to hide the cocaine on a ship rather than use couriers.

Hayden Rogers was invited by Montgomery to join the conspiracy. Rogers had once worked for Patrick Stevedores at Darling Harbour, and his contacts at the company would enable Montgomery to retrieve the drugs from the ship after docking, avoiding Customs.

Meanwhile, James contacted Morrison and flagged the proposal with him. On 19 June 2002 James left Australia to meet Morrison on the Spanish island of Majorca. A deal was agreed: 10 kilograms of cocaine would be imported by ship at a cost of $160,000. Three weeks later James returned to Sydney and confirmed the arrangements with Montgomery.

James approached his friend Bradley James Evans, who was keen to be involved. James and Evans had known each other since the 1970s and James was the godfather of Evans' third child. Evans knew of James' 1992 US drug conviction and jailing—he had written him a court reference—and through James had met Morrison in the late 1990s.

Over the next few months James, Evans, Montgomery and Rogers—with Hines in the background—honed the details of their plan. Montgomery agreed to contribute $80,000—half the importation costs—for a 50 per cent share of the profits. But Montgomery had a problem: he did not have the cash. His solution was to ask Hines who, for once, had more cash than he was used to. Hines mistakenly believed that his cut would be proportionate to the $50,000 cash he was investing—roughly a third of the total cost. What he did not know was that he was effectively funding the majority of Montgomery's share. James and Evans were to make up the balance. They were putting in $40,000 each and would share their half of the profits with Morrison.

The consignment was to be loaded in the Mexican port of Manzanillo. They chose a ship in the Wallenius Wilhelmsen line because the company docked at Darling Harbour and used Patrick's to unload its cargo.

But Montgomery couldn't wait. Wanting another quick payday, he looked up a couple of old colleagues in the drug trade: Frankie Ballis and Wayne Moore. The pair had ample supplies of ecstasy tablets and were in the process of importing more.

Around this time Montgomery met 22-year-old James Peter Gray-Spence, also known as Steve Sanders, at his favourite drinking hole, the Coogee Bay Hotel, opposite Coogee Beach. The two found they had a lot in common. Both liked a punt, both were losers and both were in the drug business. Within months of meeting, Gray-Spence was selling up to 5000 ecstasy pills at a time for Montgomery.

Later, Montgomery had Gray-Spence selling 4.5 kilogram bags of cannabis.

■ ■ ■

On 2 October 2002 Morrison's colleague and money-mover, 59-year-old Colin 'Vicker' Sidney Kemery, arrived in Sydney using the false name Jeff Spence. Morrison had met Kemery at a party in Santa Cruz, California, three years earlier. A South African, he lived in Copenhagen with his Danish wife. As Kemery waited in Sydney for the agreed $160,000, James was devising the first of several double crosses. For a start, he arranged for Morrison to increase the importation from 10 kilograms to 'between 15 and 20' without telling the others. Eventually, Kemery was given $65,000 by Montgomery and $37,500 each by James and Evans, making a total of $140,000: $20,000 short of the amount he'd been promised. The shortfall was to be paid on delivery of the cocaine. Separately, James gave Kemery a further $100,000—the balance owed on a previous importation. Kemery transferred around $30,000 into accounts in Colombia, the US, England and Denmark before leaving Australia with the rest.

After not hearing a word from Kemery for several days, the Sydney conspirators became worried. In response to their increasingly agitated inquiries, a story came back that Kemery had been picked up in Paris by French police, who had then stolen the cash. British police were also said to be hunting Kemery. None of it was true—Kemery had not gone to Paris. James was not the only one trying to double-cross his partners.

With their money gone, James and Montgomery urged Morrison to persuade the South Americans to let them have the importation on credit. After all, they insisted, this was to be the first of many. The plan was for importations every two months.

Believing the February 2003 importation would go ahead, Hayden Rogers arranged for a person using the false name Paul Johnston to take out a six-month lease on a flat in Kingsford in Sydney's eastern suburbs. It was to be the safe house where the cocaine would be stored. Negotiations for the importation dragged on while James tried to find out where the missing money had gone. Convinced that the deal was going to fall through, Johnston told the real estate agency that he would be vacating the flat. Having taken care to lease the flat in the false name, he inexplicably gave his own home address as the forwarding address. The mobile telephone number he gave for Johnston was also registered in his own name. On vacating the flat he received a cheque for the refund of the bond money made payable to Johnston. He endorsed the cheque 'Please pay [his own name]' before signing it 'P Johnston' and depositing it into one of his own bank accounts. Johnston had fatally compromised a series of potential multimillion dollar cocaine importations for the sake of a bond refund worth a few hundred dollars.

More than a month after Kemery and the cash had gone missing, James and Morrison still could not agree on what had happened to it or what they should do about the importation. On 27 November 2002 James told Morrison, 'The money's gone, you're not going to get any more.' James also demanded an explanation from Morrison as to why Kemery had taken the cash to Europe rather than directly to South America. Morrison couldn't give him an answer but he reminded James that he was not the only person suffering. 'I lost my fucking arse on that ride,' he complained.

■ ■ ■

Montgomery's anger over the lost money was at least partly mitigated by the prospect of another drug deal. In late 2002 Montgomery told Gray-Spence, 'We've got something really big happening. I've got a mate who's bringing in one hundred thousand small ones, and they'll be a better price than I've given you currently. Be patient. It's not going to happen till around Christmas.' Montgomery was talking about an importation of 100 kilograms of ecstasy tablets by Frankie Ballis and Wayne Moore. But he'd spoken too soon. Just before Christmas, Ballis, Moore and others were arrested and charged over the ecstasy shipment. (See later chapters for a full account of the Dutch syndicate's importation of large quantities of ecstasy into Australia.)

News of the arrests raced through the Sydney eastern suburbs drug scene. Fearing he might be scooped up, Montgomery went into hiding, surfacing a month later to tell Gray-Spence, 'I've been up the coast laying low. I've been really hot since this all happened . . . They pinched my little mate with the glasses [Ballis] for that massive haul in Coogee.'

Ballis may have been behind bars but importations by other members of the East Coast Milieu kept the drugs flowing and it wasn't long before Montgomery was again supplying Gray-Spence.

■ ■ ■

It was a different story for Hines. The failed cocaine importation had cost him more than just money. He had a reputation as a hard man and yet someone had ripped him off. Goaded by drugs and alcohol, Hines left Sydney on 27 December 2002 for South America, vowing to find out what was going on.

While Hines was away, the situation in Sydney changed. Montgomery, Evans and James managed to renegotiate the stalled importation. By late January 2003 Kemery was back on the scene and within weeks was able to 'find' US$20,000 of his own money as a deposit for the importation. It was a goodwill gesture, he explained, sticking to his story that he had been robbed by the French police. By mid-March Evans and James had each raised a further $14,000. This was then transferred to Morrison in California.

The quantity of cocaine to be imported was now 30 kilograms, but with much of it on credit, a higher price had to be paid. The price for bulk purchases where cash was paid upfront was between US$5000 and US$5500 a kilogram, but where it was obtained on credit the price jumped to around US$25,000 a kilogram. The Australians had no choice but to pay; there was still a good profit to be made in Sydney where a kilogram could be sold for around $140,000.

The original plan to hide the cocaine inside a container was dropped. It would now be hidden inside a car to be loaded on a vessel at the port of Manzanillo. The vessel chosen to carry the consignment was the *Tampa*, made infamous in October 2001 by its role in the so-called 'children overboard' crisis off Australia's northern coast.

A few days after the *Tampa* left Manzanillo, bad news reached Sydney: the cocaine was not on board. Morrison told the conspirators not to worry; he had already found an alternative ship, the *Tarago*. But the *Tarago*, too, sailed without the cocaine.

On both occasions the excuse given was that tighter security on the wharves had prevented the cocaine from being loaded onto the ship. James and his Sydney partners were becoming increasingly suspicious, but Morrison assured James that another ship, the *Texas*, had already been chosen and that this time nothing would go wrong. He also confirmed that the consignment would be 30 kilograms. On 25 April 2003 the operation was confirmed by Morrison as 'go, go, go', but five days later he confessed that, once again, bolstered security on the wharves had prevented the cocaine from being loaded.

By now the Sydney buyers were seriously 'pissed off', according to Evans, who asked Morrison to speak to 'the other end' to see whether they would 'put some extra [cocaine] on or knock something off the price' because of the extra costs incurred as a result of the delays. Over several days telephone intercepts picked up Morrison assuring James that everything was okay and that the cargo would be on the next ship.

On 13 May Morrison confirmed that the consignment had been loaded on board the *Tamerlane*, which was now on its way to Sydney. 'It's on. It's in a [blue Chevy] pick-up truck with Illinois plates. There are two black bags behind the seat. All you have to do is lift the seat and remove the bags.' Morrison gave James the Illinois number plate of the vehicle and described its exact location on the ship. In Sydney, the conspirators were ready to celebrate. Montgomery told Gray-Spence: 'I've got a lot of coke coming in the near future. There's a lot of it, it'll make us all rich.'

The *Tamerlane* docked at Sydney's Darling Harbour on 1 June 2003. Two days earlier Hayden Rogers had telephoned the person using the false name Paul Johnston.

After the telephone call Johnston, using his false name, hired a Hyundai Excel for seven days from Pricerite Auto Rentals at Coogee. Around midday, Hayden Rogers again rang Johnston and asked if he had 'finished'—that is, hired the car. The next day, Johnston, again using the false name, hired a Toyota Camry stationwagon for six days from the same rental company.

The following day, on Hayden Rogers' instructions, a Patrick Stevedores employee, wearing a pair of white linen gloves, drove the Hyundai to the employee car park on Hickson Road, Darling Harbour. The employee completed his night shift before driving the Hyundai from the car park to Towns Place, a small square in Millers Point, on the edge of Sydney Harbour, where he parked the car. Leaving the vehicle unlocked and the key on the floor in front of the driver's seat, he then walked back to Patrick Stevedores. (No employee of Patrick's was charged with any criminal offence in relation to this.)

Meanwhile, local police carrying out a general patrol spoke to three men sitting on the ground at nearby Observatory Park, Millers Point, overlooking the Patrick wharf at Darling Harbour. When questioned by police the three men (believed to be Hayden Rogers, Steven James and Ricky Montgomery) gave their names as Nathan Rogers, Peter James and John Adams. All three then left the park. Close to where they had been sitting, the police found a scanner for listening to the police radio. Around an hour later Montgomery was again seen by local police in a street overlooking Patrick's. About this time Hayden Rogers called a colleague from a nearby public telephone and told him they had given up their efforts to collect the cocaine.

Two days later Montgomery told James that his people had scoured every deck of the *Tamerlane* but could not find any pick-up truck. Later, Montgomery gave James the *Tamerlane*'s manifest. There was no record of the truck having been loaded. The manifest indicated that 'pallets of paper' were stored in the place where the truck was supposed to be.

James rang Morrison and told him there was no sign of either the truck or the cocaine. When Kemery was told, he appeared to be shocked, saying he had been assured by the suppliers that the cocaine and the truck had been loaded onto the vessel. James faxed the ship's manifest to Morrison, while Kemery made inquiries with the Department of Motor Vehicles in Illinois. He could find no record of the truck or the numberplate. This time, it seemed that the South Americans had scammed both their US dealers and the Sydney buyers.

A furious Montgomery told Gray-Spence: 'I've got big dramas, the coke thing has gone pear-shaped, and I mean pear-shaped.' On top of the money he'd paid for the cocaine, Montgomery had had to pay compensation to his contacts on the wharves each time the delivery was rescheduled. 'My mate has had to change his shift three times,' he explained James. 'I've had to pay him a couple of thousand dollars for compensation.' James passed on his complaint to Morrison, but Morrison dismissed it, telling him they were simply the costs of doing business in the drug trade.

During the eighteen months they spent planning the importation, the conspirators had tried to conceal their real purpose by speaking in code. The failure of the *Tamerlane* importation only increased Montgomery's suspicion that they were under surveillance. Morrison told Kemery: 'We are going to really tighten up on our code.'

The trouble was, the gang had enough trouble trying to remember the code they were already using. The ship *Texas*, for instance, had been given the codename 'George', after US President George W. Bush and his home state of Texas. Morrison, however, could not remember who Bush was or what he was code for. 'Tightening' the code could only make things worse.

On 8 June 2003 Morrison was arrested in California and charged with cocaine trafficking and other offences. Three days later Kemery was arrested in Denmark and extradited to the US. On 17 June Montgomery was arrested in Sydney and charged with unrelated passport offences.

Two weeks later state and federal law enforcement agencies, including the NSW and Australian Crime Commissions, arrested twenty members of the East Coast Milieu and charged them with supplying and importing cocaine, and other offences. Among those arrested were James, Montgomery, Evans, Gray-Spence and Hayden Rogers. Paul Johnston was not arrested.

■ ■ ■

Returning none the wiser from South America, Hines escaped arrest. On 23 July 2003 he flew to Los Angeles, determined to find out what had happened to the missing money and the aborted importations. After being refused entry to the United States because of his criminal record, he was put on the next plane back to Sydney, where his suspicions soon fell on James and Montgomery.

A year earlier, Hines had approached James and Montgomery for a false passport for a friend. James passed the request to Morrison. Kemery's connections would supply the false British passport, with Morrison acting as go-between. Hines paid a fee of $5000 but the passport never arrived. For Hines, it was the last straw. He now threatened to 'knock' James. The fact that James and Montgomery were in jail would make no difference to Hines, who had connections on the inside.

In their book, *My Brother's Keeper*, Angela Kamper and Charles Miranda describe a meeting that took place around this time between Hines and a Bra Boy they called 'Richard'. According to Richard, '[Hines] seemed agitated, looking like he'd been up the night before and he was raving. He said he'd just been deported back from the US and was really pissed off. He asked me how well I knew Montgomery. He told me he had invested a lot of money with him and that he'd been waiting far too long for a return on his investment.'

It was not long before Hines visited James in jail. Whatever he said, it was enough to frighten James, who immediately arranged for the $5000 to be repaid. Whether this would have stopped Hines from acting on his threat will never be known. On the evening of 5 August 2003 Hines was shot three times in the back of the head by a fellow Bra Boy, 31-year-old Jai Abberton. Montgomery, who was on bail at the time, had been drinking with Hines and Abberton in the Coogee Bay Hotel just before the killing. Charged with murder, Abberton was acquitted in 2005.

■ ■ ■

On 19 April 2004, a year after his arrest, Kemery pleaded guilty in the US to distributing cocaine and was sentenced to seven years and eleven months' jail followed by five years' supervised parole. He refused to help Australian authorities.

Morrison cut a plea with US authorities and was sentenced to ten years and five months' jail. Brought to Sydney, he gave evidence against Montgomery and others.

Gray-Spence and James also cut deals, rolling and giving evidence against their former colleagues in return for reduced sentences. On 22 October 2004 Gray-Spence pleaded guilty to three counts of supplying drugs and was sentenced to two years' jail.

After pleading guilty to conspiring to import 30 kilograms of cocaine, James was sentenced to ten years' jail. The sentence was widely criticised. In reaching his decision, New South Wales District Court Judge Peter Brennan explained that he had taken two factors into account: James' good behaviour and the fact that since his drug conviction in the US more than a decade earlier he had worked as a legitimate businessman. The latter, however, was not true. James had admitted to (but had not been charged with) involvement in at least four more importations during that time and Morrison had implicated him in several others.

In mid-2006, soon after the start of his trial, Montgomery sacked his lawyers and announced that he would defend himself. Claiming to be mentally ill, he underwent psychiatric analysis, only to be pronounced fit.

Montgomery's performance in representing himself at the trial ranged from canny to comical, with no one quite knowing when he was being serious and when he was putting on an act. One day, Montgomery was seen outside the court in tears and 'fairly hysterical'. Addressing the judge, Montgomery explained, 'I certainly don't understand the proceedings, Your Honour. I never got past the Higher School Certificate and I can't—the amount of information, the amount of reading, I just can't take it. I get massive migraines and then I just black out.' Another time, straight-faced and apparently serious, he asked the judge, 'How do I cross-examine myself?'

At the other extreme, his cross-examination of James was thorough and skilful. He forced James to admit to other successful cocaine importations, to perjury in other proceedings, to details of his deal with the NSW Crime Commission and how he had been able to keep most of his drug profits and increase his assets while in jail.

After a five-month trial and fourteen days of deliberations the jury was unable to reach a decision on any of the accused. All were released. Outside the Darlinghurst Court House an elated Ricky Montgomery was debating where to go for a celebratory drink when a female juror approached him, gave him a hug and a kiss and said, 'I don't know how you were able to handle the pressure. It must have been terrible for you.' The surprised Montgomery returned the compliment, saying, 'It must have been hard for you too. Thank you.' She wished him all the best for the future and walked away.

She wasn't the only juror to exchange words with Montgomery after the trial. The *Sunday Telegraph* reported that a male juror approached Montgomery, Evans and Rogers in the Crown Hotel in Elizabeth Street. According to journalist Neil Mercer, the juror 'allegedly told the men he had been looking for them for hours'. He said he had been sent there 'by the police'. He also informed the men he had been pushing for a guilty verdict and believed they should be in jail. It was a reminder of just how lucky they had been.

The police and the NSW Crime Commission were unwilling to attribute the outcome to Montgomery's lovable rogue performance in court. Suspicions of jury-tampering led to a thorough investigation of the jury. No charges were ever laid, although plenty of investigators had their doubts.

In February 2007, a few months after his hung jury trial, Montgomery began a six-month sentence for passport offences. They had nothing to do with his criminal activities and everything to do with a secret lover: Montgomery needed the passport to cover his tracks when he visited a girlfriend in New Zealand.

After Montgomery's release, he, Evans and Hayden Rogers began their retrial for conspiring to import cocaine. The retrial lasted five months. On 26 November 2007 the jury took just a few hours to convict all three, although it would be another ten months before they were sentenced.

The convictions did not go unchallenged, as lawyers for the trio questioned the relationship between James, who had rolled and become the prosecution's key witness, and Mark Standen, the then assistant director of investigations at the NSW Crime Commission. The presiding judge, Judge Peter Zahra, found that James had misled the court and that at his own sentencing hearing he had minimised his role in the importation. It was of little benefit to Montgomery, who was sentenced to eighteen years' jail. Rogers was sentenced to ten years and Evans to twelve years. Of the three, Evans was said to be especially aggrieved. According to Sydney's *Daily Telegraph*, 'A former first-grade rugby league star allegedly duped a drug importer [Evans] out of $400,000 by claiming he could get him off serious criminal charges for a hefty fee . . . [Evans] is believed to be furious about paying the huge fee for nothing.'

CHAPTER FIVE

The dreams of Frankie Ballis

Being a mid-level dealer was never going to be enough for Francis 'Frankie' Hetherington Ballis. Ballis's ambition was to become one of the high-level traffickers and importers running the drug trade in Australia and creaming the big profits.

Born on 26 September 1946, Ballis began his criminal career while still in his teens. His lengthy criminal record included possession of a pistol, possession of explosives, theft, attempt to escape and other offences. From the late 1960s to mid-1970s he was associated with the Federated Ship Painters and Dockers Union in Melbourne. In 1975 Ballis moved to Sydney, settling into the city's eastern suburbs, and soon became a trusted member of the East Coast Milieu and Hurley's Coogee Mob. Two years later Ballis joined other Australian criminals on a three-year shop-lifting and stealing spree across Europe.

Convicted of theft in the UK, Ireland and France, Ballis served jail time in Ireland and France before returning to Australia via Manila in 1983. He was smuggled into Australia aboard the ANL vessel *Australian Explorer*, an escapade organised by Dennis 'Fatty' Smith, who ran the Aussie Bar in Manila, and paid for by Melbourne's Painters and Dockers. Smith was a Melbourne criminal whose crimes are believed to have included the notorious 1976 Great Bookie Robbery of the Victoria Club in Queens Street. While the bookies admitted to the theft of about $1.4 million, the actual figure is believed to have been as high as $15 million, which Smith is said to have laundered through the Aussie Bar. About two years after arranging for Ballis to be smuggled home, Smith himself was thrown out of the Philippines. He returned to Melbourne a millionaire, bought a string of racehorses and drove a Rolls-Royce. In 1986 he was arrested and jailed for cocaine trafficking. Smith died, broke, in 2010 of a heart attack.

In the mid-1970s Ballis married Trudy Sleep, who also went by the names Joy Dale and Susan Elizabeth Bowen. Over the years Sleep's criminal record included theft, fraud and using false identification to secure the bail of a friend (a female shoplifter charged with the theft of more than $150,000 worth of property in Melbourne and Sydney). She served a short stint in jail. In 1987 Sleep paid $205,000 for a house at Bronte.

Montgomery and Ballis had been major distributors of the 12-tonne cannabis haul imported by Hurley and Malcolm Field in 1993–94. In October 1995 Ballis received $250,000 from a Liechtenstein bank account controlled by Hurley. A year later Ballis and Sleep received $200,000 in a series of transfers from the same Liechtenstein bank account. Over the next two years payments totalling more than $860,000 were transferred from the same account to the trust account of a solicitor and accountant in Victoria. A large portion of the money was paid to Ballis. For around a decade from the early 1990s Hurley and Field used the Liechtenstein bank, together with trust companies set up in the Turks and Caicos Islands, to launder drug money for themselves and their associates. The islands, in the West Indies, have gained a reputation for tourism and for their offshore banking facilities.

In the late 1990s Ballis shifted his focus from cannabis to ecstasy and any other drugs he could get his hands on, a change that led him to a Dutch-based ecstasy manufacturing and distribution network that was already operating in Australia.

Like Montgomery and Hurley, Ballis was a long-term supplier, through Tony Hines, to Maroubra's Bra Boys. By 2003 the AFP regarded Hines as being the 'syndicate head' of the Bra Boys' drug import and distribution business in Sydney's eastern suburbs. While the AFP regarded the Bra Boys as a serious threat, local New South Wales police did not. In 2001, during a City East Region Operations and Crime Review, the police commissioner, Peter Ryan, was told by local commanders that the Bra Boys were a 'loosely organised rabble and not a gang'. They were not included in a 1999 police intelligence assessment that identified 53 gangs operating across Sydney.

The AFP assessment was given unexpected support by Hurley. Worried by the Maroubra gang's capacity for violence, Hurley confided in a few close criminal colleagues and a couple of friendly police that the Bra Boys were 'prepared to shoot people' in their bid to take over Sydney's drug trade. The Bra Boys were one of three rivals Hurley was concerned about: the Montgomery crew and the [name deleted for legal reasons] crime family were the other two. His concern was not for the public, of course, but for himself and his gang.

In the early 2000s, membership of the Bra Boys was estimated at between 300 and 400, though not all members were involved in the drug trade. In late 2002 a large number of off-duty police were attending a Christmas function at the Coogee RSL when they ran into a group of the Bra Boys who were holding their own function at the club. A fight broke out and the police were given a hiding. There was no crack-down or retaliation by police. The incident showed who was in charge.

The power and influence of the gang was confirmed during the December 2005 riots that started in Cronulla and spread through a string of coastal suburbs, including Maroubra. As the government and police executive dithered about how to use reinforcements (according to an internal review of the Cronulla riots, even the police could not work out who was in charge of the police response), leaders of the Bra Boys and the Comancheros outlaw motorcycle gang, notorious for its role in the 1984 Father's Day Milperra bikie massacre that left seven people dead, met and called for peace. The message got through and the violence stopped. Revelling in the media attention, Bra Boys' leaders Jai and Koby Abberton could claim credit for achieving what the police could not. There were other benefits. Peace in Cronulla and the nearby beach-side suburbs allowed the local drug trade, which had been severely disrupted by the increased police presence caused by the riots, to get back to normal.

On 7 March 2007 the Bra Boys' self-made documentary, *Bra Boys: Blood is thicker than water*, premiered at the State Theatre in Sydney. It was a romanticised tale of battlers overcoming personal adversity to surf the world's big breaks, while always calling Maroubra home. Attended by most of the senior Bra Boys and plenty of celebrities—including the actor Russell Crowe, who narrated the documentary—and members of the South Sydney Rabbitohs, the premiere mimicked the attraction of some US celebrities to gangsta rap culture. The film bore little relation to the truth. A former head of the Gangs Squad, Detective Chief Superintendent Ken McKay, pointed out that many of the Bra Boys were violent criminals and that there was 'more than sufficient intelligence, information and connections to link them [the Bra Boys] to organised crime'.

One of those connections was to Frankie Ballis, who by the middle of 2002 was in regular contact with Dutch drug traffickers through a woman known as 'Vinnie'. As a result of intercepted telephone calls in the Netherlands to and from Vinnie, the NSW Police and the Crime Commission received information from Dutch police about ecstasy importations into Sydney.

The commission put intercepts on the private telephones of several suspects and on a number of public telephones which the suspects were known to use. Most of the suspects lived in Sydney's eastern suburbs and had years of experience with bugged telephones, but they had not anticipated the bugging of the public telephones. One of the suspects who made his calls from a series of public pay telephones and from constantly-changing mobile telephone services was Ballis.

On 24 September 2002 the police obtained a warrant to covertly search Ballis's home unit at 4/67 St Pauls Street,

Randwick. They found about 40 ecstasy tablets bearing 'safe sex' and Durex logos, and others bearing the Versace logo. The drugs were left in place, though samples were taken.

Between October and December there were numerous intercepted telephone calls between Ballis and Vinnie which, according to court papers, 'were often coded and guarded but appeared to relate to money owed, prices and expected profit, quantities, other persons assisting the enterprise and dates of forthcoming events connected to the enterprise'. In conversations about the importation Vinnie habitually referred to Ballis as 'the general manager'.

As Ballis tried to confirm arrangements for an importation, he was told by Vinnie to see 'the old assistant', 48-year-old Wayne Robert Moore. Moore was a distributor for one of Ballis's long-time Melbourne associates, 60-year-old Peter Edward Gay (also known as Peter William Johnson). Vinnie also agreed to send a representative to Sydney. Later the same day a worried Ballis called Vinnie and told her that some people he knew—he was talking about Gay—had just 'got into a lot of trouble'. Ballis stressed the need for caution and the importance of getting 'this thing right'. Told by Vinnie to 'stay with the old crew', Ballis replied: 'They're all with me . . . and they're 100 per cent loyal.' Moore also spoke to Vinnie about the 'general manager' and the 'difficult things' he was having to deal with.

The most pressing of those 'difficult things' was Gay's arrest on 13 November 2002. Gay had a long criminal record for sex, property, fraud and drug crimes. Like Ballis, he had moved from Melbourne to Sydney's eastern suburbs. Tipped off by police investigating Ballis, Drug Squad police had started investigating Gay, who was planning an importation identical to Ballis's. During October and November

2000, police intercepted telephone calls by Gay to 'Mitch' in Amsterdam about the impending importation. In coded messages Gay and Mitch discussed the disposal of an earlier shipment and the payments to be made to Mitch through his Asian money launderer in Sydney. Gay explained that he couldn't 'give him a million tomorrow . . . I can give him half a million.' Later he complained, 'I've got two and a half million out so far and I'm waiting for this money, all this money to come in, and you understand.'

'Yes, understand,' Mitch replied.

A few days later Gay complained to Mitch that the money launderer would not take the cash. 'He don't wanna take [it], I come with half a mill today, all the way into town and he wouldn't even take that. I said what about any more after that, he said no. He said, half a million, maybe another two . . . but I can't do no more than that.'

Gay told Mitch that he expected to have sold the rest of the shipment in 'another six to eight weeks' through networks in Sydney and Melbourne.

On 13 November police carried out a covert search of Gay's Coogee apartment. In two locked suitcases in the bedroom wardrobe they found around 200,000 ecstasy tablets weighing 50 kilograms, packed in 68 sealed plastic bags and worth an estimated $12 million on the streets. A third suitcase held more than $160,000 in cash. In a small vase in the hallway they found a key for a Commonwealth Bank safety deposit box. During the search Gay and his partner, 60-year-old Englishwoman Linda Rose Cowen (also known as Linda Rose Johnson) unexpectedly returned, forcing police to change their plans. Gay and Cowen were arrested and charged with drug importation and supply. When police opened the safety deposit box at the Martin

Place branch of the Commonwealth Bank, they found another $115,000 in cash and personal papers, including a false British passport for Gay in the name Johnson.

Five months later the drug charges against Cowen were dismissed at the local court. On 26 March 2004 Gay pleaded guilty in the District Court and was sentenced to ten years' jail. In jail, Gay was visited by his old friend Ursula Prendergast, the former wife of Laurie Prendergast. One of Melbourne's most violent and notorious criminals, Laurie Prendergast had been a close associate of the hit man Christopher 'Rent-a-Kill' Flannery, a central figure in Sydney's gangland war of the mid-1980s. Prendergast and Flannery were murdered within weeks of each other in 1985.

Gay's arrest reminded colleagues of the need for caution, but it did not stop Ballis, and the coded telephone conversations continued. On 9 December 2002 Moore met 62-year-old American Carl John Hinke, an environmental activist, yoga teacher and children's author who 40 years earlier had been active in the US anti-war movement. Hinke's arrival from Singapore coincided with a request by Ballis for Vinnie to send a representative to Sydney. Police telephone intercepts had recorded several conversations between Hinke and Moore. In Sydney, Hinke maintained regular telephone contact with Vinnie in the Netherlands. There was almost daily contact with Moore and several meetings between Ballis, Moore and Hinke, some of which were watched by police.

On 18 December Ballis was seen by police 'to hand over several handfuls of cash to Moore and Hinke'. Two days later Moore telephoned his mother, warning her that she might receive a visit from the police and that her house might be searched. She should tell the police that he had not lived there for ten years, Moore said. After giving her the name of his lawyer, who would contact her if he was arrested, Moore reassured his mother that he did not 'expect any dramas' and that he hoped to make 'a substantial amount of money'.

Later the same day police executed a search warrant on Ballis's new highrise apartment in Bondi Junction, seizing around $37,000 in cash and 27 ecstasy tablets. Ballis was arrested, charged and bailed.

Over the next couple of days Ballis failed to keep several appointments with Moore. The pair finally caught up at Coogee on the morning of 24 December. They walked around for several minutes before getting into Moore's car and driving for half an hour around the streets of Coogee, Randwick and Kensington. After dropping Ballis off, Moore made a telephone call and then drove to the Storage King warehouse in Denison St, Hillsdale. Instead of entering Storage King, Moore conducted what police described in court records as 'counter surveillance . . . He [Moore] continually drove down short residential streets without stopping, stopped for periods of minutes at a time on the side of the road and drove laps around the same streets several times.'

Police knew all about Moore's interest in Storage King. Two weeks earlier he had hired a small storage unit in which to stash the ecstasy shipment while it was being sold. While Moore could come and go without dealing with reception staff, he had—rather amateurishly—taken the unit in his own name, using his driver's licence as identification.

Frustrated with Ballis at what he saw as unnecessary delays in getting the ecstasy out of Storage King, Moore telephoned Hinke. The storage company shut down over Christmas and Moore was frightened of the drugs being found by the police or stolen by other criminals. Anxious to start selling the ecstasy, Moore told Hinke that he would get the shipment out of storage and take it to his place.

During late December the police had also been listening to conversations between Ballis and Hayden Rogers. On the same afternoon that Moore telephoned Hinke, Ballis called Rogers and, in coded conversation, arranged for the pair to meet. Ballis then drove a short distance to Heffron Road, Pagewood, where he found Moore waiting in his car. Rogers arrived a few moments later and spoke briefly to Ballis before both men got into Moore's car. After about an hour of cruising around 'in a circular fashion' to avoid surveillance, Moore drove to a spot near the street where Ballis's car was parked, dropped off Ballis and Rogers, and sped away.

Later, Moore rang his mother to tell her 'everything went well'. He also telephoned Hinke, assuring him that the job 'has been done' and the 'general manager' was happy. Moore urged Hinke to ring 'her' (Vinnie) and let her know everything had gone to plan.

As they listened to the telephone conversation, it dawned on the police that they had missed the transaction: the ecstasy had been delivered. Racing to inspect the security car park of Moore's home in Mowbray Street, Sylvania, they found a white Ford Econovan still parked in the lockup garage. It had not been there earlier in the day and it did not belong to Moore. The van was registered to Hayden Rogers. Inside were seven sealed cylinders containing almost one million ecstasy pills worth around $35 million. About 700,000 pills had already been sold.

Other intercepted telephone calls around this time picked up coded conversations between Hayden Rogers and

Montgomery, who was organising a 30-kilogram cocaine importation (see Chapter 4).

About 10.30 p.m. on Christmas Eve 2002, Hinke and Moore were arrested at a Cronulla seafood restaurant. A few hours later, Ballis was arrested at his home. All were charged with possessing a commercial quantity of ecstasy.

The puzzle for the police was how the importation had been carried out and how they had missed the handover. It took them some months to piece it together. A few months earlier two men had approached a large Dutch agricultural company that exported to Australia. The pair claimed to be setting up a business in Sydney and asked whether they could 'piggyback' two pallets of agricultural equipment in one of the company's Australian-bound containers. The pallets contained ecstasy tablets hidden inside plant pots. After retrieving the pallets, the two men slipped out of Australia. They were members of the Ron 'Fat Ron' Haklander syndicate (see Chapter 10).

Two years after his arrest Moore pleaded guilty to aiding the importation of the ecstasy and was sentenced to twenty years' jail.

Ballis and Hinke pleaded not guilty and were acquitted by a jury. They were free, but had spent two years in jail, their bail having been refused. Like Ballis, Hinke had faced drug charges before. In 1993 Hinke had been arrested at Courtenay on Canada's Vancouver Island and charged with possessing close to 5 tonnes of hashish with an estimated street value of C$68 million for the purpose of trafficking. Hinke pleaded not guilty and beat the charge. A co-accused was convicted and jailed for two years.

After his Sydney acquittal, Hinke's solicitor said his client would be leaving Australia and it was doubtful that he would return. In 2005, speaking from Thailand, Hinke said, 'I left the US when I was eighteen and found a good life in Canada. Still go back every summer to fish for salmon, but life is even better in Thailand.' In Thailand, Hinke became a lecturer at Thammasat University's Faculty of Liberal Arts and founded Freedom Against Censorship Thailand, which campaigns against book and internet censorship in Thailand.

Rogers was never charged over the importation. He claimed that his relationship with both Ballis and Montgomery was that of an 'errand boy' and he did not know the purpose of the 'errands' he ran. But in 2003 Rogers was arrested with Ricky Montgomery and others over the conspiracy to import 30 kilograms of cocaine. Four years later they were convicted and Rogers was sentenced to ten years' jail (see Chapter 4).

■ ■ ■

Despite Ballis having been acquitted of the major drug charge in 2004, there were still drug supply, firearm and weapons charges outstanding against him. The drug charge related primarily to his possession of the ecstasy tablets found in his Randwick unit during a covert police search. On 21 February 2006 Ballis was committed for trial on these charges. A year later the Supreme Court ruled that the covert execution of the warrant on his Randwick unit and the covert execution of two other warrants were unlawful. In 2008 Ballis pleaded guilty to supplying ecstasy and was given an eighteen-month suspended sentence. Ballis successfully argued that he only supplied his friends and this did not amount to trafficking. He was convicted of possessing a prohibited firearm but the time he had spent in jail since his earlier arrest was taken into account and no further penalty was ordered. On the prohibited weapon charge he was convicted and given a $500 fine. A year later the court found that almost $9000 in cash seized by police from Ballis's Bondi Junction unit was the proceeds of crime and forfeit to the state: around $28,000 cash was returned to Ballis.

Ballis and his wife, Trudy, split and in 2006 Ballis took up with a 42-year-old eastern suburbs woman he had known for ten years. In March 2008 the woman hanged herself in Ballis's Coogee unit after a drug and alcohol binge.

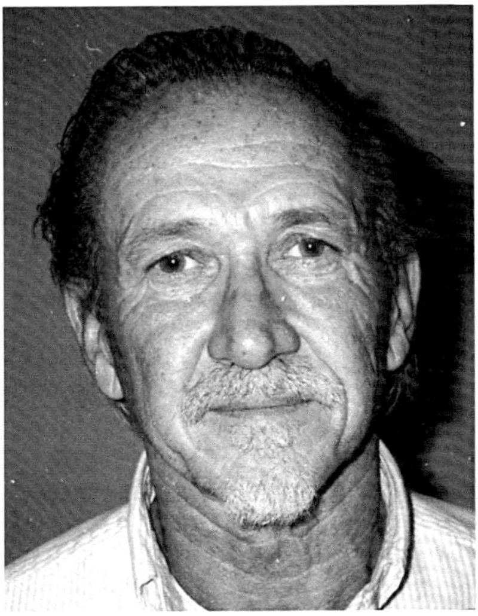

Ian Saxon, syndicate leader, arrested in 1990 after importing 10 tonnes of cannabis. (Courtesy NSW Police)

Lloyd Saxon, brother of Ian, in Long Bay Gaol Remand Centre on cannabis importation and related charges, in 1992–93.

Part of the 1990 Saxon syndicate hoard: $A5.5 million in cash seized in a Coogee garage, along with gold Krugerands, gold bars and hashish. (Newspix)

Reward poster issued after Ian Saxon's 1993 escape from jail.

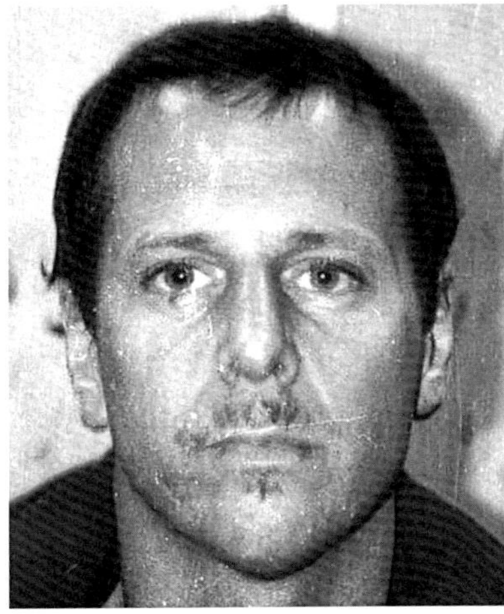

(Top left): Joey Sansom: UK citizen, international drug trafficker and member of Sydney's East Coast Milieu. (Courtesy NSW Police)

(Top right): Ronald Montgomery: US citizen, international drug trafficker and friend of Ian Saxon. (Courtesy NSW Police)

(Left): Allan McLean, a workmate and friend of Mark Standen in the Narcotics Bureau during the 1970s and 80s.

Charlie Staunton: ex-Darlinghurst police officer and associate of drug traffickers Montgomery, Saxon and others. (Newspix)

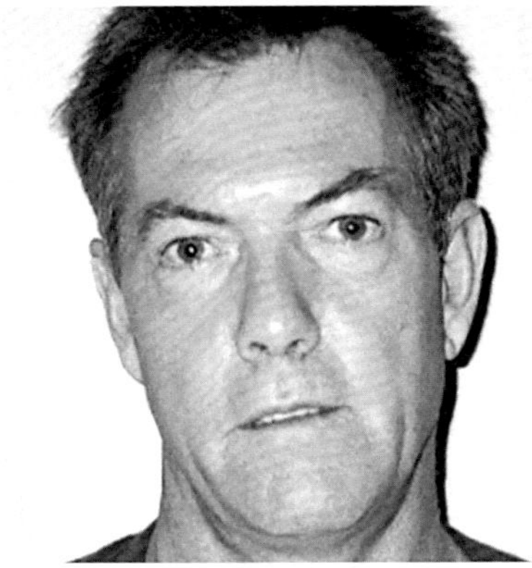

Russell Douglas Bateman: UK criminal and eastern suburbs drug trafficker. (Courtesy NSW Police)

Thomas McCaffrey: UK citizen, drug dealer and member of Bateman's crew. (Courtesy NSW Police)

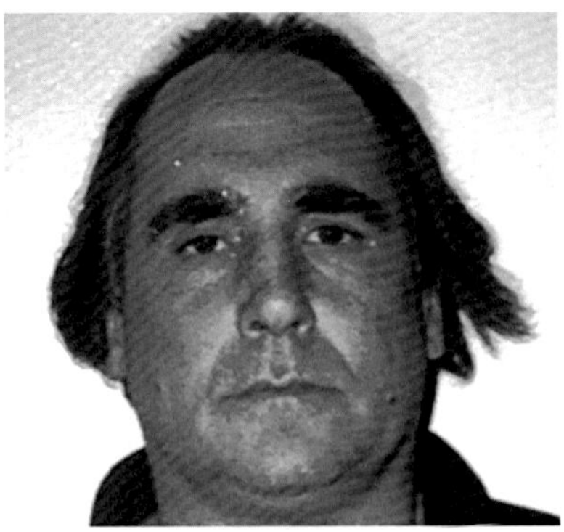

Jeffrey Allan Martin, a US sex offender who assumed Russell Bateman's name and was charged and jailed in Sydney as Bateman. (Courtesy NSW Police)

Maximiliano Diez: Colombian citizen, drug importer and trafficker, and member of Bateman's crew. (Courtesy NSW Police)

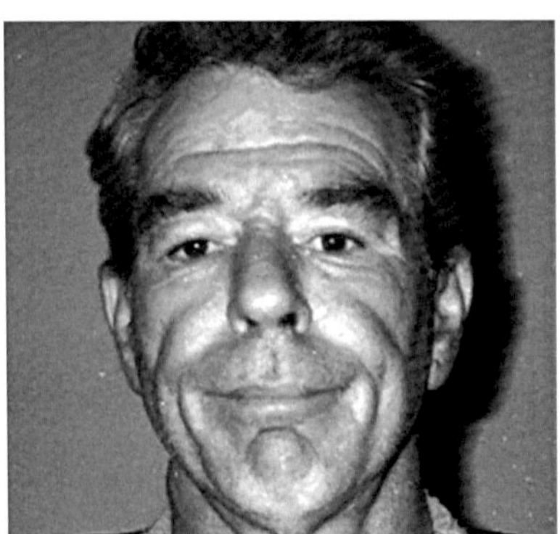

Sir Thomas Fry, a fraudster, met Bateman in jail and became a member of his crew. 'Sir' is his first name, not a title. (Courtesy NSW Police)

Part of the 500 kilograms of cocaine imported by Bateman in 1999. (Courtesy Australian Customs and Border Protection Service)

Australian Customs Service vessel *Holdfast Bay*, with Bateman's *Ngaire Wha* in tow, heading to Sydney from Patonga in 1999. (Courtesy Australian Customs and Border Protection Service)

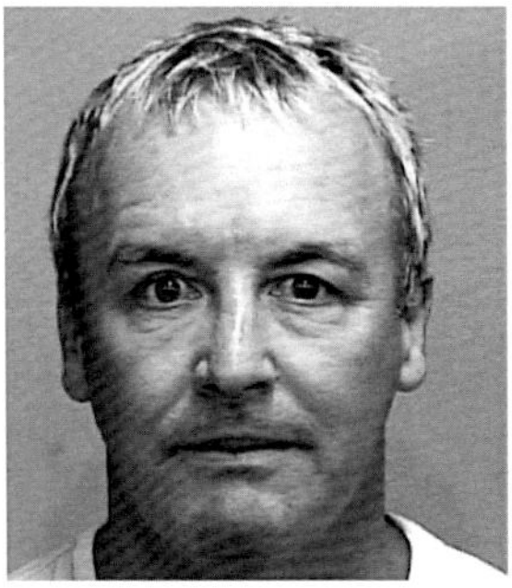

Ricky Montgomery, a prominent member of the East Coast Milieu, sold drugs for Hurley and set up his own gang. (Courtesy NSW Police)

Steven James, a long-time drug importer and friend of Montgomery, until he rolled over. (Courtesy NSW Police)

Hayden Rogers, another member of Montgomery's gang. (Courtesy NSW Police)

Bradley Evans was recruited by long-time friend Steven James to join Montgomery's gang. (Courtesy NSW Police)

Tony Hines, a violent standover man, drug trafficker and member of Maroubra's Bra Boys, supplied cocaine to Montgomery. (Courtesy NSW Police)

Wayne Robert Moore, a well-connected drug distributor in Sydney and Melbourne.

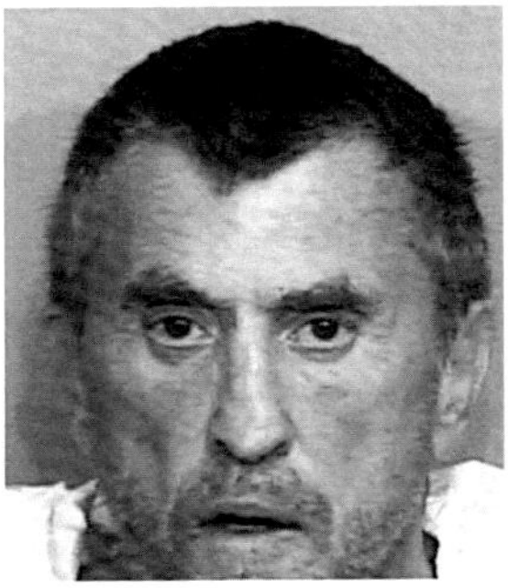

Frankie Ballis, member of Michael Hurley's mob and buyer of ecstasy imported by the Dutch syndicate. (Courtesy NSW Police)

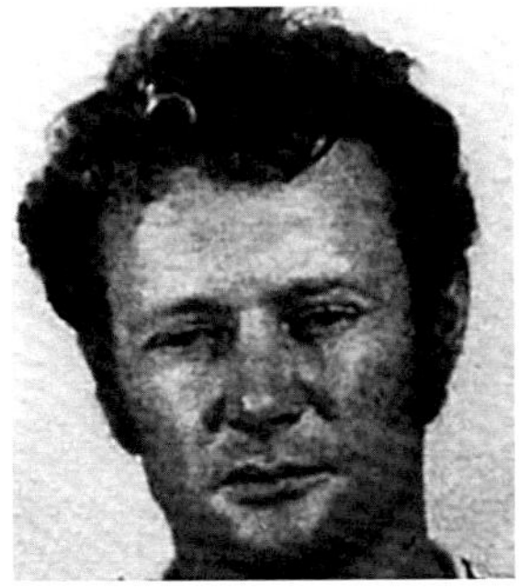

Neville Tween in the 1970s; a sex offender, Tween was also responsible for the murders of Trudie Adams and Ante Yelavich. (Courtesy NSW Police)

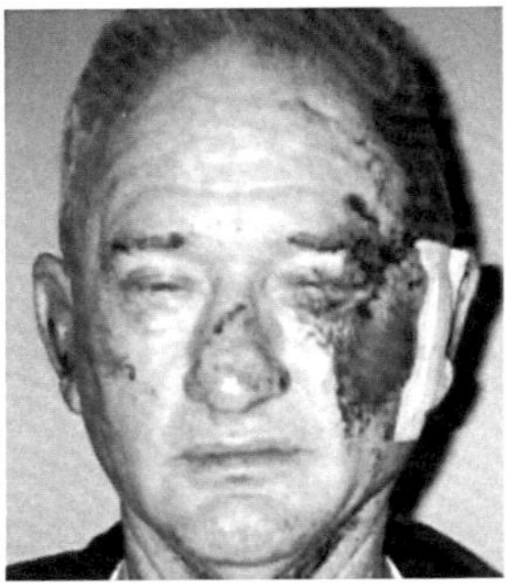

Raymond Johnson, Tween's long-time partner in sex crimes, drug trafficking, and property and other violent crimes. (Courtesy NSW Police)

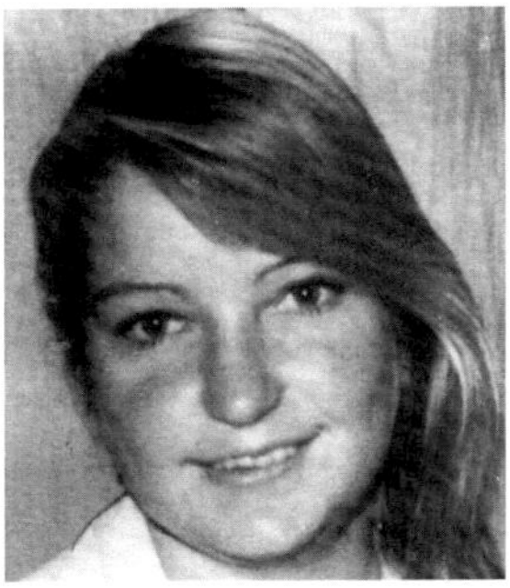

Trudie Adams, who was abducted and murdered on Sydney's northern beaches by Tween and Johnson in 1978. (Courtesy NSW Police)

Ante Yelavich, heroin importer and trafficker, last seen leaving his home in 1985 to meet with Tween at Manly. (Courtesy NSW Police)

Andrea Wharton, Yelavich's girlfriend. She went missing in 1984 while Yelavich was in jail, believed murdered by Tween.

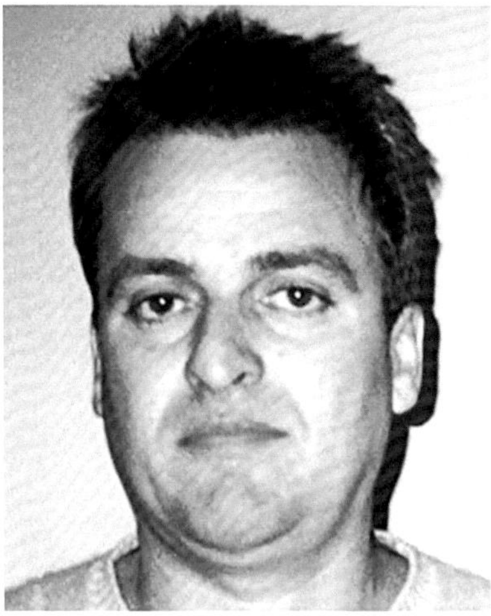

Paul Gunner: UK shoplifter, thief and drug importer with a long history in Sydney's East Coast Milieu. (Courtesy NSW Police)

Kyriakos Vassios: a Greek-Canadian and international drug importer who bought amphetamines and ecstasy from the Dutch syndicate. (Courtesy NSW Police)

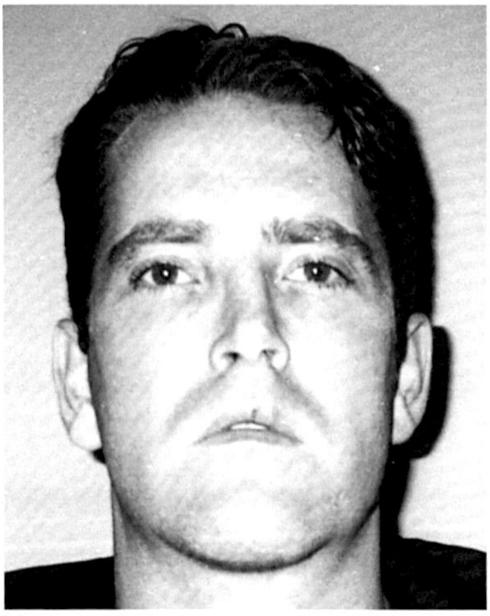

Darren Emanuel: UK criminal and drug importer. Arrested with Gunner in 2002 for supplying ecstasy. (Courtesy NSW Police)

Darren Leech: UK criminal and drug importer. Arrested along with Gunner and others in 2003 for supplying ecstasy. (Courtesy NSW Police)

New Zealand Customs recover the pod containing 18 kilograms of cocaine from the hull of MV *Tampa* in Auckland Harbour during Neville Tween's importation in June 2006. (Courtesy Australian Customs and Border Protection Service)

One of the bottles of cocaine retrieved from the pod attached to the ship's hull. (Courtesy Australian Customs and Border Protection Service)

The pod and some of the cocaine recovered by New Zealand Customs when MV *Taronga* berthed in Auckland Harbour in September 2006. (Courtesy Australian Customs and Border Protection Service)

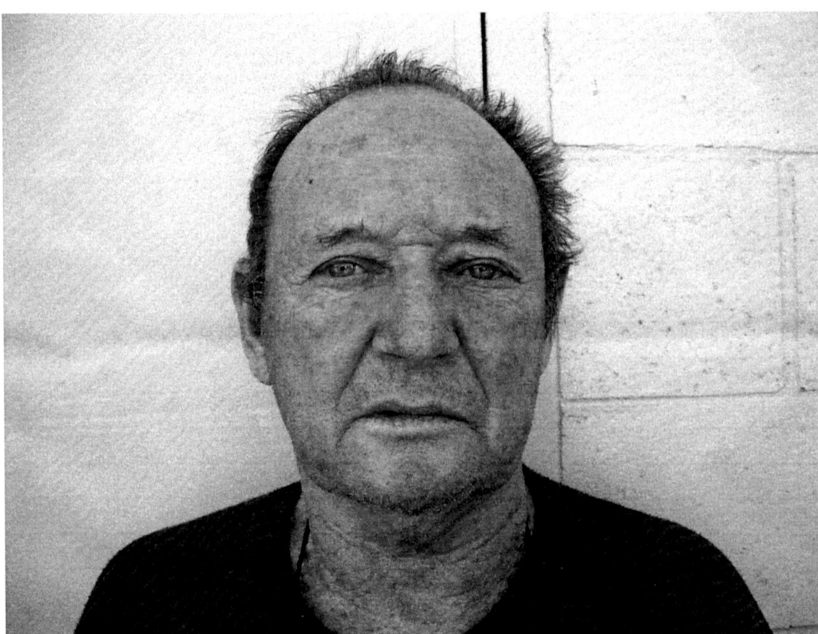

A much older Neville Tween following his arrest in 2006 for cocaine importation. (Courtesy NSW Police)

A Dutch surveillance photo. (Clockwise from top left) Loek Weerden, Fat Ron Haklander, Petrus Dekker, Thomas van den Berg and James Kinch leaving La Place restaurant in Almere, their usual meeting place during 2007–08.

Loek Weerden's company, Normi Land Systems, described itself as 'one of the leading suppliers and exporters of spare parts, equipment and complete assemblies of military battle tanks'.

The codenames used by Mark Standen, Bilal Jalalaty and James Kinch when doing business. (Courtesy *Four Corners*, ABC TV)

Standen and Jalalaty were under surveillance when meeting outside Platos Café in Sydney, near the Crime Commission.

The alleged May 2008 pseudoephedrine importation delivered to Jalalaty's warehouse was found to be rice.

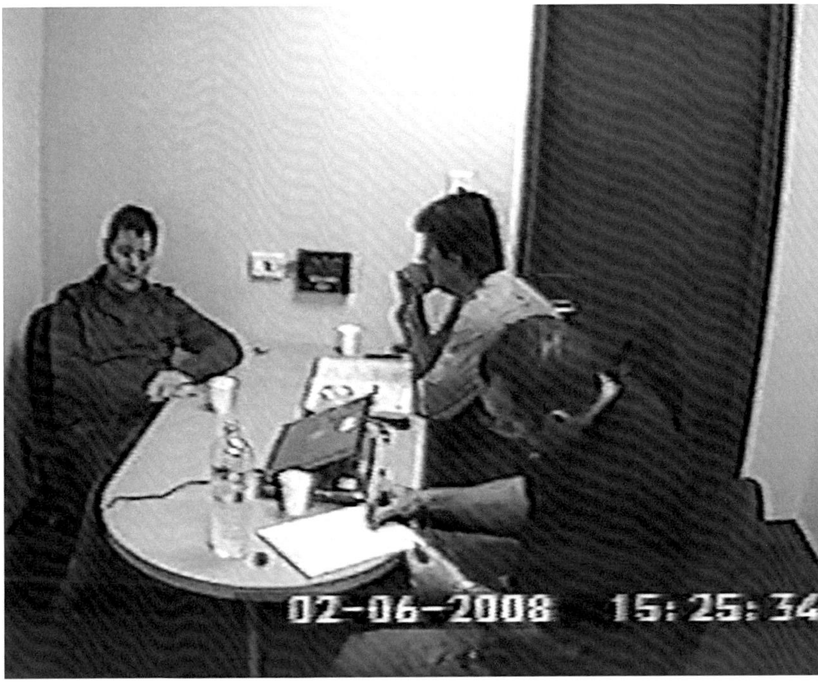

On 2 June 2008 Standen was arrested by AFP officers at the Crime Commission and taken to their Sydney HQ for a lengthy interview.

On the same day as Standen's arrest, Jalalaty was also arrested and interviewed by AFP officers before being charged.

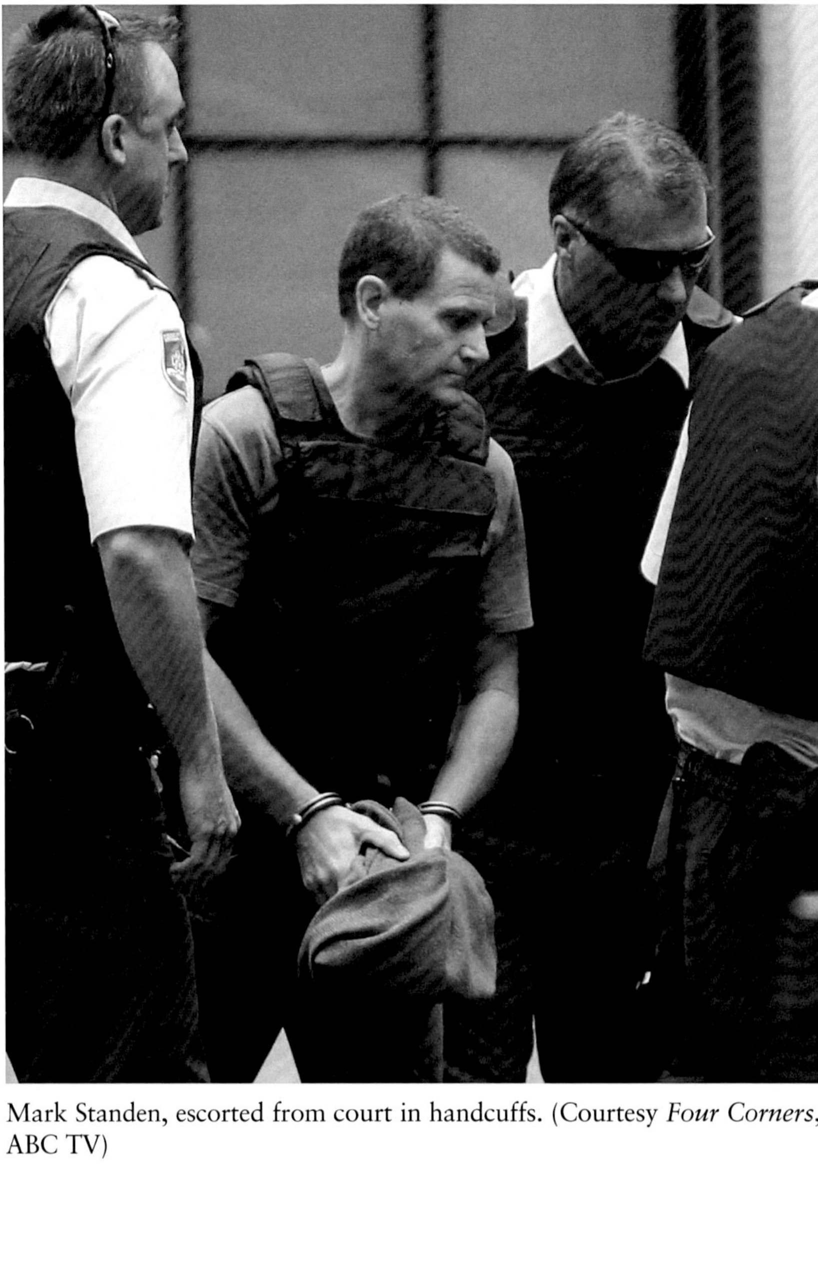

Mark Standen, escorted from court in handcuffs. (Courtesy *Four Corners*, ABC TV)

Arrested in Bangkok two days before Standen and Jalalaty, Kinch waited in a Bangkok jail for four years before being deported to Australia in 2012. On the fingers of his left hand can be seen the tattoo ACAB—'all coppers are bastards'. (Alamy)

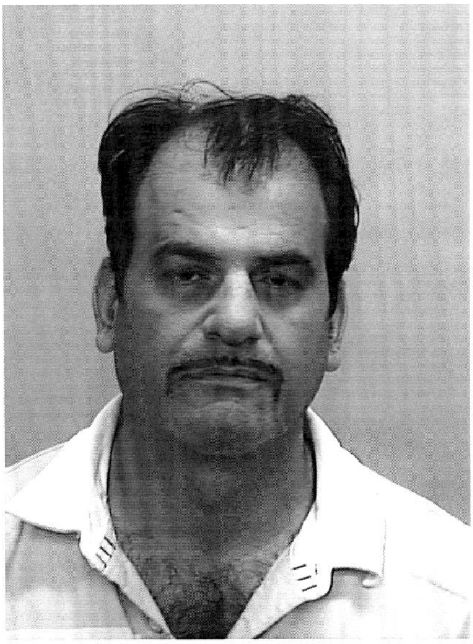

Bilal Jalalaty, after being charged by police.

AFP Deputy Commissioner Tony Negus (left), with NSW Crime Commission head Phillip Bradley (right), announce the arrest of Standen. (Fairfax)

Cees van Spierenburg, who led the prosecution of the Haklander-Weerden syndicates. (Courtesy *Four Corners*, ABC TV)

Jan Boersma, who ran the Dutch police investigation into the syndicates. (Courtesy *Four Corners*, ABC TV)

CHAPTER SIX

Painters, dockers and dealers

Keith Albert Collingburn and his wife migrated to Australia from England in the 1940s and settled in Melbourne. With his sons, Keith Albert and Neil Stanley, Collingburn senior established a reputation in Melbourne's underworld as a man to be feared and respected. But he would eventually be outshone by Keith junior (hereafter referred to as Collingburn).

Collingburn's first recorded encounter with Melbourne police occurred in 1951 when, at the age of ten, he was convicted of assault with intent to carnally know a girl between ten and sixteen years. A string of arrests and convictions followed, including numerous theft and housebreaking offences, false pretences and other fraud offences, assaults, armed robbery, firearms offences and breaches of probation.

In 1961 Collingburn and four other young men were charged with the murder of a man they had bashed in Flinders Street, Melbourne. At their first trial, the jury was discharged when a witness made a comment prejudicial to the defence; the second jury was discharged when a juror became ill. The third trial ended with all five being acquitted.

During the mid-1960s Collingburn's notoriety made it dangerous for him to remain in Melbourne; he is alleged to have fallen out with some police who suggested 'it would be in his interests to leave town'. Collingburn moved to Bondi in Sydney's eastern suburbs but he had no intention of going straight. In June 1967 he was arrested and charged with a payroll robbery of almost $6000 outside a bank at Bankstown in Sydney's south-west. Unfortunately for Collingburn and his unidentified associate, they had dropped the bag of cash in the street while making their getaway. Refused bail, Collingburn was also charged with presenting a false application for a passport. He was committed for trial on the robbery charge and sentenced to six months' jail over the false passport application. Collingburn appealed the jail sentence and in February 1968—eight months after his arrest—he was taken to the Quarter Sessions Appeals Court, Queen's Square, Sydney, where his application was listed for hearing. A few minutes before his case was to begin, Collingburn asked a constable to take him to the toilet. On the way, he bashed the constable and escaped from the building. How he did it remains a mystery.

Collingburn quickly lodged another false application for a passport which, this time, was granted. Leaving Australia for London, he joined some of his Sydney colleagues in the so-called Kangaroo Gang. For a decade and a half Collingburn, using false British passports, toured the UK and Europe shoplifting jewellery and other luxury items and holidaying in Spain, Portugal and the Netherlands. During this time Collingburn is believed to have been arrested and convicted of theft in a number of countries, his last conviction being in Paris in 1977. One of his regular shoplifting partners was Leo 'the Fibber' Callaghan, also known as Jack Warren and Patrick William Warren. The Fibber had been an ally of Sydney crime boss Lennie McPherson, and by the late 1970s was spending much of his time in the Philippines looking after McPherson's sex and gambling investments and acting as a middleman and 'Mr Fixit' for Australian drug importers and traffickers. The Fibber's help would prove invaluable to Collingburn as he established himself in the drug trade.

Collingburn had entered the British drug trade some years before, and in the early 1980s he and a number of his English colleagues were investigated by Scotland Yard over the importation of heroin in boxes of flowers from Bombay to London through the Kenyan capital of Nairobi and the Netherlands. By the mid-1980s Collingburn had £50,000 in the bank and a property worth around £100,000, and drove a Rolls-Royce and a Jaguar.

While Collingburn lived the high life in Europe, his family in Melbourne was not so fortunate. On 26 March 1971 his 28-year-old brother, Neil—a known standover man and a Painter and Docker who'd never set foot on a wharf—and two colleagues were arrested by Constables Carl Stillman and Max Gosney in the inner-Melbourne suburb of Carlton in possession of a set of golf clubs believed to be stolen property. On the way to the Russell Street Police Station there was an argument and Neil is alleged to have bashed Stillman. At the police station Neil allegedly went berserk and attacked Stillman again without provocation.

When Detective Sergeant Brian 'The Skull' Murphy went to Stillman's assistance, one of Neil's colleagues is said to have joined in the fight. The police claimed to have acted in self-defence, while Neil's companions insisted that Neil had been the victim of an unprovoked attack by the police and that he had been 'punched, kicked, jumped on, kneed and had his head rammed into steel lockers'.

Neil, although severely injured, told the duty officer that he was too scared to make a complaint. Taken to the nearby St Vincent's Hospital, he initially claimed to have fallen off a chair. After being told that his injuries were serious and that he would require an operation, Neil then declared that police had beaten him. He died two days later after surgery to repair a ruptured duodenum.

The case made headlines, with the media referring to the 'murder' of Neil. A hurried police investigation followed and ten days after Neil's death Murphy and Stillman were charged with his manslaughter and suspended without pay. In March 1972, after a three-week trial, a jury found Murphy and Stillman not guilty. Both were reinstated, although Murphy was put back in uniform.

A few years after Neil's death his widow, Rae, took up with Tommy Wraith, a drug dealer and hopeless heroin addict believed to have been responsible for the murder of two women, one in England and one in Melbourne. Wraith repeatedly beat Rae and threatened to kill her. She put up with it until one night in 1983. According to Adam Shand's book *King of the Thieves*:

> [Wraith] had been beating her as usual but she'd had enough this time. She had caught him off guard, creeping

> up behind him in the kitchen. It was too late when he realised. He had pulled his gun out but before he could shoot her, she had brought the axe down, taking his arm clean off at the elbow. Tommy looked with horror at the arm still holding the gun now lying on the floor. Then she raised the axe again and kept chopping at him until she made sure he was dead, before covering the body with a cloth 'so the kids wouldn't see'.

Rae was found not guilty of murder but guilty of manslaughter and sentenced to four years' jail.

■ ■ ■

While he was overseas, Collingburn stayed in touch with some of his criminal colleagues in Melbourne. One of these colleagues was Danny Corsetti, who in 1970 had been involved in a violent struggle for control of the Painters and Dockers. On one side of the battle was a group led by Pat Shannon, a twenty-year veteran of the docks whose wife was a primary school teacher. Behind the snappy dressing and personable exterior, Shannon was a hard man, politically 'left of the left', who surrounded himself with killers and the criminal elite of Melbourne. His team was known as the Blue Ticket. Shannon sanctioned the violence, which he saw as necessary for his survival. On the other side was a group led by Billy 'The Texan' Longley and known as the White Ticket. In the early 1960s Longley had been acquitted of attempting to murder his wife and, later, of murdering her. Longley's team included James Frederick Bazley, a violent criminal with a record for robbery and weapons possession who worked as a bouncer for an illegal casino. In 1986 Bazley was convicted of conspiring to murder the Griffith anti-drugs campaigner Donald Mackay and two members of the Mr Asia drug syndicate, Douglas and Isabel Wilson. Bazley was released from jail in 2001, aged 75.

In the lead-up to the 1970 union elections there were several violent clashes between the two groups. The ballot was scheduled for 10 December. On that day, five cars arrived at the ballot hall carrying members of Shannon's Blue Ticket, including Corsetti and Melbourne underworld figure Charlie Wootton. A gunfight broke out, and Longley and his supporters retreated. The ballot boxes disappeared. When they reappeared a short time later, the boxes were stuffed with Blue Ticket votes. Shannon's team was declared the winner. Nobody thought to report the gunfight to the police.

A few days later 50 bullets were pumped into a car belonging to a friend of Corsetti. Shannon had won the battle, but the war was just beginning. It ended three years later with Shannon's murder. In 1975 Longley was sentenced to life in jail for ordering the murder. He served thirteen years before being released.

In 1973 Corsetti and six other men were convicted for their role in the robbery, three years earlier, of Melbourne's Metropolitan Security Services depot. Nearly $300,000 had been seized by armed bandits dressed in stolen police uniforms. Corsetti and four others were convicted of the robbery, one man was found guilty of receiving money stolen during the robbery and a seventh person was found guilty of being an accessory after the fact. Corsetti was jailed for nine and a half years and the others for lesser terms. It was their fifth trial. The first had been aborted after a juror was approached to influence the verdict; the second broke down when one of the accused failed to appear; the third trial collapsed when a juror 'ran away from the court' after being empanelled (he was later charged and fined $1500); and the fourth, which lasted 50 days, was abandoned after the jury failed to agree.

After serving his sentence Corsetti formed a partnership with the Melbourne-based Calabrian godfather Giuseppe Cua to import hashish. Until 1982 Cua had concentrated on cultivating large-scale cannabis crops in Victoria and Queensland. Corsetti's role is believed to have consisted of bribing Victorian police while the Painters and Dockers took care of things on the wharves. The first importation was abandoned when a tip-off revealed that Customs had the container under surveillance. Further importations were planned and several are believed to have been successful. Some of the hash was supplied by Corsetti's old mate Collingburn (in the mid-1980s the pair was investigated in both Australia and the UK by the NCA over their involvement in the drug trade). But the risks remained high and by 1985 Cua had returned to cultivating cannabis.

Unlike Corsetti, Wootton was determined to keep a low profile, as he had done for most of his life. A rare light was shone on his criminal activities by the Royal Commission on the Activities of the Federated Ship Painters and Dockers Union, otherwise known as the Costigan Commission. Established in 1980 and headed by Frank Costigan, QC, the commission lasted for four years. In it, Wootton was described as one of the faceless men behind the docks who took a cut from the wharves and controlled illegal gambling in Melbourne; a multimillionaire with investments in trotting and drugs. In 1983 Wootton was named in a Commonwealth–New South Wales Joint Task Force on

Drug Trafficking as an associate of John Doyle, the Hong Kong-based employee of the Nugan Hand Bank and drug partner of Murray Riley, the ex-New South Wales policeman jailed in 1978 over a $40 million drug importation.

The Costigan commission found that 'Every member of the 1978–1981 executive of the Victoria Branch of the Union had been convicted at some time of a criminal offence'. The union's eleven officials had more than 250 criminal convictions while eight out of ten union members had criminal records. Fifteen murders and 23 attempted killings during the 1970s were attributed to the union's activities. Costigan noted that 'Large-scale theft on the wharves is endemic. Yet less than 5% is reported to the police, and then only some days or weeks after it has occurred. The rate of solution of those reported is miniscule.' In addition there was 'a large number of major armed robberies'. The prospect of these crimes being solved, Costigan wrote, was no more than a 'remote possibility'. The union, at least in Victoria, was 'an organised criminal group' that 'treat[s] the law with contempt'. He concluded: 'With such a history of violence, murder and maiming, there can be little doubt that this union in Victoria is regarded with considerable fear.' Collingburn's criminal interests were a natural fit with those of the Painters and Dockers but his circle went beyond the corrupt waterfront union.

■ ■ ■

In 1966 the Fibber's son, eighteen-year-old Barry, already an accomplished shoplifter, had accompanied his father to England. For a decade the Fibber and Barry were active members of the Kangaroo Gang, but by the mid-1970s both had turned their attention to the drug trade.

A heroin addict, Barry moved to Bangkok, Thailand, where he was involved in importations to Australia. Talk of Barry's Australian drug connections (which consisted mainly of his father) reached Phil Sparrowhawk, an English cannabis trafficker based in Thailand, who in 1981 offered Barry a load of 4 tonnes of cannabis that had unexpectedly become available. In his book, *Grass*, Sparrowhawk describes how Barry successfully imported the shipment into Australia. (Sparrowhawk claims to have made $2 million on the deal.) Almost immediately Barry agreed to another importation, this time of 500 kilograms of Kashmir hash, but before it could happen Barry died in a Bangkok hotel of a heroin overdose.

After his son's death, the Fibber visited Sparrowhawk in Bangkok. Both saw the benefits of further cooperation. Taking Sparrowhawk to Manila, the Fibber introduced him to a new client, 'Joe Smith'. 'Smith' was Lawrie McLean. Over the next few years McLean and Sparrowhawk would import several shipments to Australia.

Sparrowhawk wasn't the only partner McLean was introduced to by the Fibber. Another was Collingburn. The pair had a lot in common. Both started out as Melbourne criminals before moving to Sydney and eventually leaving Australia as wanted men; both had spent some lucrative years with the Kangaroo Gang; and both were now international drug traffickers (Collingburn had links with a Dutch–US–Canadian drug syndicate) with strong underworld credentials.

While Collingburn was not averse to dealing directly with Sparrowhawk and McLean, his preferred partner was the Fibber, who obtained his own supplies from the same pair. In 1986 Collingburn returned to Australia and joined several of his old mates, the Fibber among them, at a luxury apartment on the Gold Coast.

The next year an investigation by the NCA and the AFP into the Fibber and several of his drug associates collapsed after a tip-off from corrupt Queensland police caused $8 million in cash to vanish through a firm of Queensland solicitors and a Gold Coast bank to accounts in London, Bangkok and Washington. It was Collingburn who masterminded the transfer of the cash before he too 'disappeared' back to the UK. Damaging as the tip-off was, the NCA was close to making arrests when, in the words of journalist John Silvester, 'internal squabbling caused the investigation to slowly fall apart'. The drug importations continued.

■ ■ ■

In 1996 a yacht named *Sea Mist* was forced to dock at Cork, Ireland, after it was blown off course during a freak storm. Searched by Customs, it was found to have 599 kilograms of cocaine worth an estimated £80 million hidden on board. The boat's skipper, an American named John Ewart, was arrested and jailed for seventeen years. While the rest of the crew was acquitted, it was to be the beginning of the end for an international drug ring with interests in Ireland, the Caribbean, the United States, Mexico, Venezuela, Australia, France, South Africa, Switzerland, Spain and Cyprus. Over almost a decade the syndicate carried out at least another five importations to the UK worth more than £230 million.

In February 1999, 472 kilograms of cocaine imported by the syndicate was seized from a lockup garage in Leigh-on-Sea, Essex, and from a farm in Laleham, Surrey. Several arrests followed, but the ringleader, 52-year-old Irish-born

Brian Wright—known as 'the Milkman' because he always delivered—and two other gang members escaped. In 2005 Wright, who is believed to have entered the drug trade during the 1970s, was finally arrested in Spain. By 2007, eight years after the first arrests, nineteen members of the gang had been jailed for terms ranging from two to 30 years. Wright, who received the longest sentence, was described as 'a gambling-mad drug baron' whose syndicate was one of the most successful ever to target Britain.

Among the conspirators who escaped arrest was Collingburn. The yacht *Moonstreak*, which carried out cocaine importations into Britain in 1997 and 1998 worth a total of at least £80 million, had been owned by Collingburn before being 'sold' just before the first importation. British police believed the sale was a sham to enable Collingburn to distance himself from the vessel's real purpose.

Around the same time, Collingburn's name came up in an investigation by the US DEA into an international syndicate that had been smuggling multi-tonne shipments of cannabis to the UK, Australia, the US and Canada since the early 1980s. One of its leaders was the naturalised US citizen David Kulik (see Chapter 1). Once again, Collingburn was able to avoid arrest, but pressure from British police and immigration authorities was making life in the UK difficult for him. For a short time Collingburn moved to Curaçao, one of the five islands making up the Netherlands Antilles, off the north coast of South America. (In 2010 Curaçao became an autonomous country within the Kingdom of the Netherlands.) His Caribbean idyll came to an abrupt end after a local man was arrested with 5 kilograms of cocaine. The address he gave led the police straight to Collingburn, who quickly left the island. In early 1999 Collingburn moved to Australia—although there is no record of him entering the country—and joined the Fibber and other criminal colleagues from the Kangaroo Gang and the drug trade on the Gold Coast. Before long Collingburn approached a man in the foyer of the highrise apartment building in Surfers Paradise where he was staying. 'I'm Keith Collingburn', he said. 'You're Jack Sparrow, aren't you?' Although the pair had never met, Collingburn and 73-year-old John Victor 'Jack' Sparrow knew each other by reputation. It was the Fibber who had engineered the meeting.

During the following weeks, Sparrow and Collingburn met almost every day. Sparrow's criminal record, unlike Collingburn's, was mostly for relatively minor offences, beginning in 1939 with a conviction for break, enter and steal. This was followed by occasional convictions in Melbourne and Sydney for gambling and receiving stolen property. After the early 1960s there was a twenty-year lull before more convictions for gambling and possessing an unlicensed pistol. Not all Sparrow's problems were with the law. In 1961 the Australian Jockey Club Committee had banned all horses owned by Sparrow from racing. Eleven years later Sparrow was declared bankrupt.

The lifetime he had spent around racetracks had introduced Sparrow to some colourful people. One of these was an Irishman named Richard Kennedy. Born in Dublin, Kennedy had migrated to Australia in 1963 but retained his Irish citizenship after being granted permanent residency. He had an agricultural machinery business in Sydney. Kennedy had known Sparrow for around a decade through their common interest in the races and the pair would often catch up 'for a coffee' when Sparrow was down from Surfers Paradise. In May 1999 Sparrow rang Kennedy and asked him to come to the Gold Coast, where he introduced him to Collingburn. According to evidence later given in court by the AFP, the meeting marked the start of a drug conspiracy. Sparrow's role was to introduce a number of willing participants to Collingburn, who ran the operation. The initial conversation, as Kennedy remembered it, went like this:

> Collingburn: 'I have connections in Europe and South America and we can supply the market here at various times with speed, ecstasy, hash and coke. However, we need someone who can bring the stuff into Australia for us on an ongoing basis. Would you be interested in helping out?'
>
> Kennedy: 'I do business in Europe, but I have no business links to South America.'
>
> Collingburn: 'Well you might be able to help us in moving our stuff from Europe to Australia. What quantities could you handle?'
>
> Kennedy: 'That would depend, hash is bulky and would be difficult to move so I guess powder or tablets would take up less room and be easier to move. I would need more information and time to think about it.'
>
> Collingburn: 'Okay, but we need to know as soon as possible.'

Before his meeting with Collingburn, Kennedy had put his long-time colleague, 60-year-old Thomas Thompson, on notice that there might be a 'job' for them and arranged to meet him at Jupiter's Casino after speaking with Collingburn.

Thompson was born in Scotland and, like Kennedy, had kept his British citizenship after migrating to Australia in 1967. He ran a company selling farm equipment in the Brisbane suburb of Darra. As colleagues in the agricultural business, the two men regularly travelled overseas together, visiting exhibitions in Europe and the United States. This would provide valuable cover for the importation. At the casino Kennedy told Thompson about the proposal and he 'agreed to assist'. Thompson confirmed Kennedy's account of their conversation, adding, 'I don't recall being told how much I would be paid for participating, but I believe mention was made of needing expense money if I was to participate.' Later, Thompson was given $50,000 to cover the costs of arranging the importation. Like Kennedy, Thompson had known Sparrow for about ten years, but had met him only occasionally.

Over the next couple of weeks Kennedy and Thompson discussed possible methods of importation. According to Kennedy, 'the idea of using . . . hydraulic rams as a means of concealing narcotics was conceived. We chose this method because the circumstances as we knew them . . . seemed to suit this method. . . . [We] had a conversation about the rams needing modification to increase their internal capacity [to secrete the drugs] . . . it was agreed that Thompson would have the modifications made.'

In September 1999 Collingburn and Kennedy left Australia separately for the UK. From there they travelled to a rendezvous in Amsterdam. After making some inquiries about the size of the importation, Kennedy returned to Sydney. A month later Kennedy left Sydney again, supposedly to spend ten days in the UK, but really to meet Collingburn in Amsterdam. By now a number of hydraulic rams had been modified to allow the drugs to be hidden inside. Thompson arranged for 38 of the rams to be sent to a firm in Coventry in the English West Midlands to await collection by him. Leaving Australia a week after Kennedy, Thompson flew to London. After collecting the hydraulic rams in Coventry, he loaded them into a van which he then drove to Amsterdam. He was met by Kennedy, who took him back to a house where they waited for Collingburn.

According to Kennedy, Collingburn arrived at the house later that day with seven or eight 'soft-sided sports and travel-type bags of different sizes and styles.' Kennedy asked Collingburn 'How much is here?', only to be told 'I'm not sure myself.'

The answer didn't satisfy Kennedy. 'What if there is a shortfall later on?' he asked. 'I can't be responsible if I don't know what's here.'

'Don't worry,' Collingburn replied nonchalantly. 'I trust you.'

Kennedy and Thompson then got to work packing the drugs into the hidden compartments in the hydraulic rams.

Collingburn and Kennedy returned to Australia, leaving Thompson to finalise arrangements for importing the hydraulic rams into Australia. The consignment was shown as having originated in the UK.

During the first week of November, AFP surveillance teams watched meetings between Collingburn and two alleged fellow conspirators, 51-year-old Edward Michael Monahan and 39-year-old David Peter Cain, at a golf club on the Gold Coast. A few weeks later Sparrow rang Kennedy and asked him to return the unspent portion of the $50,000 he had been given. Over the following days Kennedy made a series of cash deposits into Sparrow's bank account totalling $15,000.

By now Cain was in Spain. In an intercepted telephone conversation with Monahan, Cain spoke about money they owed to their Spanish co-conspirators—apparently from a previous drug importation. 'I promised them two hundred [thousand] now I'm down two hundred and twenty-five,' Cain said, explaining that he was 'terrified' of the violence that might result from not paying. He went on: 'How's Silver [Collingburn] going because I gotta, I gotta, if I don't dig up a hundred and twenty-five that house has to go to auction.'

'Now listen,' said Monahan, trying to calm him down, 'we're still gunna be all right out of it.'

On 27 November 1999 the vessel *Nedlloyd Kobe* sailed from the Dutch port of Rotterdam with its container load of hydraulic rams stuffed with drugs. In Singapore the container was transferred to the *Haruna Maru*, which was to go on to Brisbane. The alleged conspirators continued to meet, both in Sydney and on the Gold Coast. There was talk about a 'Christmas party'—a reference to collecting the drugs. After the ship docked on 29 December Collingburn spoke to Cain and Monahan about a $100,000 'introduction fee' for Sparrow. (Sparrow later claimed that he first heard of the intended 'gift' during the court proceedings.)

In early January 2000 the container was unloaded from the ship, but the AFP and Customs Service were waiting. Customs found the drugs, removing most of them, and replacing them with substitute powders and tablets. The consignment was now under 24-hour AFP surveillance.

On 7 January the container was delivered to Thompson's warehouse in Darra, where it was unloaded and the hydraulic rams transferred to a rental van. Thompson called Kennedy and told him he would be driving to Sydney in the morning. The next afternoon, around 5 p.m., Thompson arrived at Kennedy's factory in Enfield, where the van and its cargo were secured for the night.

On the morning of Sunday 9 January Kennedy and Thompson began unloading their cargo. Unscrewing the collar at one end of one of the hydraulic rams, Kennedy saw what he believed to be the drugs hidden inside. He picked up the ram and poured the contents onto the factory floor. Realising straight away that this was not the substance he and Thompson had packed in Amsterdam, he tipped out the contents of another ram. Thompson tasted the white powder; it was sugar. Thompson opened another hydraulic ram. This one contained tablets, not powder, but the 'tablets [were] significantly larger than those I had placed into it.'

Had they been ripped off by the Dutch supplier or was it a police sting?

Locking the factory, Kennedy and Thompson fled but were quickly intercepted by AFP officers, arrested and taken to AFP headquarters in Sydney. A search of Kennedy's factory uncovered 4.5 kilograms of ecstasy tablets, a number of hydraulic rams containing narcotic-like material substituted by the AFP in place of the real drugs and almost $260,000 in cash. At Kennedy's city apartment police found nearly 4.4 kilograms of ecstasy tablets, presumably from a previous importation, while a search of Thompson's warehouse in Darra found $90,000 in cash and documents relating to the importation of the drugs. Confronted by the evidence, the two men agreed to roll on their co-conspirators.

Meanwhile, Collingburn and Monahan had driven overnight from the Gold Coast, arriving in Sydney mid-morning and booking into the Novotel Hotel in Brighton-Le-Sands in southern Sydney. Under police supervision Kennedy rang Collingburn from a public phone. They arranged to meet that evening at the Sheraton on the Park Hotel in the city. At the meeting Kennedy asked Collingburn, 'What time do you want to do this tomorrow?'

'Let's make it here at 2 p.m.,' Collingburn replied. 'Are you okay for money at this stage?'

Kennedy said that Thompson would 'call you about that in a couple of days' and then asked, 'Have you spoken to Jack [Sparrow]?'

'Yes,' said Collingburn. 'He's okay. But he talks too much on the bloody phone.'

Monahan lurked nearby but was careful not to approach. The conspirators left the hotel separately and Kennedy returned to AFP headquarters.

The next morning Monahan was arrested by the AFP near his home in Kensington, in Sydney's east. In the house police found 129 ecstasy tablets, scales, an electronic money counter, several mobile telephones in false names, two fake Queensland driver's licences and materials for the manufacture of amphetamines.

At 2 p.m. Kennedy drove to the Sheraton and parked outside the entrance. As he waited by his car Collingburn emerged from the lobby. The two men spoke briefly. As Collingburn went back into the hotel, Kennedy took three large blue bags from the boot of his car. Moments later, Collingburn returned. Kennedy asked, 'Have you got a car?'

'Someone's bringing it,' said Collingburn. 'Someone' was 39-year-old David Peter Cain.

Kennedy was eager to be gone. After giving him a business card with a new telephone number, Collingburn picked up the three bags Kennedy had taken from the boot and put them on the footpath to wait for the car. The Sheraton on the Park is a busy hotel and the constant movement of luggage, together with the pedestrian traffic on Elizabeth Street, made the handover less conspicuous.

Soon afterwards, Cain was arrested by the AFP as he drove into the World Square car park in Goulburn Street, Sydney. In his car were the three bags of narcotic substitutes. Electronic scales, mobile telephones in false names and gemstones were discovered in his Botany home. Collingburn and another man, 46-year-old Rowan Scott Edwards, were arrested near the World Square car park. A search of Collingburn's Gold Coast apartment uncovered documents related to a hotel in Amsterdam. Sparrow was arrested on the Gold Coast and returned to New South Wales.

All seven were charged with offences relating to the importation of 7 kilograms of cocaine worth an estimated $3.5 million; 9 kilograms of ecstasy powder worth an estimated $3.4 million and 66 kilograms of ecstasy tablets worth an estimated $11.2 million.

The trials did not go as the AFP had hoped. In 2002 the charge against Sparrow of conspiring to import drugs was dropped by the Commonwealth Director of Public Prosecutions. Collingburn was acquitted at trial of two charges of conspiring to import drugs. Cain was acquitted of aiding and abetting the importation of drugs. Edwards was acquitted of having goods in his custody suspected of being stolen or otherwise unlawfully obtained. Charges against Monahan of taking part in the supply of drugs and possessing drugs were dropped. Monahan pleaded guilty to two charges of opening an account with a cash dealer in a false name. On each charge he was given a suspended jail sentence on entering into a three-year good behaviour bond. Monahan's criminal record went back to the 1980s and included fraud, theft, burglary and drug charges for which he received a four-year jail sentence. Thompson and Kennedy each pleaded guilty to two charges of aiding and abetting the importation of drugs and were jailed for five years and seven years and six months respectively.

This was not the first time Kennedy had been sentenced to jail for importing drugs. On 20 May 1978 he and 35-year-old Dennis John Carter were arrested in Sydney Airport trying to smuggle 10 kilograms of heroin, with an estimated street value of more than $5 million, inside luggage from Kuala Lumpur. Forty-three-year-old Keith Arnold Wilson—described as 'the manager of the Malaysia operation'—was arrested when he returned to Sydney. The court was told that the importation 'probably would have been successful if it had not been for a dog which sniffed out the heroin'. (It was one of the first large importations detected by sniffer dogs.) Kennedy, Carter and Wilson were sentenced to jail terms of twenty years, six years and fourteen years respectively.

Sources with some knowledge of the 1999–2000 importation claim Collingburn had planned to import only ecstasy tablets and powder. The cocaine belonged to Kennedy and Thompson, who had secretly negotiated with another syndicate to add it to the consignment.

In 2003 Collingburn's old partner in crime Danny Corsetti, then 72, was jailed in Melbourne for four years over his role in a cannabis distribution network that extended from Adelaide to Sydney. In sentencing Corsetti, the judge described him as being the 'prime mover' in a conspiracy to transport 111 kilograms of cannabis hidden in the legitimate cargo of two trucks to Sydney. 'You had contact with all the co-conspirators . . . telephone intercepts demonstrate that you are the man who gives direction to others,' the judge said. Four other conspirators were also jailed.

That same year, the Fibber died of cancer. Sparrow delivered one of the eulogies at his funeral on the Gold Coast. Despite the millions of dollars he had earned during his life of crime, particularly once he became involved in the drug trade, the Fibber died broke. Four years later Sparrow spoke at Michael Hurley's funeral. Hurley had spent his last days under police guard in the Prince of Wales Hospital in Sydney's eastern suburbs. He had been arrested a year earlier over the importation of 10 kilograms of cocaine from South America and had been awaiting his trial when he died of cancer. In 2010 Stan 'The Man' Smith who, with Lennie McPherson and George Freeman, had ruled Sydney's underworld, died at his home. Speaking at his funeral, Sparrow described Smith as 'one of the finest human beings I have had the privilege of being able to call my friend.'

The next year Sparrow celebrated his 88th birthday at Limoncello in Double Bay. Formerly known as Eliza's, the restaurant had for decades been the favoured haunt of some of Sydney's most notorious gangsters. Among the guests who had come to wish Sparrow a happy birthday was Thomas Anthony 'Tony' Vincent, a key figure in the Kings Cross underworld during the 1970s and 1980s. In 2004 police had raided his club, Lady Jane's, variously described as a restaurant, gentlemen's club, strip joint and sex club, and arrested Vincent on charges of supplying cocaine. Twelve months later he and ten others were charged with an international $150 million superannuation fraud. The fraud had been quickly spotted and all but $3 million had been recovered. In February 2007 Vincent was sentenced to ten years' jail for supplying drugs. Later he was sentenced to three years' jail after pleading guilty to a lesser charge relating to the superannuation fraud. He was released in

2010. David Freeman, the son of the late George Freeman, was also present at the birthday celebrations, as was Bruce Hardin, who had operated an illegal gambling club under Freeman's protection during the 1970s and early 1980s, but was now running a pole-dancing bar.

■ ■ ■

Collingburn never faced trial for the Bankstown armed robbery that was still outstanding at the time of his escape in 1968 from Sydney's Quarter Sessions Appeals Court, nor did he serve the six months' jail he had been sentenced to over the false passport application. He was never charged with escaping from the court or assaulting the police officer in order to escape. The cases were too old, witnesses had died and other evidence had long since been destroyed.

Collingburn had been broke when he returned to Australia in early 1999, having squandered millions of dollars in drug profits through his extravagant lifestyle and his (and his partner's) heavy addiction to cocaine. His plan was to rebuild his fortune away from the gaze of the British police. But Collingburn's addiction made him careless—a dangerous characteristic in an international drug trafficker. A fortnight after his acquittal, Collingburn met some old mates for a low-key farewell lunch in Sydney's eastern suburbs. He returned to the Gold Coast for a short time before leaving Australia for Europe. Collingburn was active for some years in the Dutch drug trade before dying 'peacefully' in September 2016.

CHAPTER SEVEN

Vaso Ulic and the Balkan network

One of the major players in Sydney's Balkan drug network was Vaso (also known as Vasa) Ulic. Ulic was born in Titograd in the Federal Republic of Yugoslavia (now Podgorica, the capital of Montenegro). He migrated to Australia in 1979 at the age of 20, lived in Sydney's western suburbs and became an Australian citizen in 1989. By that time Ulic was well established in Sydney's drug trade and was a familiar figure in Kings Cross.

On 7 September 1990 Ulic and Arben 'Benny' Puta were arrested by an undercover cop and a police informant codenamed 'Franko' in a 'buy-bust' heroin sting. The sting had begun at a motel in Bondi and, after a series of anti-surveillance measures, ended in Wentworthville in the western suburbs. The undercover cop and Franko were to pay Puta $2000 for about 57 grams of heroin, which they had bought previously from him, and $118,000 for heroin they were to buy that night. As they were about to close the deal, Ulic and Puta told them that they could only supply 226 grams of heroin—half of what was promised—but that the rest would be available the next day. Sixty-five thousand dollars was handed over in exchange for the 226 grams, which had a street value of $432,000. Ulic and Puta were arrested and charged. Puta was a well-known drug trafficker who was on bail at the time for a 1989 murder (he was acquitted of the charge in 1992) and who was found by the Wood Royal Commission to have paid corrupt police to 'green light' his heroin network, particularly in Kings Cross.

On bail, Ulic and Puta resumed and expanded their sale of heroin and other drugs. In March 1992, seeking to protect his drug activities from unwanted police attention, Ulic went to meet a detective who could help. He was accompanied to the meeting by Puta's associate Hedegko 'Ned' Pikic (also known as Nedjelko 'Ned' Bikic), a major drug trafficker in Kings Cross and Sydney's western suburbs. Three years later, the detective rolled over to the Wood Royal Commission and was given the pseudonym WS14. Describing his meeting with Ulic, WS14 said: 'Vaso wanted us [WS14 and a colleague] to drop off, leave him alone, stop following him, working on him, and we were given a TAB ticket; it was a trifecta ticket . . . It was worth about $3000 . . . Ned Pikic actually gave us the trifecta ticket.' WS14 said that the two detectives accepted the ticket on the understanding that they would stop investigating Ulic. The ticket was cashed and split between WS14, his colleague and a former detective who had facilitated the meeting.

Fifteen months later, on the morning of 18 June 1993, Europa Sio, a 32-year-old bouncer, was shot in the men's toilets at JJ's nightclub in Darlinghurst Road, opposite the Kings Cross police station. Ulic and Pikic had gone to the nightclub around 6 a.m. that morning. Two hours later Ulic and Sio argued over an outstanding debt owed by Ulic. (It was said to be either a gambling or drug debt.) The argument continued on the footpath outside the nightclub, where Sio pushed Ulic onto the bonnet of a parked car, saying, 'You bastard, you owe me $6900.' Ulic was heard to reply, 'Yes, I will pay. Leave me alone.' With that, Sio let Ulic go, walked back into the nightclub, picked up his bag and left. Ulic rejoined Pikic in the nightclub and denied owing Sio the money.

About half an hour later Sio returned to the nightclub and sat down at the table next to Pikic and Ulic. Sio and Pikic went to the bar where they had a conversation before entering the men's toilets, where Ulic was waiting. The barman heard what sounded like a firecracker going off and turned to see Pikic and Ulic standing in the doorway. Ulic was holding a pistol in his right hand and, after firing another shot, he turned and pointed it at the barman's head, saying, 'I'll shoot you, you saw nothing. Say nothing or I'll come back and shoot you too.' Pikic and Ulic ran from the nightclub. Sio had been shot twice with a .25 calibre handgun and died later that day.

At the Wood Royal Commission, WS14 explained what happened as the police searched for Ulic. He had heard that Ulic was planning to leave the country with more than $200,000 in cash. He discussed this with two other detectives and it was decided that 'We were going to try and intercept him . . . we were going to steal the money . . . we followed him, followed him all the way down to . . . Rockdale . . . because we thought he might have been, you know, [going to] pick the money up somewhere along the line, but it looked like he was just going straight to the airport, so we stopped him . . . He didn't have that money.' WS14 said that he and one of the other detectives held Ulic while WS14 'threatened to push him over onto the railway line, you know, to reveal where the money was'. Ulic refused to say and eventually the detectives gave up and 'sort of brushed him off and sent him on his way to the airport' where he boarded a plane and left the country, despite being wanted for murder.

Pikic was charged with the murder of Sio, but the charges were withdrawn in August 1993.

On 22 February 1991 Ulic and Puta had been committed for trial to the New South Wales District Court for supplying heroin. The following year Puta pleaded guilty to five charges of supplying heroin. He was sentenced to a total of seven years' imprisonment.

In mid-1995 an application for Ulic's arrest and extradition was made to the Federal Republic of Germany. Ulic was arrested in Dusseldorf in possession of Belgian passports and driver's licences in the names of Mario Romeo and Daniel Do Jong. They revealed that since fleeing Australia he had visited the Netherlands, Italy, Belgium, Germany and Yugoslavia. Extradited from Germany, Ulic appeared at the Central Local Court in Sydney on 5 December 1995 on the murder and drug charges. Seven months later, after a number of adjournments, the New South Wales Director of Public Prosecutions dropped the charges and costs were awarded against the police. The earlier corruption had damaged the prosecution in both the murder and drug charges.

Back on the streets, Ulic was soon selling drugs again. After meeting 22-year-old Fabian Quaid and a number of his associates in Perth in the late 1990s, Ulic expanded his business in Western Australia. Quaid quickly came to be a central player in Ulic's criminal activities and saw Ulic as a father figure. Born in India of Persian descent, Quaid had moved to Australia with his family when he was six. He represented Australia in tae kwan do at the Sydney Olympics in 2000 before settling in Sydney as a personal trainer. In court Quaid was described as a person who 'apart from honing his martial arts skills and collecting debts for a bikie gang . . . was never one to pursue a career working with his hands'. He admitted having 'facilitated travel for organised crime figures' and claimed that despite having 'little or no legitimate income' he had the ability 'to access large amounts of cash quickly'.

Ulic made several trips to Podgorica, strengthening existing connections and developing new ones. In early 2000 Ulic was named, along with Quaid and Ray Spadina, on listening device and other warrants and on a target list for Operation Mascot-Boat, a joint investigation by the NSW Police and NSW Crime Commission into drug trafficking and police corruption, centred largely on Sydney's north shore.

In December 2003 Quaid flew to Rome and met Ulic. Quaid returned to Sydney in February the following year, making contact with many of Ulic's criminal connections and money men. His role consisted of organising the movement of large amounts of cash to Sydney, setting up importations with Ulic, collecting the cash to pay for the importation and sending it to Ulic. The drugs would be landed in Sydney, either by plane or ship, and would then be driven across the country for distribution in Perth by outlaw motorcycle gangs.

It was while Quaid was visiting Ulic that the Australian Crime Commission established Task Force Schumacher to investigate major criminal networks in several states. Over the next eighteen months 41 arrests were made and 102 charges were preferred. About $40 million worth of drugs was seized together with almost $1 million in cash and proceeds of crime worth around $2 million. In November 2005 officers from the Australian Crime Commission raided the Adelaide offices of Ulic's financial services firm, but the commission's actions were immediately challenged in the Federal Court, limiting the investigators' ability to analyse the material seized. The firm, however, was about to sink under a mass of bad loans.

Around mid-2004 Ulic had received a tip-off that police were closing in on him. He left the country for Podgorica where he remained out of harm's way while continuing to organise large shipments of ecstasy into Australia.

Before leaving Australia, Ulic had recruited two countrymen; 69-year-old Antonio Mauceri and 41-year-old Djelos 'George' Nikolic. Neither had a criminal record. Mauceri's furniture business was intended to provide cover for an ecstasy importation. He travelled overseas with others involved in the venture; acted as go-between with the supplier of the furniture and with the money men; arranged the necessary shipping and importation documentation and liaised with shipping and Customs agents. Nikolic remained in Australia and, among other things, recruited insiders on the wharves to remove the ecstasy from the shipping container and the wharf before the container could be inspected by Customs.

In November the cargo carrier CSLC *Jakarta* sailed into Port Botany, Sydney. On board was a secret cargo of 161 kilograms of ecstasy, worth $40 million on the streets. Unluckily for the conspirators, the Australian Crime Commission had been covertly observing Nikolic, Mauceri and others as they awaited the arrival of the shipment. As the container was landed the commission arranged for it to be secretly moved from the wharf and examined by Customs. It was found to contain furniture and two large wooden crates. When the crates were opened, ecstasy was discovered hidden in sealed bags bearing labels for Horizon Espresso Coffee. The shipping container had been sent from a Belgian furniture company and was addressed to TMM Antiques—a business name previously associated with Mauceri. After the drug had been substituted the container was delivered to an address used by Mauceri in connection with his furniture business.

Mauceri and Nikolic were arrested and charged with conspiring to import ecstasy. Mauceri pleaded guilty and in December 2005 was sentenced to sixteen years' jail, reduced to eight years for 'assistance to authorities'. Nineteen months later Nikolic was convicted at trial of the same offence and was sentenced to sixteen years' jail.

Others involved in the importation, including Ulic and Quaid, escaped arrest. Mauceri and Nikolic had been taking orders from Ulic, while Quaid had, this time, been responsible for arranging the transportation of the ecstasy to Perth for distribution. Not long after the ecstasy seizure, information was picked up by investigators that Quaid had lost another drug shipment. This one consisted of 50 kilograms of ice being sent from Indonesia.

In 2007 Ulic and Quaid agreed to import a shipment of 3,4-methylenedioxymethamphetamine (MDMA) powder which they would use to produce ecstasy for sale throughout Australia. Quaid travelled to the inner-Perth suburb of Subiaco, where he met 60-year-old Rade Ljuboja, who was to handle the landing of the drug and organise a safe house fitted out with a pill press, scales and other equipment and materials used in making ecstasy tablets.

Arrangements were made by conspirators in Sydney, Melbourne and Perth for the production and distribution of the ecstasy. On 16 April 2008 the MSC *Monica* docked at Fremantle after sailing from Mauritius. Around 2 a.m. the next morning a small vessel approached its stern. A member of the crew was waiting and bags containing 60 kilograms of MDMA powder were taken off the *Monica* and loaded onto the smaller vessel. Around 44 kilograms was delivered to the safe house. Sixteen kilograms was taken elsewhere and 'disappeared'.

Unknown to the syndicate, Australian federal and state law enforcement agencies had been watching and listening. In late May 2008 they began to make arrests. Ljuboja and two others—the intended 'cooks'—were arrested in Perth while Quaid was arrested in Sydney and extradited to Western Australia. Ljuboja and Quaid were imprisoned for 25 years and seventeen years respectively. The 'cooks', one from Queensland and the other from Victoria, were imprisoned for seventeen years and fourteen years.

In 2013 Fabian Quaid's 38-year-old brother, Marc, was arrested by Western Australia Gang Crime Squad police at his luxury villa in Northbridge, an inner-city suburb of Perth. Detectives seized $212,000 cash. A week earlier police had raided a warehouse in the Perth suburb of Malaga and seized almost 13 kilograms of methamphetamine valued at $45 million. Quaid was charged with two counts of possessing the drug for the purpose of supply and other related drug charges, while his driver and courier, 51-year-old Roberto Zanon, was also charged with supplying the drug.

In May the following year Quaid and Zanon were convicted of the methamphetamine charges in the District Court. At his sentence hearing, Quaid was described by the prosecutor Linda Petrusa as being near the top of a 'sophisticated' drug-dealing operation and 'prolific, persistent and consistent' in his dealing; referring to emails revealing the movement of nearly 13 kilograms of methamphetamine, 1 kilogram of cocaine and 3000 ecstasy pills in just over two weeks. In another email, Quaid wrote that he believed he could have sold 40,000 ecstasy pills at two music festivals over one long weekend. District Court judge Bruce Goetze agreed with Petrusa, describing Quaid as being in the 'worst category of offenders' before handing him sentences of twenty and fifteen years for the two charges. The sentences overlapped, giving Quaid an effectively sentence of 23 years' jail. Zanon was jailed for fourteen years.

The former business partners in Sydney who introduced Ulic to corrupt police networks had problems of their own. On 5 April 1998 two men were lured to an address in Bankstown leased by Puta and shot dead as they entered the house. One was shot seven times at close range with a .45 calibre Ruger pistol and a .357 Magnum revolver; the other was shot twice in the neck and the head with a 9 millimetre pistol. Both men had been brought to the house to teach them a lesson after one had pointed a gun at Pikic and threatened to kill him. In an attempt to create an alibi for himself, Puta was shot in the thigh so that he could claim to have shot the pair in self-defence. In 2001 Puta was convicted and given an effective sentence of eleven years' jail for the manslaughter of the two men and for contempt of court. The same year Pikic was given an effective sentence of seventeen years' jail for the manslaughter of one person and the murder of the other. Five other men were also jailed over the killings.

On his release from prison Puta went straight back to his old habits. In 2010 police discovered a clandestine 'ice' drug lab in a Ramsgate Beach unit in south Sydney that was later linked to Puta. In 2012 he was arrested and charged with manufacturing a drug and exposing children to the process, selling an unauthorised firearm and seventeen counts of dishonestly obtaining financial advantage by deception. He had been using stolen credit card details to pay his electricity bills, phone bills and parking fines. In mid-2013 Puta was convicted of the seventeen charges of deception at the Central Local Court in Sydney and sentenced to twelve months' imprisonment. The following year Puta pleaded guilty at the Sydney District Court to one charge of taking part in the manufacturing of a drug. On 16 September he was sentenced to six months' imprisonment, but the sentence was suspended, with Puta entering a good behaviour bond for the same period.

At the time of writing, Ulic is believed to be a principal in an expanding, European-based drug network supplying as much as 6 tonnes of cocaine and ecstasy a year to Australia. He is still wanted for the 2008 drug importation with Fabian Quaid. Ulic is also wanted by the Montenegrin police for questioning over the attempted assassination of the Serbian opposition leader Vuk Draskovic in June 2000. The politician was watching television at his seaside home in Budva, Montenegro, when two shots were fired through the lounge window, clipping his ear and the left side of his head. Ulic had been an important player in Sydney's Balkan drug network but in his absence another significant figure would emerge: Radoslav 'Ray' Spadina (see Chapter 17).

CHAPTER EIGHT

Blood relations

In 1999, as violence between Middle Eastern crime gangs exploded on the streets of Sydney, NSW Police completed a damning report on the Sukkar crime family. The report identified certain members of the Sukkar family as being heavily involved in 'heroin, cocaine and firearms trafficking, amphetamine manufacture and trafficking, violence, fraud and money laundering in Sydney, Melbourne and elsewhere'. The principal targets of the assessment included 27-year-old Steven Sukkar (then a practising solicitor), 34-year-old Paul Sukkar and their close ally, 26-year-old Korean Hyeon Joon Choi, known as John Choi.

The Sukkars were assessed to be 'the largest and most feared family within the Lebanese community'. They arranged legal representation for people arrested while working for them and paid compensation to those sentenced to jail—provided they kept their mouths shut.

At various times since the 1980s the Sukkars had either been in 'business' or 'at war' with the murderous Kings Cross criminal Danny Karam and his gang, Danny's Boys. During the late 1990s Danny's Boys and their heroin-addicted leader were involved in shootings, kneecappings, drugs and protection in Kings Cross and the southern suburbs of Sydney. Grievances over money and resentment at the way Karam treated the Muslim members of his gang came to a head in December 1998, when the gang murdered its boss. Leadership passed to Michael 'Doc' Kanaan, but his reign ended six months later after a shootout with police. Kanaan was jailed for life and other members of the gang were given long jail sentences.

The Sukkar family migrated from Lebanon to Sydney in 1966. In the late 1970s and early 1980s Steven and Paul's father spent time in jail over his role in the cultivation and distribution of cannabis. In March 1984 his wife, Salma, and their son Joseph, then 23, were involved in the attempted supply of 90 kilograms of hashish oil. The drug had been imported into Australia on board a Lufthansa flight in the luggage of Interpol undercover agents working with the AFP. On arrival, the 'couriers' booked into a Sydney hotel and were contacted by Joseph who, with Salma, met them and negotiated payment for the consignment. At first the Sukkars wanted most of the consignment on credit, but terms were eventually agreed and over the next few days Joseph paid 'large sums of money' to the couriers in return for 60 of the 90 kilograms imported. The balance of the consignment was to be handed over once the Sukkars had sold the first 60 kilograms and had the money to pay for the rest. Joseph collected the hashish oil and was arrested. His mother was arrested soon afterwards.

The whole importation had an estimated wholesale value of $1.4 million.

Joseph pleaded guilty to possessing hashish oil, being knowingly concerned in the importation of hashish oil, conspiracy to supply hashish oil and attempting to possess hashish oil. He was jailed for eight years on each charge and the sentences were to be served concurrently. In 1986 Salma Sukkar was convicted of conspiring to supply hashish oil and sentenced to nine years' jail. According to court records, it was Salma who was in charge of 'all negotiations and arrangements' relating to the purchase of the drug.

On his release from jail, Joseph went straight back to the drug trade, and by the late 1990s he and other members of his family were importing ecstasy tablets supplied by the Dutch syndicate of which the Englishman James Kinch was a member (see Chapters 10 and 18). At first the syndicate dealt with Joseph through Antoun El Hani in Lebanon, but later Joseph dealt with the Europeans directly. The El Hani and Sukkar families had known each other in Lebanon—their homes were only 5 kilometres apart. Speaking of the Sukkars, El Hani said: 'They have got arms. They carry guns all the time. They go to church carrying guns.' El Hani's wife said of the family: 'Joseph Sukkar is a danger. It's very dangerous for [her husband to give evidence against the Sukkars] and for me and for my children. I'm all alone, I haven't got any family of mine in Lebanon, my only strengths, my only help is my husband . . . They can take revenge.' El Hani's daughter said: 'They are well-known in Lebanon, family Sukkar. During the war—the civil war—they are like a party, you know they have guns and they still have this mentality for revenge, eye for an eye and tooth for a tooth, they live in the mountains, they're [a] very well-known vengeful Mafia sort of family.' Her family, she said, had already been threatened by 'Joseph and his brother'.

In 1999 John Choi, who had migrated to Sydney from South Korea, formed a company called CJ Trade Consultants Pty Limited, of which he was the principal shareholder and director. Steven Sukkar and another brother, Louis, were also appointed directors. The company was first used as a cover for the importation of drugs into Australia in late 2000, when their Dutch supplier hid 400,000 ecstasy tablets in refrigerator parts shipped from Antwerp. The drugs arrived in Sydney in February 2001, were cleared by Customs, collected in early March and sold through the Sukkars' drug network over the next few months.

As the consignment was being delivered, El Hani flew to Sydney to meet Joseph and Choi. El Hani was to confirm the safe arrival and receipt of the drugs and, above all, to ensure the consignment was paid for. As a result of the successful shipment a second importation using CJ Trade Consultants was planned and agreed. Again, El Hani was to act as intermediary. Returning to Lebanon on 18 April 2001, he spoke to his Dutch contacts, putting in train arrangements for the next shipment.

Meanwhile, Choi persuaded Simon Sunal Prasad, the brother of Steven Prasad, an officer and employee of CJ Trade Consultants, to help with the importation. The collapse of his import and trading business had left Simon Prasad in serious financial trouble. Both he and the company had large debts; Prasad owed Choi $100,000. Choi promised Prasad $50,000 for his role in the conspiracy and agreed to forego the debt. Torn over whether to accept, Prasad sought advice from a business associate, 43-year-old Brisbane commodity trader Morris Charles Shepherd, who told him that he had little choice but to agree to Choi's offer. Shepherd had his own reasons for advising his colleague to join the conspiracy: Prasad also owed him money. To Shepherd, the importation represented an opportunity not just to get his money back, but to make a hefty profit. For $25,000—half of Prasad's share—Shepherd agreed to join the plot. His role would be to arrange for the clearance of the proposed consignment—using forged documents—through Australian Customs. Choi also arranged for the shipment to be stored in a Brisbane warehouse for a short time before it was driven to Sydney.

As he had done with the previous importation, Choi arranged through his company for the purchase and shipment of refrigeration equipment from Belgium to Brisbane. The equipment consisted of a cool room packed in three crates containing 48 modular plastic columns, four modular doors and a number of panels. For this, Choi was to be paid $300,000 by Joseph Sukkar.

On 18 April 2001, while Choi was setting up the Australian end of the importation, Joseph Sukkar left Australia. Over the next few months he confirmed arrangements with the suppliers, travelling to Lebanon, the Ukraine and the Netherlands where, on 26 April, he and El Hani met 'Jeff' (Josef Faas) and 'Eric' (not further identified) to discuss the importation. Joseph then flew back to Sydney, arriving on 3 August. Two months later Joseph was back in the Netherlands to make last-minute arrangements for the supply and importation.

In October 2001, within days of Joseph leaving Australia, a shipping container with the refrigeration equipment organised by Choi was loaded aboard the *Rotterdam Express* in Antwerp, Belgium, for consignment to CJ Trade

Consultants in the Port of Brisbane. Hidden in the equipment were 480,000 ecstasy tablets. In Singapore, the container was transferred to the *Tauranga*, which landed the shipment in Brisbane on 17 November 2001. Three days later Customs officials examined the container and discovered the ecstasy tablets. Most of the drug was removed and replaced with substitute tablets, leaving around 13,000 of the original ecstasy tablets.

Prasad and Shepherd arranged clearance of the importation, presenting shipping documents; paying freight, duties and other charges; and organising delivery to a warehouse in Brisbane leased by Shepherd. Meanwhile, in Sydney, Louis hired a truck using a false name, and with a man named Glen Bourke drove to Brisbane to collect the container from Shepherd. Choi and Louis then followed Bourke back to Sydney. Near Kempsey, Louis swapped places with Bourke and drove the truck to his home at 84 Consett Street, Concord West, a property owned by Steven Sukkar.

Later that day (24 November) Louis, Steven and Joseph Sukkar (Joseph had flown back from Europe the day before) unloaded the refrigerator parts. Opening several of the columns, they realised that these were not the tablets they had ordered. Louis ate three of the tablets and confirmed that they were not ecstasy. The three brothers argued. Was it their Dutch suppliers who had ripped them off, or had the drugs been stolen in Belgium en route to Australia? Had Choi stolen the ecstasy tablets? The possibility that they had been detected and replaced by Customs was considered and, surprisingly, dismissed. The brothers reasoned that if the police had discovered the shipment, they would already have been arrested. Choi was less certain. Telling Louis to 'get rid of that shit', he hurriedly left Sydney and flew to South

Korea for 'business reasons'. Inevitably, his rapid departure aroused suspicion.

Over the next couple of weeks there were meetings between the Sydney buyers and the Dutch suppliers, who were also suspicious of the claim that the drugs were 'missing'. Joseph telephoned El Hani, who was in Brazil. He told El Hani of the missing drugs and indicated that the problem was at the Dutch end. El Hani disputed this and promised to speak to his contacts, Jeff and Eric. While the Dutch and Sydney groups instinctively blamed each other, both remained suspicious of Choi. Louis pored over the paperwork in an attempt to identify where the shipment could have been interfered with, but to no avail. As the days passed, Choi looked increasingly like the culprit. Louis told his brother Steven he would 'kill Choi if that were true'. Louis's distrust of Choi was fuelled by the Dutch and by El Hani, who assured Joseph that the problem was 'at his [Sukkar's] end', adding that he and some of his Dutch colleagues were coming to Sydney to investigate.

Meanwhile Steven, Louis, Joseph and Paul Sukkar held a meeting at Joseph's house in Concord West. They removed forty-eight columns and four cool room doors from the garden shed where they were stored and loaded them onto a hire truck. Louis and Paul then drove the truck to a warehouse in Granville where they hid the apparatus. Back at the Concord house, Louis, Paul, Joseph and Steven separated the real ecstasy tablets from the substitutes, retrieving the 13,000 tablets (worth more than $200,000) left untouched by Customs.

The next day, 3 December 2001, El Hani, travelling alone, arrived in Sydney. He went to the Concord house where he met Joseph. Together they inspected the substituted tablets. Amid the confusion Louis was overhead in a telephone conversation with 'Shane' (a major distributor for the Sukkars). There were supposed to have been half a million tablets, Louis told Shane, so 'basically we've had fourteen million worth of things go missing'. (Louis was not far out. Federal authorities estimated the wholesale value of the tablets to be up to $12 million and its retail value to be up to $33 million.) The cash loss to the Sukkars was devastating. In another telephone conversation, Louis told Choi, who was still overseas, that Joseph had no money: 'We all done our arse here, mate, you know we're in the shit.'

Despite their suspicions about Choi, the Sukkars continued to talk to him. Financially, they were being squeezed on all sides: the Dutch suppliers were demanding to be paid for the missing shipment, while Prasad and Shepherd pressed them for the $25,000 each they had been promised.

Somehow, as they fended off their creditors, the Sukkars found time to discuss further importations. In a telephone conversation between Louis and Joseph, Louis asked whether the Europeans would be willing to send another ecstasy shipment, to which Joseph replied that if it happened, he would supervise the shipment in person. In another conversation Steven stressed to Joseph the importance of keeping onside with their Dutch colleagues because 'they'll appreciate what you are doing and then just get started on the next one'. Steven went on: 'Once we cover that gap [i.e. the money owed to the Dutch suppliers] that's it; we say it's not our end then we just get onto the next [ecstasy importation].' In yet another conversation, Joseph told Steven: 'We'll do one more [ecstasy importation],' and later, 'Believe me you'll do very nice money in the next two months.'

This time, however, it was not just ecstasy that Joseph had in mind. He told Steven: 'We're talking about a tonne of cocaine from Brazil.' In a later discussion with Louis and Steven, Joseph spoke about the Brazilian cocaine deal as well as doing 'another [ecstasy] importation'. Paul Sukkar told his three brothers they would do it 'the way we did the last one . . . [but it will be an] . . . even bigger one.'

On 5 December 2001 Louis met Joseph and El Hani at the Concord house. Soon after leaving the house, Louis was arrested. He was present when police broke open the garden shed at the back of the property and found plastic bags containing the substitute tablets and a few of the ecstasy tablets that had been missed. Louis claimed to know nothing about the bags or their contents.

The other brothers along with El Hani, Prasad and Bourke were quickly arrested. On 7 May 2002 Choi was arrested in South Korea and sentenced to three months' jail for smoking cannabis and another nine months for possession of cannabis. He was extradited to Australia on 2 September 2003.

El Hani pleaded guilty and was sentenced to fifteen years' jail.

Louis Sukkar was sentenced to eighteen years' jail over the importation and to six years' jail on a charge of offering to supply ecstasy.

Steven Sukkar was convicted and sentenced to fourteen years' jail (he was also struck off the roll of solicitors).

Simon Prasad was convicted and sentenced to fourteen years' jail. Shepherd pleaded guilty and was sentenced to eleven years six months' jail.

Paul Sukkar went to trial but the jury could not agree on a verdict. He eventually pleaded guilty to being an accessory after the fact to possessing ecstasy and was sentenced to fourteen months' periodic detention.

Glen Bourke was acquitted of all charges at trial.

Joseph Sukkar and Choi received the heaviest sentences, each being jailed for twenty years. Choi claimed that he believed they were importing diamonds and that it was only after the shipment had been opened at the house in Concord that he discovered the truth. According to Choi's story, Louis told him that ecstasy tablets were put inside the columns because diamonds were unavailable.

During 2004 Joseph was tried over his involvement in the first ecstasy importation which was alleged to have occurred between 22 September 2000 and 16 July 2001. The case was largely circumstantial, based on telephone conversations intercepted during preparations for the second importation. Joseph's defence at the trial was that there had been no 'first' importation; rather, it had been a 'dummy run' for the later importation. He was acquitted of the charge.

Paul's 2004 sentence to periodic detention was not his first conviction. His criminal record began at the age of thirteen. During the next eight years he was convicted of possessing a prohibited drug, supplying heroin and other offences. In mid-2005, while still serving his periodic detention, Paul negotiated the sale of 25,000 ecstasy tablets for $325,000, or $13 a tablet. The buyer was an undercover cop. On 25 August 2005, as the sale was about to be made, Paul was arrested in possession of the drugs. Pleading guilty, Paul claimed to be only a middleman who stood to earn $10,000 for introducing the buyer and seller. The court heard that the value of the drugs on the street was more than $1 million. In February 2007 he was sentenced to eleven years and six months' jail. Paul appealed against his sentence but the appeal was dismissed.

Around two years after his arrest, information considered reliable gave an insight into Paul's drug activities in 2005. According to the informant, just before his arrest Paul had been involved in the importation of 300 kilograms of ecstasy tablets. It was alleged that 120 kilograms was returned to the suppliers after Paul's arrest. It is likely that the 25,000 ecstasy tablets Paul was trying to sell at the time of his arrest were part of the importation.

As well as the ecstasy, Paul was said to have played a significant role in importing and selling up to 400 kilograms of cocaine, although it had not been a good batch. There were complaints that the cocaine 'burnt people's noses' when they sniffed it.

■ ■ ■

In the years leading up to the 2005 arrest of Paul Sukkar, the Dutch syndicate had taken a battering both in Australia, where costs were exceeding profits, and in the Netherlands, where key figures in the syndicate faced prosecution. In February 2005 Joseph Sukkar and Antoun El Hani gave evidence against their Dutch contacts, Jeff and Eric, via an audiovisual link with the Netherlands. Jeff and Eric were convicted and jailed.

Paul's arrest was said to have been the trigger that caused the Dutch syndicate to finally 'shut up shop' in Australia, at least temporarily. According to an informant, '[M]embers travelled to various countries: one syndicate member, "Matty", [a UK citizen and member of what is known in the UK as the "Chelsea crime group"] is currently in China, some others are in Spain and another called "Nigel" [a UK citizen usually resident in Sydney] went to England to get married.'

For a while the Dutch syndicate retired to lick its wounds but its business in Australia was far from over.

CHAPTER NINE

Gunner for hire

From the day he was born, the Englishman Paul William Gunner seemed destined to live a life of crime. His father was a career criminal and through his mother he grew up mixing with several of London's most notorious crime families. By the age of around thirteen, Gunner was shoplifting with members of the Kangaroo Gang. He showed such promise that one old-time Australian criminal (a close mate of crime 'head honcho' Michael Hurley) 'sponsored' visits to Sydney during the 1980s for a series of highly successful crime sprees.

During one visit to Australia in 1989 Gunner began a relationship with Lee Ashby, who was on close terms with several members of the East Coast Milieu, including Frankie Ballis, Ricky Montgomery and Hurley. Two years later Gunner and Ashby had a child. The same year Gunner and a few of his mates stole Westpac Banking Corporation traveller's cheques with a face value of $32 million from a warehouse in the inner-western suburb of Homebush. Within months, several million dollars' worth of cheques had been presented and cashed both in Australia and overseas. In April 1992, six days after being granted permanent Australian residence, Gunner left Australia with Ashby and their child, aware that he was under suspicion for the theft of the traveller's cheques. Arrested soon after arriving in England, Gunner spent six months in jail fighting extradition to Australia. He was returned to Sydney in October and two months later was granted bail.

Perhaps deciding that he had little to lose, Gunner spent the next fifteen months on a crime spree. Working in pairs, Gunner and his gang preyed most weekdays on trucks delivering goods to large retailers in the Sydney and north shore central business districts. They stole computers, printers, cameras, jewellery, watches, shoes and other goods. By December 1993 Gunner and his colleagues suspected their activities were attracting the attention of police. Over the next three months Gunner had several meetings and telephone conversations with a police officer to whom he gave the codename 'King'. In return for money, King gave Gunner information about police activities and revealed that someone was informing on him. Court papers describe King as being 'a New South Wales police officer at the time seconded to the NCA [National Crime Authority]'. While at the NCA, King had been involved in Gunner's arrest for the theft of the traveller's cheques.

King returned to the NSW Police. No action was taken against him and he was later promoted.

On 2 March 1994 Gunner was arrested, along with three accomplices and several others involved in similar crimes, and charged with seventeen counts of theft totalling around $150,000. This represented only a small fraction of both the number of thefts and the total value of goods stolen. Three months later, on 23 June, Gunner pleaded guilty to conspiracy, theft, bribery (of King) and passport offences, for which he was eventually sentenced to a string of jail terms, some of which were to be served concurrently, that added up to six years' jail. Lee Ashby was charged with being an accomplice to the theft of the traveller's cheques—she had arranged for cheques with a face value of $16 million to be stored at her grandparents' home on the NSW Central Coast—and in 1994 was convicted and sentenced to 300 hours' community service work.

Of the $32 million in stolen traveller's cheques, around half the haul was destroyed by a co-offender, while cheques worth $9 million were recovered in England and Australia. Cheques worth several million dollars are still unaccounted for.

With Gunner safely locked up, the Australian government set to work on having him deported. Gunner put up a stubborn fight and at various times not only won, but had costs awarded to him. However, in July 1998 the Federal Court found against him, approving his deportation and awarding costs to the government.

While in jail Gunner learnt that his partner, Lee, had fallen for Glen Roderick Flack, former partner in crime and now avowed enemy of the notorious career criminal and murderer Arthur Neddy Smith. Gunner appeared to cope with the fact that his wife had left him, but the news provoked trouble outside the jail. An agitated Bobby Chapman—another of Smith's former partners in crime until Smith sold him out in the mid-1970s—approached Lee at a

Kings Cross nightclub. 'I've heard you've taken up with that arsehole Flack. Is that right?' he asked. A few more words were exchanged and Chapman grabbed Lee, indecently assaulting her. 'Tell that arsehole Flack what I did and that's what I think of him.'

A fortnight later, on Good Friday 1995, Chapman was found bashed and shot dead a few streets from his home in the south-western Sydney suburb of Raby. No one was ever charged with the murder. Chapman was disliked by police and crooks alike—neither was sorry to see him dead.

Released from jail in March 2000, Gunner was deported to England, but this didn't stop him re-entering Australia soon afterwards to supervise an importation of amphetamines organised by his English colleagues and supplied by a Dutch syndicate.

On 17 December 2001, 44-year-old Greek–Canadian Kyriakos Vassios, also known as 'Sandy' and 'Eddy', entered Australia on a false British passport in the name of Brian Timothy Flock (Flock had died in 1980 of natural causes at the age of seventeen), to receive a shipment of amphetamine powder in Sydney. A few months earlier Vassios had placed an order for the amphetamines—believed to be several hundred kilograms of powder—with the Dutch suppliers. They had sent the drug to Greece where Vassios arranged for it to be hidden in a consignment of olives bound for Sydney. It arrived around Christmas 2001. After selling most of the amphetamines, Vassios returned to Europe in early January 2002 and quickly placed another order. The method of importation would be identical but this shipment would consist of amphetamine powder and ecstasy tablets. On 24 April 2002 Vassios, using the same false passport, returned to Sydney to receive the second consignment of 'olives'.

This time, however, things did not go so smoothly. There were problems with both the sale of the drugs in Australia and the flow of cash to the Dutch suppliers. Anxious for their commission, the English intermediaries asked Gunner to sort the matter out.

Gunner obtained a false British passport in the name of Timothy Charles Williams and arrived in Sydney on 20 May 2002. After speaking to Vassios and others involved in selling the drugs, Gunner told his English bosses that buyers were hesitating because the amphetamines were 'made differently to what they were used to in Sydney'. He insisted he was 'negotiating with prospective purchasers and had provided samples of the drug to them'. Gunner told them he 'had collected some monies in relation to supplies . . . and that he was going to ask for $40,000 per kilogram'. It would be the last time Gunner spoke to his English bosses.

On the evening of 21 June 2002 Gunner was arrested and charged with supplying drugs, possession of a false passport and possession of $5000 cash.

At the same time, Vassios and a female friend left room 501 at the W Hotel in inner-city Woolloomooloo carrying four bags. They took the bags to the hotel car park and put them in the boot of a car. As they were about to drive away, they were stopped by the police. The four bags were found to contain $2.1 million in cash, as well as a 9 millimetre semi-automatic pistol and two loaded magazines containing 24 rounds of ammunition. The serial number on the pistol had been filed off. Another $859,605 in Australian banknotes, $13,280 in euros and $2640 in Thai baht were found in room 501. Both Vassios and his companion refused to answer any questions. International inquiries confirmed that the man travelling under the name Brian Flock was in fact Vassios.

Over the next three weeks five more men were arrested. Thirty-two year old Mark Wright was arrested in a Perth hotel in possession of 18 kilograms of amphetamines and $19,000 in cash. He told police that he had had the amphetamines in his possession for five weeks and had been guarding them for other people. He also said that he had travelled from Queensland to Western Australia and been involved in various discussions about the drug with 32-year-old Darren Joseph Leech and 33-year-old Darren Ricky Emanuel, both of whom had minor criminal records in the UK. The pair were members of the British arm of an Anglo-Dutch syndicate, represented by James Kinch in Australia, involved in the importation and distribution of ecstasy (see Chapter 10). Wright claimed to have been paid 'about $25,000' for the five weeks' work. Also arrested were Leech's and Emanuel's main Australian buyers, 32-year-old James Longhurst of Bondi Junction and 31-year-old David McCoy of St Ives on Sydney's north shore.

In October 2003—fifteen months after the arrests—police dug up a further 70 kilograms of amphetamines that had been buried at the southern end of Sydney's Long Reef Beach. The drug cache, with an estimated street value of $3 million, had been buried by Longhurst before the July 2002 arrests.

Gunner was convicted of supplying drugs and jailed for nine years. Emanuel pleaded guilty to supplying drugs and was jailed for four years and four months. Leech pleaded guilty to supplying drugs and was jailed for six years. McCoy pleaded guilty to supplying drugs and was jailed for two years and three months. Longhurst pleaded guilty to supplying drugs and was jailed for eighteen months. Wright pleaded guilty in the Perth District Court and, after an appeal by the

Crown against the leniency of his sentence, was jailed for nine years.

Vassios forfeited the $3 million cash to the Crown and was jailed for sixteen months for possessing an unauthorised firearm. On his release Vassios was deported to Canada, where he faced serious drug trafficking charges. He was convicted and sentenced to several years' jail. A US citizen, Vassios had a history of trafficking drugs in Europe, the United States, Canada and Australia. His criminal record in the US included charges in Philadelphia of theft and receiving in 1978, supplying drugs in Gloucester in 1985 and shop-lifting and conspiring to possess the synthetic drug PCP in Philadelphia in 1987, for which he was eventually jailed for twelve years. In the mid-1990s, after serving his sentences in the US, Vassios moved to Canada.

Some of the men who had participated in Vassios's second amphetamine shipment into Sydney managed to escape arrest. One of these men was James Kinch.

CHAPTER TEN

Little Jimmy Kinch

James Henry Kinch, also known as Derek Woevenden, Seamus Kinch, James McCarthy and 'Little Jimmy' (Kinch is 167 centimetres tall) was born in Ireland on 6 July 1958. He had a long criminal record in the UK, beginning in Manchester when, aged eleven, he was convicted of burglary and theft and placed on probation. Over the next 23 years he incurred at least another 30 convictions for burglary, theft, stealing a motor vehicle, handling stolen property, fraud, firearms and other crimes. His last conviction in the UK was for robbery and brought Kinch an eleven-year jail sentence. On his release from jail in the mid-1990s Kinch entered the drug trade.

Through his criminal activities and connections Kinch was introduced to a Pakistani family described by British police as 'one of the biggest heroin dealing families in the Birmingham area', and another crime family based in

Manchester. The latter had been involved in the drug trade since the 1970s and in the large-scale importation and distribution of drugs since at least the early 1980s. By the early to mid-1990s both the Birmingham and Manchester families were linked to a network of British criminals—several of whom lived in Spain or Portugal—and, through them, to criminal syndicates in the Netherlands. These syndicates had access to state-of-the-art laboratories capable of producing huge quantities of ecstasy and were eager to expand their share of the British market. With these two crime families as his suppliers, Kinch began distributing drugs throughout the UK. His success soon saw him recruited by the Dutch-based syndicate of Fat Ron Haklander, whose speciality was high-quality ecstasy tablets.

Haklander was not the only one to take an interest in Kinch. His success had drawn the attention of the British police, whose efforts to crack down on him were causing problems for the syndicate. His notoriety was starting to cost the syndicate money. A way was needed to make use of Kinch's talents while taking the heat off the British operation. In the late 1990s, at the syndicate's request, Kinch moved to the United States. Settling in Miami, Florida, Kinch was soon busy setting up 'storage facilities, organising methods by which [drug] imports can be cleared, received, transported and stored, along with establishing and liaising with prospective and arranged purchasers'. He organised several large ecstasy importations into the US and made good profits for the syndicate before deciding he 'did not like the US'. One reason for his dislike was that there was believed to have been a rollover in the US operation, and drugs had been lost in Miami. According to a senior member of the Dutch syndicate, the syndicate sent 'a hit man to Miami to find those responsible. It resulted in fourteen people being shot, three of whom died.' Back in Britain, Kinch arranged the trafficking of ecstasy tablets across Europe and the UK. Around 2000 he heard about the syndicate's importations of ecstasy into Australia. It was a market he was eager to exploit.

The Dutch syndicate wanted Kinch to take charge of its Australian operations, supervising the security and sale of importations and collecting money. At the time the Australian trade was concentrated in the hands of independent importers, most of whom were buying through the Birmingham and Manchester drug families. Most importations came through Sydney. The new arrangement would bypass both families. As well as giving Kinch a more important role within the syndicate, it would entitle him to a bigger share of the profits from importations. In addition, it would cut out the Pakistani family that Kinch believed owed him money.

In late 2001 Kinch was sent to Australia to establish a permanent base for the distribution of drugs on behalf of the Dutch syndicate. Kinch spent his first few months setting up storage facilities, mostly in Sydney's eastern suburbs, for incoming and future importations, organising the delivery of ecstasy to customers and otherwise managing importations he had organised, and laundering the proceeds of importations back to the Netherlands. When selecting storage facilities Kinch would conduct surveillance of the facilities and note such things as the number of staff opening and closing the depot; whether or not surveillance cameras were in use and whether people were filmed entering or leaving the premises; and the procedures, including documentation, for hiring and using the depot. He would install voice-activated tape recorders in the offices to determine whether employees spoke about him after he left. Three sheds were used for each importation: one for unpacking the drugs after delivery, another for storing the drugs and a third for storing the cash. Different sheds were also used for each importation. Kinch also rented apartments as 'safe houses' in various hotels in Coogee, Bondi and in the Sydney CBD.

Several successful importations were carried out. However, one importation led to the 2002 arrests of Paul Gunner, Kyriakos Vassios and other members of their network (see Chapter 9), while another led to the December 2002 arrests of Frankie Ballis, Wayne Moore and Carl Hinke (see Chapter 5).

During 2002 and early 2003 Kinch left and re-entered Australia on false passports at least seven times. In February 2002 Kinch and another member of the syndicate working in Sydney (we will call him Charlie) were summoned to Bali for a meeting with Haklander. Charlie was to be reprimanded by the syndicate for attempting a rip-off. Having partly completed the rip-off, Charlie had changed his mind and confessed to Kinch. Following the reprimand, Charlie was allowed to remain with the syndicate, but with a 'babysitter' assigned to him to ensure that he did not waver again. Two months later Kinch met up with Haklander in Sydney to discuss the opportunities available.

In Sydney, Charlie and Kinch devised a secure method of delivering drugs to buyers. Arguably the riskiest part of the operation, it was also the part that brought in the cash. The method involved Kinch giving the buyer's telephone number to Charlie, who would ring and arrange for the three of them to meet at the Moore Park Supa Centa in the city's eastern suburbs, where Charlie and Kinch would walk the buyer through the delivery. The complicated process involved Charlie, Kinch and the buyer, but the three would never be seen together in the same place. It would begin with the buyer driving a van or similar vehicle to the top car park level of the Supa Centa. After leaving the keys in the van, the buyer would meet Charlie in a café on the top level of the Supa Centa. Charlie would then drive the vehicle to the loading dock of a self-storage unit in Waterloo where Kinch would be waiting with the drugs, which were hidden inside PVC pipes. After Kinch had loaded the pipes into the van, Charlie would drive back to the Supa Centa, leaving the keys in the vehicle for the buyer, who was waiting in the café. When the drugs were paid for depended on how well Kinch knew the buyer and how much was being bought. Sometimes payment was required immediately; sometimes it was made a few days later. After the handover was completed Charlie would use a payphone to report to the syndicate in the Netherlands. Several successful deals were carried out in this way.

All of the importations entered Australia through Sydney, although Kinch also dealt with buyers in Melbourne.

During 2002 Dutch law enforcement authorities stepped up their investigations into the syndicate. Intelligence soon led them to the group's overseas distributors. Kinch and his colleagues were now high-priority targets in both the Netherlands and Australia, where Kinch was assessing the risks of expanding the syndicate's role in Sydney's drug trade. On 22 January 2003 Kinch flew to the Caribbean island of Aruba—part of the Kingdom of the Netherlands—where he assured his bosses, including Haklander, that the potential profits justified the risks.

In late 2002 Australian authorities had received information that Kinch was preparing to import 500,000 ecstasy tablets into Australia and that he had access to 200 kilograms of cocaine stored in Panama.

On 4 March 2003, in a combined operation involving state and federal law enforcement authorities and the NSW Crime Commission, police searched a storage unit at Rent-a-Space Self Storage, 42 O'Dea Avenue, Waterloo, and found $500,000 cash. The unit had been rented by Kinch in December 2002 and had been accessed eight times in the four weeks before the search. The next day, a police search of Kinch's unit at Quay Apartments in Phillip Street, Sydney, found $8000 cash, five mobile telephones and keys for four safety deposit boxes at the Commonwealth Bank. An electronic money-counting machine was found in a storage locker linked to the apartment. The safety deposit boxes contained $30,000 in cash.

Unaware that he was under investigation and that his telephone had been intercepted, Kinch complained to his suppliers in the Netherlands that he was having trouble selling the previous importation as 'the quality was poor when compared with other [ecstasy] pills on the market, or [those which had been] provided in the past'. Despite having tried the pills and finding them to be 'satisfactory', Kinch wanted approval to reduce the price and indicated that he had 'paper to return to Holland'—a reference to the $500,000 in cash at Rent-A-Space Self Storage (Kinch was unaware that police had already found the money).

On the afternoon of 12 March 2003 Kinch went to the reception area of the storage shed at Waterloo but immediately became suspicious and did not enter the shed. Three hours later Kinch called his one-time house cleaner, Kirsty Chambers. Kinch told Chambers that he wanted to see her straight away and then called again to say that meeting him would be 'worth more money to you . . . I'll definitely give you . . . thousands.' That evening the pair met at Bondi.

Kinch asked Chambers to go to his unit at Quay Apartments and remove a suitcase and clothing, move a sports bag from one locker to another and get rid of a plastic bag that was hidden in a cavity behind a brick wall in the car park.

Chambers did as she was told. After removing the plastic bag from the cavity, she put it inside another bag and threw it from the car park into the laneway below. Unfortunately for Kinch, the noise of the bag hitting the road alerted a security officer and a doctor who was parking his car. The doctor recognised the contents of the bag as drugs and called the police. They found sixteen ecstasy tablets of various brands inside the bag as well as a small quantity of cocaine.

Two days later, on 14 March, Chambers was interviewed by police and confessed to her role in attempting to dispose of the drugs. The same day Kinch was arrested at Manly on Sydney's north shore and charged with supplying and possessing drugs and engaging in money laundering.

Kinch sent police to another apartment (this one leased in Chambers' name) at the Crown Plaza Hotel in Coogee, where $227,000 in cash was seized, and then to another self-storage unit in Waterloo, where they found 72 kilograms of ecstasy tablets. The tablets were later identified as belonging to the importation carried out by Frankie Ballis and Wayne Moore (see Chapter 5). The unit was within metres of two others searched by police a month earlier as part of the ongoing Ballis–Moore investigation. As far as Kinch was concerned, its security had already been compromised by the earlier search. In allowing the police to find the ecstasy, Kinch was making a gift of something that he had already abandoned. The tip-off that cost him nothing was to be a model for Kinch's future dealings with the police.

Mark Standen and the Crime Commission were heavily involved in the operation, but it was the NSW Police who arrested and charged Kinch: the case officer was plainclothes constable Chris Symons of Special Crime and Internal Affairs (SCIA). Kinch rolled at once, or so it appeared. Constable Symons and Mark Standen became his handlers.

Almost from the moment he was arrested, Kinch was described as 'a ten out of ten' informant, although he was not registered as such for seven months. During this period Symons had about 25 contacts with Kinch; most were in company with Standen and all were documented. Standen, meanwhile, had about 300 contacts with Kinch, most without Symons' knowledge. Very few of these were officially recorded.

Despite the frequency of these contacts and the detail of the information said to have been provided, it was not until October 2003 that Symons completed a 'NSW Crime Commission Informer Registration' application for Kinch, who was described as 'well placed within an international drug importation syndicate . . . [and with the] . . . syndicate's representative in Australia'. Kinch was said to have 'provided accurate information which has been independently corroborated'. The registration was signed by Symons as the 'case officer' and Standen as the 'informer co-handler'. Two senior New South Wales police officers—one a detective inspector and the other a detective superintendent—also signed the application form. One signed as a 'co-handler' and the other as 'a senior supervisor'. Constable Symons had never handled an informant before he met Kinch, yet was given little in the way of advice or support from his superiors at SCIA. There was no mention in the application that Kinch had told lies, that much of his information had come to nothing, or that he had refused to hand over more than $1 million in drug profits.

Given the assessment of Kinch's importance in the internal drug trade as a 'ten out of ten' rollover, it is difficult to understand how senior police in SCIA could justify nominating Symons as Kinch's handler. This is not intended as criticism of Symons, who was doing as he was told, but of the senior officers who gave such responsibility to an untrained and inexperienced senior constable, who had never before had dealings with an informant, let alone one of such experience and importance as Kinch. There is no doubt that these failures enabled the development of a corrupt relationship between Standen and Kinch. Similar failures—inadequate supervision; the use of incorrect procedures; defective record keeping; and the appointment of officers not equipped, through lack of training or experience, to do the jobs they were expected to do—had been identified in numerous police investigations going back several years.

CHAPTER ELEVEN

Mark Standen—a man on the make

Mark Standen was born in Strathfield in Sydney's inner west. After receiving a good education at a local independent school, he joined the Australian Customs Service at the age of eighteen. Standen showed promise and two years later was assigned to the Narcotics Bureau, which was then a branch of Customs. (In 1979 the Narcotics Bureau merged with the Commonwealth Police and the Australian Capital Territory Police to become the AFP.) It was at this early stage that Standen began to exhibit signs not only of flaws in his character, but of the extraordinary luck he would ride for much of his career in law enforcement.

On his transfer to the Narcotics Bureau, Standen met the more senior Allan Gregory McLean. A habitual gambler, McLean could never earn enough to get out of the debts he incurred by his gambling. Standen, too, became a problem gambler. A former colleague who knew Standen in those days described him as someone who 'gambled in bursts'. He would gamble until his money ran out, then stop, perhaps for a few months, until he had built up another 'bank' which he could then gamble away. 'He was compulsive,' the former colleague said, 'but he was able to exercise some restraint. Not like Allan [McLean], who couldn't miss a bet.' McLean and Standen socialised and shared betting tips. Their gambling habits signalled that they were risk-takers—it was almost inevitable that this trait would spill over into their professional lives.

In May 1979 Standen and two other narcotics agents raided a house in Sydney's Bondi, where they found eighteen silver foils of hashish. Three years later Standen was hauled before the Royal Commission of Inquiry into Drug Trafficking (the Stewart Royal Commission). Standen admitted to the commission that several weeks after the Bondi raid he and his colleagues had flushed the hash down a toilet, falsified entries in the bureau's log book to indicate that nothing was found in the raid and then destroyed a signed statement from the occupier of the house confessing to his ownership of the drugs. Asked by the Royal Commissioner, Justice Donald Stewart, if he and his colleagues were 'really trying to obliterate all traces of this incident', Standen responded, 'That is correct.' Standen told the commission that they had destroyed the hashish and the paperwork because the drugs weighed less than 500 grams and charges could not be brought under federal laws.

But AFP Chief Superintendent John Reilly, who investigated the matter after a complaint was made by the NSW Police, told the commission that Standen and the other agents had given a different version of their actions. According to

Reilly, they told him there had been problems with charging the owner of the drugs because of a lack of cooperation from local police and they then became embarrassed about having held on to the hashish for more than two weeks. Years later Standen told a colleague, 'I flushed the drugs on the advice of my supervisor as they had been mouldy and sitting in my drawer for over three months and he didn't know what to do with them.'

As a result of Reilly's inquiry, Standen and another agent had been charged under the Public Service Act and recommendations were made that both be barred from joining the AFP when it merged with the Narcotics Bureau later that year. Reilly told the commission that he had twice taken Standen's name off the list of officers to be transferred to the force, but the ban had been dropped because of 'indecision by members of the Department of Administrative Services and what was then Business and Consumer Affairs'. Reilly agreed with the Royal Commissioner's remark that 'There is no question that what Mr Standen did in concert with the others was dishonest'. Yet to the 'amazement' of the bureau's director of operations, Brian Bates, the men were transferred to the federal police. Bates told the commission that the earlier decision to refuse them employment had been made by an acting assistant commissioner and approved by the commissioner, Sir Colin Woods.

A fortnight later Labor senator Nick Bolkus raised the matter in Federal Parliament. On behalf of the Minister for Administrative Services, Senator Tony Messner replied that the matter was 'currently under investigation by the Stewart Royal Commission of Inquiry into Drug Trafficking, who will no doubt report to government on the matter in due course. Accordingly, it would not be appropriate for me to comment at this time.'

But Stewart did not report on the matter and Standen's corruption was 'forgotten' for 26 years. No explanation has ever been given, at least to the public, for the decision to override the AFP Commissioner Sir Colin Woods' ruling that Standen should not be appointed to the AFP; or for the fact that on at least three occasions Standen's name was reinstated after being removed from the approved transfer list; or for Justice Stewart's failure to report on a matter which he had personally described as 'dishonest'. Were they cock-ups, or were they the result of something more sinister?

Standen's workmate, McLean, had also been adversely mentioned during the Stewart Royal Commission. Born in England during World War II, McLean had been a member of Her Majesty's Customs and a narcotics officer in London before migrating to Australia in 1974. Like Standen, McLean had moved from his job in the Narcotics Bureau to the newly created AFP. He spent time in the Sydney office of the drug squad before returning to Customs as a senior investigator.

In Sydney McLean had been a regular at Tati's restaurant in Oxford Street, Paddington, owned by the Argentinian Roberto Fionna. An avid punter and racegoer, Fionna played host to fellow gamblers Robert 'Aussie Bob' Trimbole, James 'Diamond Jim' Shepherd (a senior member of the Mr Asia drug syndicate) and others in the drug trade. Tati's became a meeting place where Fionna organised introductions and sometimes acted as go-between in drug deals. Before long McLean was acting as a 'runner' for Trimbole, placing bets and making something on the side.

In March 1980 McLean was the officer in charge of an AFP search of Fionna's Paddington flat, where 3.6 grams of heroin was found in a wall cavity. Fionna insisted that the heroin had been planted on him by McLean but did not understand why. In evidence to the Royal Commission of Inquiry into Drug Trafficking, Fionna's wife, Mabel, gave evidence that McLean did not pay for the meals and drinks he had at Tati's restaurant. McLean said the opposite. Another witness, the Mr Asia accountant Robert Scott, reported Fionna telling him that McLean had to be bribed to stop the drug prosecution. This, too, was denied by McLean.

Despite the strong whiff of corruption surrounding McLean's connection with Fionna, McLean escaped relatively unscathed from the Royal Commission and was not pursued by either the AFP or Customs. By then, McLean himself had entered the drug trade. In 1985 Scotland Yard detectives received information that London criminals were in contact with a 'friendly' Australian Customs officer. That officer was McLean. The London connection was his brother-in-law, Archie Davis. McLean made two trips to England to discuss drug importation into Australia and hosted several British criminals on their visits to Australia, paying their hotel bills with his American Express and Diners Club credit cards. The deal with the British fell through, but McLean became involved in the importation of heroin with a Sydney-based syndicate.

In 1987 McLean was arrested and admitted to his role in six importations (of both heroin and cannabis) worth around $14 million since 1982. On average, he said, he received about $10,000 for each kilogram imported. McLean was convicted and received an effective sentence of 24 years' jail. Several other members of McLean's group received long jail sentences.

As McLean began his jail sentence, his former colleague Mark Standen was making his name with the AFP. In the late 1980s and early 1990s Standen took part in the investigation of the Ian Saxon syndicate and several other major organised crime groups. In 1993 Standen resigned from the AFP, where he held the rank of sergeant, and took up a position with the NCA, then Australia's prime repository of organised crime intelligence. Given his earlier record and Sir Colin Woods' decision that he was not a fit and proper person to be an officer in the AFP, it was an extraordinary appointment that gave Standen access to all federal, state and territory organised crime data.

In 1994 the NCA and the AFP merged. NCA employees were sworn in as AFP officers with the same powers. At the time of the merger, Standen was being paid the equivalent salary of a superintendent in the AFP and he retained that rank. Again, no account was taken of his dubious past. Standen remained with the AFP, though on loan to the NCA, for two years. During this time he again became involved in the investigation of Ian Saxon, who had escaped from jail and was the subject of an international search. In 1995 Standen helped track Saxon to the US city of San Diego. This resulted in Saxon's extradition to Australia and a long jail sentence (see Chapter 1).

Standen resigned from the AFP in 1996 and was appointed to the position of chief investigator with the NSW Crime Commission. Before appointing him, the commission obtained letters from the AFP, the NCA and the NSW Police Special Branch, and was advised that none possessed information to indicate that Standen was unsuitable. He was later promoted to assistant director of investigations; equal third in charge of the commission.

At the time he resigned from the AFP, Standen owed a lot of money to bookmakers, most of them illegal. A former colleague recalled, 'He had been in debt for a long time and he just kept gambling and losing. His debts had to be cleaned up before he could join the Crime Commission and it was arranged that he would cash in his pension contributions.' Standen had been in the same federal pension fund since he had joined the Narcotics Bureau. 'I think he owed about $230,000 and he used all his superannuation entitlements and long service leave to pay them out, but he was still a couple of thousand short and I think he had to borrow some money from a bank.'

Another former colleague recalled, 'Standen was always complaining about money, from as early in our association as I can remember. He never put his hand in his pocket to pay for anything; he would never buy a coffee.'

Money problems would continue to weigh on Standen's mind over the next twelve years as he worked on cases involving some of the state's most notorious organised crime figures, among them Michael Hurley, Frankie Ballis, Ian Saxon, Ricky Montgomery and Paul Gunner. Crucially, Standen also led investigations into the English and Dutch crime syndicates that, by the mid-1990s at least, had become major players in Australia's illegal drug trade.

CHAPTER TWELVE

Family friends

James Kinch was not the first criminal befriended by Mark Standen. In 1994 Standen moved to the Central Coast and bought a house not far from Neville Brian Tween. The pair became friends; they visited each other's homes and would go away together on 'family getaways'. During the early 2000s Standen and his family lived with the Tweens. But Standen's relationship with Tween was not just social. Tween was a violent career criminal who used at least eight aliases and Standen was a police officer who, over several decades, had investigated him. Tween was said to be one of Standen's informants. Both men were active in the drug trade.

Born in 1940, Tween spent his early childhood in the Western Australian gold town of Kalgoorlie before the family moved to the Riverina in New South Wales. By the age of ten Tween had a record for at least seven break, enter and steal offences. After leaving school at fourteen, he was sent to Mount Penang Boys' Home on the Central Coast and later to Tamworth Juvenile Justice Centre. He spent the next few years living off crime while trying to keep one step ahead of the law.

In the early 1960s Tween went to New Zealand where he committed numerous burglaries, some of which involved the blowing or cutting of safes. In late 1963 he was arrested, convicted and jailed for five and a half years for burglary and possession of burglary instruments. On 2 June 1964 he escaped from Christchurch Prison and fled to Victoria. Five months later he was arrested in Melbourne in possession of explosives, firearms and some partially burnt banknotes that appeared to have been salvaged from a blown or cut safe. Tween was convicted of possessing the explosives and jailed for three years. Released in 1967, he was returned to New Zealand to serve the balance of his 1964 sentence. He was also convicted of escaping from custody. Tween remained in jail until 1970, when he was deported to Australia.

Back in Australia, Tween settled in the northern beaches area of Sydney before moving to South Australia, where he changed his name to John David Anderson; the name he still goes by today (for the sake of consistency we will continue to call him Tween). In July 1971 he was arrested and jailed for three years for breaking into hotels, theft and related offences, including possession of firearms. While in jail he married his probation officer. South Australian police noted, 'This is considered a marriage of convenience for the purpose of influencing the Parole Board and to have someone "on the outside" to run errands for him.' On his release in October 1974 Tween and his wife settled in Terrey Hills, near Sydney's northern beaches, where they had two small children.

Tween's principal partner in crime was Gary James Batt (also known by the name Charlie Brown), whom he had met in 1955 while at Mount Penang Boys' Home. Batt is believed to have been an accomplice in the South Australian jobs committed by Tween in the early 1970s. After 1974 Tween and Batt committed a number of safe robberies and supplied drugs in Sydney. Both were drug users.

In July 1975 Tween told Batt to bring nineteen-year-old Paul Milton Whittaker, a local drug dealer and user, to a clearing in the Ku-ring-gai Chase National Park, not far from Tween's home in Terrey Hills. Tween believed Whittaker had cheated him in a $200 drug deal, by cutting the marijuana with parsley. Batt thought they were just going to give Whittaker a 'backhander' as punishment, but when they arrived at the clearing Tween 'went crazy'. He was wearing a motorcycle helmet and was armed with a submachine gun with a bayonet attached. Tween forced Whittaker to dig his own grave, strip and dress in women's underwear, then took photographs with a Polaroid camera while Batt sexually assaulted Whittaker. When he was eventually released, Whittaker reported the matter to police, telling them that, after the attack, Batt had said to him, '[Tween] is mad, he picked up two sheilas hitching, took them up there and we got a lot of good pictures of them.' At the clearing where Whittaker had been attacked, police found female underwear, a bag containing two pairs of replica handcuffs, a spent 9 millimetre cartridge shell and several bottles of wine and spirits.

Batt and Tween were convicted of procuring a male person with intent to perform an indecent act and sentenced to six months' jail. On his release from jail Batt fled to Melbourne, terrified of Tween and his new partner in crime, Raymond Johnson, after a fallout in jail. 'If you don't disappear,' Tween had threatened him, 'I'll make you disappear.' According to Batt, his fear of Tween dated from the assault on Whittaker. 'I knew he was a [sexual] deviant . . . He was pretty crazy.'

Born in Balmain in 1946, Johnson was a mate of future crime boss Michael Hurley. Johnson had fourteen convictions by the age of fourteen and 34 convictions by the time he teamed up with Tween in the mid-1970s. His crimes included assault and robbery; possession of explosives; break, enter and steal; possession of safe-breaking implements and house-breaking implements; and theft. Tween and Johnson robbed safes in various New South Wales country towns.

On 24 June 1978, eighteen-year-old Trudie Adams left the Newport Surf Life Saving Club and was seen getting into a Holden panel van on Barrenjoey Road. She was never seen again. Her disappearance was widely reported and led to a major police investigation. Fourteen young women came forward with accounts of abductions and rapes around the northern beaches during the 1970s. When police interviewed the women, they found a number of similarities between their stories. Tween was a suspect for the murder of Adams and the abduction and rape of at least some of the other women.

A second line of investigation centred on the 'Roseland lads', a group of more than fifteen young people who hung around the Roselands Shopping Centre in south-western Sydney, some of whom had been heard to make comments implying their involvement in Adams' murder. Other members of the group reported these comments to police.

In late 1979, after six years of bashings and violence, Tween's wife left him. In 1982 Tween married his second wife. They divorced eighteen years later but remained 'best mates'.

From the time of their arrival on the Central Coast, Tween and Johnson were heavily involved in the importation, manufacture and supply of drugs, most of which were sold in Sydney's northern beaches and eastern suburbs.

On the evening of 2 September 1985, less than three weeks after his release from jail, 28-year-old Ante Yelavich—also known as 'Tony' and 'Nails' as he had worked in a beauty parlour doing manicures—disappeared after leaving his parents' home in Manly on his bike. Friends of Yelavich told police that he had arranged to meet Tween at 11 p.m. outside the Manly International Hotel, which had been recently renovated and renamed the Manly Pacific Hotel by its owners, the Kalajzich family. (The Kalajziches would make the headlines themselves a few months later when Megan Kalajzich was murdered in her bed—a crime for which her husband, Andrew, was later convicted.) One of Yelavich's relatives said that on the day he disappeared Yelavich had told him he was 'going to score an ounce of heroin' from Tween that night. Curiously Yelavich's bike was found on his parents' front lawn the next morning.

Yelavich grew up in Manly where he surfed and played rugby league at school. He started using drugs in his mid-teens and heroin when he was about eighteen, and quickly became an addict. Originally a drug supplier, he was soon a heroin importer who, according to a friend, 'did over ten runs to Thailand to obtain drugs'. Flying home via Bali, Yelavich would hide the drug inside his surf boards and would 'dirty the boards up' to make it appear they had been used. At some stage he met and married a Thai girl and they had a child. From then until the early 1980s he would send money to support them.

At eighteen Yelavich had been arrested in Fremantle, Western Australia, and given two years' probation for possession of heroin. In June 1979 he was fined $2000 and placed on a supervised five-year good behaviour bond for possessing heroin. After returning to Sydney he worked as a drinks waiter at a Kings Cross nightclub and continued to deal drugs. Among his suppliers and customers were Tween and Johnson.

In 1980 Yelavich was arrested at Manly for supplying and possessing nearly 60 grams of heroin. While on bail he fled to Queensland's Gold Coast where he lived the life of a successful drug trafficker. He is also believed to have begun carrying a gun. His new girlfriend, twenty-year-old Andrea Frances Wharton, shared his addiction to heroin, having been a user since she was sixteen. While in Queensland Yelavich made at least one drug run to Thailand, bringing back 2 kilograms of heroin. As well as selling drugs locally, he continued to do business on Sydney's north shore. On 10 September 1982 Yelavich, who was using the name Anthony Allard, was arrested by the AFP Drug Unit after returning with his girlfriend to his home at Burleigh Heads. Yelavich was arrested and extradited to Sydney.

On 17 March 1983 Yelavich was convicted at Sydney District Court of supplying heroin and false passport charges. His sentence was deferred on his entering a recognisance of $1000 to be of good behaviour for five years; accepting probation and parole supervision; surrendering his passport and not travelling outside Australia. Just three months later Yelavich was arrested and charged in Burleigh Heads with possession of a replica pistol and cutting instruments. On 16 September the New South Wales Criminal Court of Appeal quashed the deferred sentence and re-sentenced Yelavich to three and a half years' jail for supplying drugs.

While serving his sentence, Yelavich continued to use heroin and other drugs and was involved in a jail drug network with 40-year-old Godfrey Jonassen Sadaraka, commonly known as John Sadler, a friend of Tween's from the early 1960s when both were doing time in New Zealand's Mount Eden jail. Sadaraka controlled much of the drug trade inside Long Bay and other jails. Among the couriers he used to smuggle heroin and other drugs into the jail were Tween and Johnson, who also acted as his debt collectors. Visits from Tween and Johnson also enabled Yelavich to maintain his north shore drug network.

On 18 January 1984, Yelavich was found to have the drugs Serapax and Lomotil in his possession and was confined to his cell for 48 hours. On 4 June 1984, still in custody, he appeared at Waverley Court and was sentenced to two months' imprisonment for carrying cutting weapons. On 14 September 1984 he was paroled.

Yelavich was not free for long. On 11 March 1985 he was arrested and charged with breaking, entering and stealing from a property at Cromer, in northern Sydney, and returned to Long Bay Remand Centre to serve the remaining three months of his non-parole period. As police later observed, 'It was a sloppy attempted break and enter in Cromer during which he was heavily affected by Rohypnol and managed to lock his keys inside the getaway car.' Placed on recognisance for five years to be of good behaviour, Yelavich was released from jail on parole on 14 August 1985.

On at least two occasions while in jail, Yelavich had begged friends on the outside to pay his drug debts of $1000 and $500. They were paid, but he continued to run up debts. Within days of Yelavich's release, Sadaraka had sent a debt collector to someone close to Yelavich with the message that his boss (Sadaraka) was 'a tough guy that you didn't fool around with'. Within hours Sadaraka backed up the threat by phoning from jail to demand $7000. The debt was paid.

Although Yelavich continued to deal drugs, his relationship with Tween and Johnson had soured. Tween was rumoured to have stolen nearly 300 grams of heroin belonging to Yelavich while at the same time demanding Yelavich pay outstanding drug debts to other prisoners.

For some time after Yelavich's disappearance Tween and Johnson continued to supply heroin to a number of his female clients in return for sex, just as they had when Yelavich was alive.

Sadaraka, originally from Auckland, had a long criminal record in New Zealand. He figured prominently in the 1965 Mount Eden jail riots during which prisoners burnt much of the jail. After his release, Sadaraka moved to Australia, where he was later convicted and jailed for the 1975 murder of his brother-in-law in Sydney. Released in 1992, Sadaraka was deported to New Zealand. A year later he was arrested and charged with the killing of 49-year-old marijuana grower Ken Forbes at Waiotemarama, near Opononi, in the Northland region of New Zealand. Forbes had been bashed and cut with either a knife or machete. The court was told that it was likely that Sadaraka took 'a degree of pleasure' extracting information from Forbes about his stash of drugs. At the time Forbes had a crop of around 600 plants under cultivation. In 1994 Sadaraka was convicted of murdering Forbes, but a decade later a retrial saw the conviction changed to manslaughter. Sadaraka was released from jail in 2003 and died of natural causes three years later.

After Yelavich was arrested in 1982 his girlfriend's life fell apart. She continued to use drugs, particularly heroin, and made several drug runs to Sydney. On 19 February 1984, while Yelavich was in jail, Wharton left her parents' Gold Coast home following an argument. Ten days later she sent a letter to her mother saying she was confused and planned to stay away for another month. The letter was post marked Darlinghurst, Sydney. Wharton was never heard from again. Her car was found at Coolangatta Airport. At the time of her disappearance Wharton was under Queensland probation and parole supervision for drug-related offences. In September 2012 the Deputy State Coroner found 'on the balance of probabilities that Andrea Wharton, a missing person the subject of this Inquest, is dead, but I am unable to determine the date or place of her death, nor the cause or manner of her death.' Tween and Johnson are prime suspects in her murder.

In 2012, 26 years after Yelavich's disappearance, the Deputy State Coroner, Carmel Forbes, found 'on the balance of probabilities that Ante Yelavich, a missing person, the subject of this Inquest, is dead, but I am unable to determine the place or manner or cause of this death which occurred sometime after 2 September 1985'. A $100,000 reward for information about the murder of Yelavich has never been claimed.

Johnson's relationship with Tween was lucrative but volatile. In January 1988 Johnson was the explosives man when a gang led by Michael Hurley broke into the National Australia Bank in Sydney's Chinatown and emptied more than 80 safety deposit boxes of cash, gold and jewellery said to have been worth millions of dollars. In the early 1990s Johnson and Tween are believed to have been involved in up to three drug importations through Western Australia. Not long afterwards the pair fell out, each man accusing the other of cheating on a drug deal. They never spoke to one another again.

In 2001 Johnson was arrested in Sydney for having possession of a semi-automatic 9 millimetre pistol, a shotgun, a stun gun, ammunition, a police identification badge signifying the rank of inspector, housebreaking implements, a knife and goods stolen or otherwise unlawfully obtained, and for resisting police in the execution of their duty. On his release from jail in April 2006 Johnson moved to Queensland where he died of natural causes in October 2010.

In September 1994 Tween was one of three people arrested over a 1200-plant hydroponic marijuana crop inside a warehouse at Gosford. Sentenced to three years' jail, Tween was released after eighteen months.

A decade later Tween and his 29-year-old son from his first marriage, Michael Anderson, were involved in a plot to import cocaine to Australia from Panama, via New Zealand, using watertight containers attached to the hulls of ships. In mid-October 2005, 29-year-old Anderson travelled to Panama, South America, followed a week later by his father, who was travelling under the false name of Victor Patrick Harris. Before leaving for Panama, Tween had tried to send his son at least US$7500, but the money was seized by US Customs. Anderson stayed with his father in Panama until early November when he returned to Australia, followed five weeks later by Tween.

On 7 June 2006 the MV *Tampa* departed Panama, reaching Auckland Harbour in New Zealand on 25 June. A routine inspection of the ship's hull by divers engaged by the New Zealand Quarantine Service discovered a watertight aluminium container attached by chains to the hull of the ship below the waterline. The container was removed and found to hold 14.4 kilograms of pure cocaine. New Zealand

Customs, Australian Customs, the AFP and the NSW Police began a joint operation to catch the culprits.

As the NSW Crime Commission learnt of the investigation into the Panama cocaine importations and discovered the names of the importers, Standen found himself in a difficult and compromised situation. Not only was his mate Tween the organiser, but Standen himself was receiving money from another drug importer, James Kinch, and was in the process of organising his own importation.

Johnson and Tween had already been the subjects of numerous state and federal investigations. Between 1991 and 1996 both were named in operations by the NSW Police, the AFP and the NCA. Most involved the importation and trafficking of drugs. Mark Standen took part in several of these operations, initially as an AFP investigator, later as a member of the NCA, and finally in his role at the NSW Crime Commission. He knew all about Tween's ongoing association with major organised crime figures and his record as a murderer, sex offender, drug importer and trafficker. But Standen could not have warned Tween even if he had wanted to, as Tween and his son were now under close physical and electronic surveillance by federal law enforcement authorities.

On 26 June the MV *Tampa* left Auckland Harbour for Brisbane before sailing on to Sydney and then Fremantle in Western Australia. Unable to inspect the hull in either Brisbane or Sydney, Tween telephoned his son and left a coded message on progress of the importation as the MV *Tampa* sailed to Fremantle: 'The lady's birthday is on or about the 9th so if, er, you could make, get her present and that by about Thursday or Friday . . . say Friday the 7th or the 8th. Make sure that we don't miss giving her presents. Okay, bye for now.'

Tween and his son travelled separately to Perth. Tween arrived first, bringing flippers, a mask and a wetsuit and hiring a car in Perth as well as two oxygen cylinders and two weight belts from a dive hire shop in Fremantle. He also bought an inflatable dinghy, a Honda outboard motor, stern light, foam float, rope and folding anchor. On 8 July Tween met his son at the airport. The next day they were observed carrying out surveillance close to where the MV *Tampa* was to be moored.

During the evening of 10 July they were seen travelling to Gilbert Fraser Reserve in North Fremantle where they inflated their motorised dinghy and loaded it with diving equipment before heading down the Swan River to the MV *Tampa*'s mooring near Stirling Bridge in Fremantle Harbour. Tween's son dived overboard and was detected on sonar swimming around the hull of the vessel. After about twenty minutes he returned to the dinghy, unable to find the container of drugs. The pair then motored away. The next day Michael Anderson returned to Sydney. Tween followed two days later, having left their diving equipment in Perth with a friend.

Seemingly undeterred, Tween set about arranging another importation using the same method but this time without his son. On 12 September 2006 the MV *Taronga* left Panama and a fortnight later docked in Auckland Harbour. Later that day divers inspected the vessel and found a metal container attached to the hull similar to the one attached to the *Tampa*. Inside was nearly 6 kilograms of pure cocaine. The drug was substituted by New Zealand authorities and the *Taronga* was allowed to sail for Brisbane.

From the next month Tween was in constant contact with 'Jamie' in Panama. They discussed the progress of the importation, referring to vessels as '*señoritas*'. From intercepted telephone conversations it became apparent that Tween realised all was not going well. His son was not there and there was nobody else who could help him retrieve the container from the hull.

On 25 October, the day after his last conversation with 'Jamie', police raided various properties and vehicles connected to Tween and his son, finding boats, diving equipment and travel documents used on trips to Panama, as well as cocaine. Traces of the drug were also discovered in containers similar to those taken from the *Tampa* and the *Taronga*, suggesting an earlier and successful importation.

The combined street value of the cocaine found on both vessels was more than $11 million. Tween and his son were arrested and charged with the attempted July 2006 importation. While in jail awaiting his trial, Tween had a visit from Mark Standen, during which he is said to have given an alibi statement. The AFP, who were running the case, were not told of Standen's visit.

Tween's son pleaded guilty and was sentenced to ten years' jail while Tween was convicted at trial and sentenced to eighteen years' jail.

Tween appealed against his conviction, claiming to be suffering from a range of physical and psychological conditions and arguing that he did 'not have significant criminal tendencies at the present time' and had only 'a moderate risk for recidivism'. At the time his criminal record had more than 30 entries, including possessing explosives, a machine gun and an unlicensed pistol; supplying drugs; indecent assault of a male; safe breaking; break, enter and steal; larceny; receiving stolen goods; and escaping lawful custody. His appeal was dismissed.

Tween spent a significant part of his sentence in the Long Bay Correctional Centre's aged and rehabilitation hospital ward, alongside Neddy Smith.

For many years Tween was registered at the NSW Crime Commission as Standen's informant. There is no known record of any useful information provided by Tween to either Standen or the commission during that period. The registration is believed to have been a cover to enable both men to explain their relationship if questions were ever asked. In many ways the relationship between Standen and Tween foreshadowed Standen's later relationship with James Kinch.

In 2007, during a NSW Police review of unsolved homicides, Manly detectives investigated the Yelavich murder while the Homicide Squad looked again at the disappearance of Trudie Adams. The two teams liaised and Detective Senior Constable Jayson Macleod of Manly contacted Standen at the NSW Crime Commission. For several months Standen repeatedly told Macleod that he knew of no holdings or human sources (informants) that could benefit the Yelavich murder investigation. Standen claimed to have had dealings with Tween and Johnson over many years because of their suspected involvement in the drug trade. He had 'a similar rapport' with both men, he said, without elaborating. Standen told Macleod that the Crime Commission was interested in helping and asked for a comprehensive overview of the Yelavich investigation, which Macleod supplied. But despite three months of negotiations, Standen offered nothing useful in return. Given Standen's close personal relationship with Tween it was no surprise, perhaps, that the Yelavich investigation stalled.

Three police investigations had already been conducted into the disappearance and believed murder of Trudie Adams when, in January 2011, the Deputy State Coroner, Scott Mitchell, began an inquest into her disappearance. Adams was described as being 'an outgoing, intelligent and well-educated young woman'; 'a happy and feisty girl with lots of friends and her whole life to look forward to'; 'part of an extremely strong network of girlfriends'; 'talented' and 'very warm and likeable'.

Between January and March more than 50 witnesses appeared before the Coroner, who noted that there had been two main lines of inquiry, namely the 'Roseland Lads' and Tween.

He found that Adams' disappearance had been 'a matter of great interest' among several in the Roseland Lads group and that they had 'made boastful, stupid and callous claims of knowledge of or responsibility for her fate'. Some who heard these claims had reported them to police, 'but even they probably didn't believe the substance of what was being said'.

Batt gave evidence at the inquest of his criminal association with Tween, including the sexual assault of Paul Whittaker. He told the inquest that he was scared of Tween, whom he regarded as 'well over the top', 'crazy,' 'capable of murder' and 'mad', and that he had severed relations with Tween in late 1976 after his release from jail over the Whittaker matter.

Two victims of the 1978 attacks were shown police photographs and identified Tween and Johnson as the men who had abducted and sexually assaulted them. Two other victims identified Tween as being 'very similar' to one of the men who attacked them. However, Counsel assisting the Coroner, Peter Hamill SC, observed that the process used when carrying out photographic line-ups would not pass muster in a courtroom today.

While the 1975 attack on drug dealer Whittaker by Tween and Batt had many similarities to the attacks on the women, the Coroner noted that in the former case the victim, Whittaker, was male and the motive related to a drug deal gone wrong.

Tween was brought from the hospital at Long Bay jail to give evidence to the inquest. He denied involvement in the murder of Adams and in any abduction and/or sexual assault, but admitted to having owned a mustard-coloured Holden panel van similar to the vehicle used in the abductions. Of the crime against Whittaker, Tween showed no remorse and was dismissive when questioned about it at the inquest, saying, 'There was no violence or harm done to him.' Tween refused to answer some questions and was twice sent to the cells at the Glebe Coroner's Court to consider his position.

It was noted at the inquest that the sexual assaults began soon after Tween moved to Sydney's northern beaches in June 1970 and stopped while Tween was incarcerated between 1971 and 1974 and between 1975 and 1977, then stopped altogether when Tween moved to the Central Coast after Adams' disappearance.

Swabs had been taken from some of the fourteen women in a bid to identify the offender's blood type but around 2009, when then Detective Gavin McKean sought to use the swabs to test for DNA, he found they had been disposed of in the 1980s.

McKean and a number of other police who gave evidence at the inquest expressed the view that Tween was either responsible for the disappearance of Adams and several other crimes of violence or was a strong suspect. Johnson was also named by some as Tween's partner in these crimes.

On 1 April 2011 the Deputy State Coroner found 'on the balance of probabilities that Trudie Jeanette Adams . . . died shortly after 12.30 a.m. on Sunday, 25 June 1978 in or near the northern beaches area of Sydney or in the surrounding bushland as a result of a criminal act or acts or misadventure associated with a criminal act or acts by a person or persons unknown'. He referred the case to the Commissioner of Police for further investigation 'in accordance with the cold cases protocol'. The Adams case is among around 200 unsolved cases allocated for further investigation by the Unsolved Homicide Team.

Despite the NSW Government having, in 2008, offered a $250,000 reward for information leading to the arrest and conviction of her killer, the case remains unsolved.

In September 2013, Tween died of natural causes in jail without shedding any light on his crimes.

Several detectives and former detectives who worked on Tween between the 1980s and the 2000s believe he and his accomplices were often tipped off when they were being targeted by police and that, on several occasions, this enabled him to avoid arrest.

After Tween's arrest in 2006, his former second wife was heard to complain to a drug-trafficking mate of Tween about Standen, explaining that they had 'looked after' him for years: he had moved into their home, they had provided him with financial support, and they had found him a new home.

In the mid-2000s Standen's son applied to join the NSW Police, listing Tween as a reference. The job application and reference were rejected. In 2008 one of Standen's children described his and Tween's families as being 'very close'.

Twenty months after Tween's arrest, Standen himself was behind bars.

CHAPTER THIRTEEN

The game

From the moment James Kinch was arrested on 14 March 2003 the 'game' began. It was one familiar to police and criminals around the world. The rules go like this: a big-time criminal is caught. He is an old hand in the international drug trade and knows how it works. His cooperation could inflict serious damage on parts of the drug trade. For the police, the aim is to get as much information as possible, even if it means doing a deal: putting in a good word for him at his sentencing to get his jail time reduced or, if his information is valuable enough, indemnifying him against prosecution and placing him in a witness protection program.

For the criminal, on the other hand, the goal is to create the pretence of cooperation and the illusion of valuable information (including the possibility of ongoing cooperation and information). You might tell the police what they already know, thereby confirming their suspicions (even if those suspicions are wrong), or what they are likely to discover anyway. You might tell them where to find a stash of drugs, knowing (or at least suspecting) that police have the location under surveillance, or give them information they might have already picked up from telephone intercepts or listening devices. Now and then the cooperation will extend to giving up some 'small fish' who cannot harm the criminal or his network or, better still, a competitor.

For both sides, the object of the game is the same: to gain more than you give.

In the game between Kinch and the police, the police started in front. Kinch was under arrest and his bail had been refused. The police were still gathering evidence against him and his associates, both in Sydney and in the Netherlands, and the deeper they probed, the stronger the evidence would be. The courts would take a dim view of Kinch's British criminal record and, if convicted, he was likely to do significant jail time. But Kinch had two things going for him. One was his long history of arrests in the UK: it meant that he was well versed in the game and knew exactly how the police played it. The other was the almost naïve eagerness of the police and the Crime Commission to offer him a deal in return for information. Almost immediately, Kinch began to provide useful information—or did he?

Not long after his arrest, Mark Standen described Kinch as 'extremely reliable', providing 'frequent, high-quality information to the Commission'. While singing his praises, Standen was more than happy to take Kinch at his own word: '[Kinch] said that whilst we may find it hard to believe, he is a man of his word and will do for us what he said he will do.'

Meanwhile, the AFP noted that Kinch dealt 'direct with M Standen and [it] is unlikely that he will communicate with other law enforcement officers in Australia'.

Given the closeness of their relationship, it was perhaps not surprising that Standen soon began to argue for the charges against Kinch to be dropped.

In the days immediately after his arrest, Kinch provided information that led to the seizure of large amounts of cash and drugs. But the authorities had already seized much of the cash and knew the whereabouts of more; as inquiries progressed they would almost certainly have found it without help from Kinch.

Was it a case of Kinch playing the 'game'—or was there another, more intriguing motive behind his 'cooperation'? A person who knew Kinch and was close to the case has suggested a different motive: Kinch knew he was in trouble and was trying to flush out signs of police corruption that he would be able to take advantage of. When he directed the police to the drug money, Kinch knew exactly how much cash was there. If the police making the seizure claimed to have found less, it meant they had kept the remainder for themselves. Kinch would then have known that one or more of his captors was corrupt—and potentially corruptible. If this was the plan, it didn't work—the drug money was properly accounted for and Kinch's ingenious ploy failed.

The flow of seemingly high-quality information continued. As well as leading the authorities to 72 kilograms of ecstasy tablets—the previously undetected portion of the Ballis–Moore importation (see Chapter 5)—Kinch told them about a planned importation of more than 200 kilograms of ecstasy tablets. But this importation had already been detected by Customs.

Between late April and mid-May 2003, just six to eight weeks after his arrest, Kinch told Standen an extraordinary story; that a hit man sent to Australia by the Dutch drug syndicate had visited him in jail 'to attend to any of his needs'. These 'needs' could include an escape plan and, if necessary, the murder of his one-time cleaner, Kirsty Chambers, whose evidence was critical to Kinch's prosecution. Kinch claimed that he 'told the person that the girl was to be left alone, that he had matters under control and that things were not as bad as they first appeared'. He also claimed 'that the same person, and an unknown accomplice, had visited his lawyer, William 'Bill' O'Brien, and demanded a copy of the brief of evidence and other information known to O'Brien'. According to Standen, Kinch said that 'O'Brien had been terrified by this visit and subsequently told Kinch that if he wanted "special things done", he would need to find another lawyer. O'Brien has not reported this incident to the commission.' Eight years later plainclothes constable Chris Symons said he had been present when Kinch made these claims, yet no contemporaneous notes were taken. The first written record appears to have been the notes made by Standen after a conversation on 23 May 2003 with the Crime Commissioner, Phillip Bradley, and the then Deputy Director of Public Prosecutions, Greg Smith, about dropping money-laundering charges against Kinch.

Given Kinch's importance to the Haklander syndicate, there is every reason to believe that the proposed assassination might have been considered and could have been carried out. Yet Chambers was left at risk, without protection. If Kinch had told the truth, then a professional killer remained (and possibly still remains) at large, either in Australia, the Netherlands or elsewhere. If, on the other hand, Kinch had lied about the hit man or the offer of escape, that would have raised serious questions about his value as an informant, the very basis of his relationship with the Crime Commission. Yet these claims were never tested.

Not all of Kinch's information was accepted at face value. Soon after his arrest, he spoke of a person we will call 'Nick'. Kinch claimed that he worked for Nick but suspected that Nick and another colleague had stolen $1 million in drug proceeds that was supposed to have been split between the three of them. However, the minutes of a meeting between the NSW Police and the Crime Commission report that 'according to Mark Standen, Kinch has been lying about his role in this matter. Kinch claimed that he was working for . . . [Nick] . . . but information from TI [telephone intercepts] indicated otherwise.'

Over the following months Kinch continued to talk. Despite the evidence that Kinch had been 'lying about his role in this matter', Standen continued to describe Kinch's information about Nick and his associates as being 'reliable'. Standen would later dismiss this discrepancy by saying it was 'commonplace for people to give an isolated piece of information in the hope that it might assist them. It's unusual for someone to give what appears to be a complete download of everything they know.'

Kinch went on to give deliberately vague information about impending large-scale importations of cocaine (up to 100 kilograms); ecstasy (up to five million tablets) and other drugs; about previous importations and rumoured cash hoards of several million dollars belonging to the Dutch syndicate; about a planned new ecstasy laboratory in the Netherlands and about the ringleaders of the syndicate and its activities. Little came of these 'tip-offs'. As one senior police officer commented, 'The information was no different to saying George Freeman was a crook. So what's new?'

There was one occasion when a tip-off from Kinch did produce a result. Nearly 160 kilograms of ecstasy was seized from a container on a wharf and several people were arrested, but neither they nor the drugs were connected to Kinch or his operations.

As Kinch 'talked' and pushed for deals, Standen complained to the then head of the Crime Commission, Phillip Bradley, that the money-laundering charge was 'the stumbling block to our confiscation settlement and further debriefing of Kinch'. In May—just two months after Kinch's arrest—Standen prepared a submission that outlined Kinch's value as an informant and claimed that '[Kinch] indicated that he would be prepared to plead guilty to the drug charges but sought to have the money-laundering charge withdrawn.'

Two weeks later Standen complained that 'the DPP girl' was sending lengthy requests, which 'seems like a big fat waste of time if we're not going to proceed on money laundering'. A few days later, at Standen's urging, Bradley wrote to the then Deputy Director of the Office of the Director of Public Prosecutions (ODPP), Greg Smith, about advice given by Standen at a meeting with the ODPP. At the meeting Standen had confirmed that 'Kinch has indicated a willingness to plead guilty to the drug charge in return for the DPP not proceeding on the money-laundering charge' and that 'Kinch has provided and is continuing to provide substantial assistance in relation to a number of matters'. Bradley's letter noted that a 'custodial sentence [on the drug charges] is likely to be imposed and the assistance [given by Kinch] will not be brought to the attention of the sentencing judge'. The usual practice of providing 'a letter of comfort' to the judge explaining how the defendant had assisted police was considered to be too big a risk for Kinch. Bradley argued that Kinch 'cannot be otherwise recognised and he may continue to assist, and the public interest would be served by encouraging him to do so'. Two days later the money-laundering charge against Kinch was dropped. The court was told of this decision on 3 June 2003. Three weeks later Kinch was granted bail and released.

Despite Standen's assurances, both verbal and in writing, that Kinch would plead guilty to the drug charges, Kinch stuck to his plea of not guilty. Asset confiscation proceedings, which were to be resolved once the money-laundering charge had been dropped, also remained outstanding. Assets totalling $1.3 million had been restrained within weeks of Kinch's arrest. A total of $300,000 was later deducted to cover his legal fees. The confusion increased when Standen informed the ODPP that, although the Crime Commission had told Greg Smith that Kinch would plead guilty to the drug charges, 'Mr Kinch has stated that he did not give such an undertaking and that we were mistaken.'

According to Standen, Kinch had said he would 'plead guilty to "the right charge", being a charge reflecting what he actually did. It is unclear what this means although he has discussed an offence . . . [of] . . . hindering the discovery of evidence concerning a serious offence by another person.' Standen added, 'It is fair to say that the money-laundering case was far from strong.'

In the months after his arrest, Kinch told authorities that during the years 2002–03 he had sent to European suppliers about $60 million collected from wholesale ecstasy buyers in Australia, while other syndicate members based in Sydney had sent back many more millions of dollars. Among the methods he described were physically carrying the cash out of the country in luggage, hiding cash in air cargo and telegraphic transfers. Most, however, was sent through money launderers using the *hawala* system (see Chapter 14). Around September 2003, just weeks from his committal, Kinch told authorities that he had access to $1.5 million in cash that the Dutch syndicate wanted him to 'get out of Australia' and send to them in the Netherlands. According to Kinch, those who had been minding the money for him had become impatient and had brought the money from Melbourne to Sydney where it was collected on his behalf. The $1.5 million was made up of $50 and $20 bills, he said, and he could 'access the money within two hours'. A few days later his story had changed. In the new version $300,000 was being held by a Sydney drug gang and a further $100,000 had been put aside for legal fees in another case. Getting hold of this $400,000 would take a little longer.

Asked to give the cash up to the Crime Commission, or at least to tell them where it was, Kinch refused. He agreed, however, to take part in a controlled operation, supervised by the police, to transfer some of the funds to the syndicate, provided he was protected from prosecution for any offence he might commit in the process. The protection was given. The cash for the operation—$250,000—was to come from the Melbourne money.

One day in early October, Kinch produced a black Puma bag containing $300,000 cash in various denominations (there was no explanation for the extra $50,000, which was apparently accepted by the Crime Commission without question). After the cash was counted and its serial numbers recorded, Kinch went to the Exchange Point, a business known to provide foreign currency and money-laundering services, and handed over the $300,000. A few weeks later Kinch told authorities that the transfer had been 'successful': the money had been received by his colleagues in the Netherlands (see Chapter 14).

Unconcerned by the disappearance of the $300,000, authorities began talking about further 'controlled' money-laundering operations. But having whetted their appetite, Kinch again backed away from his earlier promises, refusing to cooperate until his outstanding drug matters were resolved. (His committal proceedings were about to begin.) This time he added two new demands: the return of his passport and the removal of travel restrictions preventing his departure from Australia. Kinch explained that he wanted to return to the UK to see his family and friends over Christmas. He would return to Sydney in the New Year to face the outstanding drug charges.

Kinch then changed his mind again, saying that he would not participate in any more controlled remittances until his application for variations to his bail was resolved. Invited to leave the remaining $1.2 million cash (the story of how much money Kinch could lay his hands on changed constantly) with the Crime Commission to 'encourage his return', Kinch refused, insisting that the money was not his to give away.

In October 2003 Kinch's committal proceedings on the two drug charges began. Both the prosecution and defence were aware of problems with the case. Four months earlier, Stephen O'Connor, a solicitor at the ODPP, had interviewed Kirsty Chambers, who made serious allegations about Mark Standen and his role in preparing her statement. In accordance with the prosecution's duty of disclosure, O'Connor had written to Kinch's lawyer, O'Brien, describing his interview with Chambers. He had asked Chambers 'if she agreed with everything in her statement, i.e. was it true,' to which she answered, 'No.' Chambers didn't agree with the part that read, 'In particular some keys on the hall table.' She claimed that 'Mark [Standen] put that in and said to her they were the keys to the safety deposit boxes.' According to Chambers, 'Jimmy [Kinch] just told her to grab everything on the hall table, he didn't specifically say the keys, they were there but it was not what Jimmy said.' O'Connor went on: 'She [Chambers] said she protested that wasn't what he said but they said don't worry about it and she signed it anyway.'

O'Connor's letter explained that he had discussed with Chambers the circumstances that led to her making the statement. 'She said it was all very intimidating and embarrassing. She was asked to go with them to answer questions, which she did . . . Mark really came the heavy with her . . . it was like *L.A. Law* stuff. He kept saying to her "this is big, Kirsty, we are talking about Spain, Portugal, this is really huge. We know what you have been doing, who you have been doing it with", etc.' Chambers told O'Connor that Standen then asked if she had a family. 'When she said yes he then said "well we can make things very difficult for you".' Chambers got the impression that the 'threat', as she put it, was coming from Mark that 'if she didn't tell them everything he would make life very difficult for her and her family . . . they really came the heavy with her. She asked [Standen] if she needed a lawyer and [Standen] said no.'

Four months after making her claims about Standen, Chambers entered the witness box as the main prosecution witness against Kinch. As expected, Chambers' evidence was not the same as that given in her statement. She repeated her claim that not everything in the statement was true, that she had felt threatened by Standen and that he was the one who had inserted the untrue claims about Kinch into the statement.

Chambers' story changed several times during the committal hearing and at one point she told the court that she was too scared to give evidence. The prosecution declared Chambers to be a hostile witness, while the Magistrate observed that 'The ramifications [of Chambers' claims] for all are terribly important'. In response, the prosecutor, Roger Kimbell, told the court that Standen would be called to answer the allegations. However, Standen was not called and the prosecution closed its case. Despite the 'ramifications' of Chambers' claims and Standen's failure to give evidence, Kinch was committed for trial.

Within days Kinch was up to his old tricks with the Crime Commission. An application by Kinch's lawyer for a 'No Bill' (effectively a request for the charges to be dropped) was filed with the ODPP and rejected.

Meanwhile, Standen ignored requests from the ODPP to prepare a statement in response to Chambers' claims. In a letter dated 28 November 2003 to the Crown prosecutor, Roger Kimbell, Standen apologised 'for not having confirmed my comments in writing prior to today'. He recalled that, during their telephone conversation of 17 November, they had 'discussed the key prosecution witness, Kirsty Chambers, and agreed she is a problem in that she has now provided several versions of her dealings with Mr Kinch.' Standen went on: 'I note you require a statement from me concerning the taking of the original statement. I will provide that in the next week or so. As you are in the best position to assess her reliability I do not intend to say more about Ms. Chambers.'

Noting that the ODPP had rejected the defence's 'No Bill' application, Standen emphasised Kinch's value as an informant, stressing the importance of the information he had already provided and of other information he was offering, and that Kinch 'now feels he has been assisting the authorities without due recognition of his efforts. He agrees that the [dropping of the] original money-laundering charge was some recognition but was of the view that the chance of a successful prosecution for that offence was unlikely.' According to Standen, Kinch believed that 'he has provided considerable and ongoing assistance that has not been recognised. He has indicated that the risks attached to his working with the authorities are extreme. It is difficult to disagree. He is presently disinclined to continue his assistance.'

Despite Standen's own promise to provide a statement 'in the next week or so', it was never provided. No further effort appears to have been made to get it, nor to interview police who were present when Chambers was detained or who might have been present when she was questioned. Her allegations against Standen had effectively been brushed aside.

During six months of so-called 'cooperation' with Standen and other law enforcement officials, Kinch had never mentioned his boss, Fat Ron Haklander, the head of the Dutch syndicate. In September 2003, acting on information provided by Dutch police, Standen and plainclothes constable Chris Symons had asked Kinch about a person known as Fat Ron, who was suspected of being the head of the syndicate. Admitting that he had met Fat Ron, Kinch provided some typically vague information about him. When shown a picture of Yaron Abraham, an international drug boss, Kinch falsely identified him as Fat Ron. Two months later Dutch police advised their Sydney colleagues that 'Fat Ron is not one and the same as Yaron Abraham' and that they had 'a strong suspicion as to his true identity [Ronald Haklander]'.

Told of the Dutch suspicions, Kinch equivocated. A note records that he now 'seems to concur'. At no time did Kinch admit to knowing Fat Ron to be Ron Haklander. Nor did Kinch admit that after his arrival in Australia in late 2001 he had kept in regular contact with Haklander. Kinch also failed to mention that in February 2002 he had flown to Bali to meet Haklander and other senior members of the syndicate to discuss drug operations in Australia, or that he had socialised with Haklander in Sydney in April 2002. As they searched for Haklander, Dutch police asked Standen: 'Can our friend [Kinch] tell something about the place where he stays?' Standen replied, 'I have not had contact with [Kinch] lately and he is less and less interested in passing information . . . However, the other day he told me that Fat Ron has gone back to Spain.' Standen was lying: at the time he was seeing Kinch almost daily.

■ ■ ■

In late 2005 Dutch and US law enforcement authorities arrested 37 members of Yaron Abraham's drug network in the Netherlands and the US. Dutch court records show Abraham was suspected of making more than $100 million from trafficking ecstasy. The same records link him to drug and money-laundering activities in Australia (see Chapter 14). He was jailed for eleven years.

As the ODPP considered whether or not to proceed with the Kinch trial, federal law enforcement authorities received information from the Netherlands that 'since January 2003 a Dutch-based criminal syndicate headed by

Ron Haklander . . . has stockpiled over 4000 kilograms of MDMA in Australia. The syndicate is well known to Dutch authorities and considered to be a major player in the Australian MDMA market.' Emphasising the size of the syndicate, the report concluded: 'The syndicate is suspected of having the resources and capability of affecting the supply of and the price of MDMA in Australia.'

Standen paid no attention to the warnings from the Dutch authorities. During January 2004 he continued to discuss with Kinch the possibility of controlled operations, but Kinch refused to become involved. He also turned down another request to hand over the $1.2 million, telling Standen and Symons that he no longer had control of the cash and that some of it had already been sent out of Australia. He claimed not to know how or who had sent it. In effect, Kinch was admitting that while 'cooperating' with the Crime Commission to have the money-laundering charges against him dropped, he had contrived to launder an untold amount of cash (anywhere between $300,000 and $1.5 million) back to his drug syndicate bosses in the Netherlands.

Fearing for her safety, Chambers 'disappeared' after Kinch was committed for trial, leaving Australia on 17 January 2004 for New Zealand. Ten days later the ODPP dropped the two drug charges against Kinch. In return he agreed to settle a proceeds of crime action by the Crime Commission in the sum of $1.3 million, less $300,000 in legal fees. Kinch's passport was returned to him and on 14 February he left Australia. Although prohibited from returning for five years, Kinch quickly got to work meeting the needs of the Australian ecstasy market.

Kinch had played the game and won. He had beaten all the charges, remitted $300,000 to his syndicate bosses with the authority of the commission and up to $1.5 million while 'working for the commission' but without their knowledge, and still had at least $1 million in Australia. The drugs he had surrendered to the authorities were simply part of the costs of business in the drug trade, and those people he had named were either already known to authorities or of little consequence to the syndicate. Kinch's legal fees had been paid for out of assets seized and forfeited. Those assets represented only a fraction of his drug fortune: he had laundered at least $60 million profit in Australian drug deals in just two years before his arrest and had continued to profit from the drug trade while on bail. Importantly, Kinch had emerged with a 'new friend'—Mark Standen—who appeared only too happy to help him. Standen would later say of his relationship with Kinch: 'We were friendly and friends at that point.'

As he left Australia Kinch was still playing the game. The importations would continue and the $1 million that he had not handed over to the Crime Commission would be used two years later to bribe Standen and to fund another importation.

Kinch has several tattoos, but the most revealing is the one on the fingers of his left hand, which spells 'ACAB'. The letters stand for 'all cops are bastards'. The implications of that tattoo went unheeded by the law enforcement authorities in Australia.

CHAPTER FOURTEEN

Follow the money

For all his lies, reliable intelligence about the Dutch syndicate's drug activities in Australia suggests that Jimmy Kinch's claim to have sent $60 million back to his bosses in the Netherlands may well be accurate. In the eighteen months before Kinch's arrest in March 2003 at least 23 members of Fat Ron Haklander's syndicate are known to have visited Sydney to handle the delivery and sale of eight or more importations of ecstasy into Sydney. The importations, more than six million tablets in all, had a street value of at least $240 million. Yet Kinch's $60 million represents less than 1 per cent of the annual amount laundered in Australia. In 2004 the Australian Institute of Criminology estimated that up to $6.3 billion of criminal profits—much of it from the drug trade—was laundered here each year, the bulk of it using the *hawala* (an Arabic word meaning transfer) system.

In its simplest form, *hawala* is a system of transferring money between financial institutions without the physical movement of cash. A customer in country A approaches the money broker (or launderer), known as a *hawaladar*, and requests that money be 'transferred' to country B. The hawaladar contacts their associate in country B (or the next point en route to country B) and eventually the money is made available in local currency out of the *hawaladar*'s funds in country B. There is no paper trail and the money is paid to the person giving the password for that transaction. Numerous transactions occurring over weeks and months between *hawaladars* in various countries ensure accounts are balanced. (Although it was not known by the name *hawala*, a similar method was used to transfer millions of dollars in drug money during the late 1970s by the notorious Nugan Hand Merchant Bank on behalf of clients including the Murray Stewart Riley heroin syndicate and the Mr Asia heroin syndicate.)

In October 2003 James Kinch organised the transfer of $300,000 in drug money from Sydney to his bosses in the Netherlands under the noses of state and federal police. Although the money itself vanished, the operation led to a major money-laundering investigation that targeted the very money-exchange business used by Kinch.

During the early 2000s the Dutch syndicate used at least four *hawaladar*-type outlets to launder Australian profits. The Exchange Point in Sussex Street, Sydney, operated by Abdul Azees Mohamed Ansari ('Azees') and his brother, Hajamaideen Mohamed Ansari ('Haja'), was one such outlet. The Ansari brothers were born in India and moved with their family to Singapore, where they lived for about a decade before migrating to Australia in the mid-1990s.

Both brothers settled in Sydney. In 1994 Azees found work in foreign exchange with a local finance company. Six years later he opened the Exchange Point with his brother Haja. Before long the brothers had a list of clients eager to launder money through the Exchange Point.

In mid-2003 Doran Yona, a 51-year-old Israeli national, was introduced by his nephew Yossi to someone named Roni, who offered to pay Yona to fly from Europe to Sydney to do a job for him. The job was to get a large amount of money out of Australia. For his troubles he would be paid all expenses plus US$10,000. Roni was part of a large European drug syndicate—the same syndicate to which James Kinch belonged. Yona agreed.

Arriving in Sydney on 3 October, Yona received his instructions by phone from Roni in Europe. He went to an apartment in Bondi, where he found more than $2 million in cash inside a floor safe. The apartment had been rented by an unidentified woman and the safe had been shipped to Sydney a few months earlier from Antwerp. Its false back had been used to hide a shipment of ecstasy; now it contained the proceeds of that importation.

Over ten days Yona delivered the cash by hand to the Ansaris at Exchange Point, who deposited it into various bank accounts in sums of less than $10,000. Meanwhile, Yona hired a removalist to take the safe to a storage depot and then flew back to Europe.

After receiving the money, the syndicate sent Yona back to Sydney do it all over again. The fee was the same: US$10,000. Yona arrived in Sydney on 23 June 2004 and went straight to the Exchange Point, where he met the Ansari brothers. While discussing the transfer of cash out of Australia, Azees asked, 'Any idea how much?' to which Yona replied, 'Two, maybe three [million dollars].' This time the transfer was to take place over a longer period of time and 'involved more steps than on the previous occasion'. The cash was to be handed to Yona over several weeks. As Yona received each instalment, he would deliver it to the Exchange Point.

Yona booked into the Swiss-Grand Hotel, Bondi Beach, hired a Holden Commodore and, using a false name, leased a mobile phone. Over the next few days, telephone conversations between Yona, the Ansari brothers and others (including his overseas contacts) were intercepted by the police.

Among the people Yona had been told to contact was a man named Tim Kauwenberghs, a 27-year-old Belgian national who had arrived in Australia via Hong Kong on 29 May 2004 and booked into the Mercure Hotel in George Street, Sydney. Kauwenberghs had a criminal record in Europe that included intentional battery and wounding, robbery with violence, fraudulent destruction of goods and possession of psychotropic substances. He was serving a suspended sentence at the time he flew to Australia.

Six weeks earlier, a Belgian named 'Koen' had offered Kauwenberghs $20,000 to install a 'safe' at the premises of one of his business associates in Australia. The safe had been dispatched from Belgium and shipped to Sydney, arriving on 18 February 2004. After being cleared by Customs it had been taken to a unit at Storage King, Eastgardens. According to Kauwenberghs, it was while the safe was in storage that he received a phone call from Koen in Belgium telling him that it contained a large quantity of ecstasy tablets, and that he would be paid $150,000 to collect the safe and take it somewhere.

On 9 June Kauwenberghs retrieved the safe and the drugs from Storage King. Three days later he and his girlfriend, who had accompanied him to Australia, drove to the Central Coast and rented a house at 17A Hargraves Street, The Entrance North, in the name 'Koen van Pratt of 48 Arrolsenstraat, Ieper, Belgium, 8700'. At first Kauwenberghs stored the drugs in the laundry, but then he buried them in nearby sand dunes at Tuggerah.

Two weeks later, on Koen's instructions, Kauwenberghs met 'Dave' at The Entrance and handed him around 90,000 ecstasy tablets. It was the first supply of the drug to a major buyer. Dave has not been identified, but Koen must have known and trusted him. Later Dave warned Kauwenberghs that he was probably under police surveillance.

On 24 June Kauwenberghs received a telephone call from Koen, who told him to expect a call in about an hour and a half from a man who would arrange to give him the keys to a car into which he was to put another 230,000 ecstasy tablets. The call was from Yona (the pair had never met). Yona named a street in Bondi where he would be waiting with the car, a rented Holden Commodore. Kauwenberghs arrived for the rendezvous and drove the Commodore back to The Entrance. Over the next two days there were telephone calls between Kauwenberghs, Yona and Koen. It was agreed that Kauwenberghs would leave the Commodore containing the ecstasy tablets in the car park of the Swiss-Grand Hotel at Bondi for Yona to collect. The delivery was made on 26 June.

The following day Koen rang Kauwenberghs and told him to deliver another 100,000 ecstasy tablets to Yona. Kauwenberghs hesitated, telling Koen that he had 'done enough'. A few hours later, however, he left The Entrance and drove to Bondi with the drugs in another rented car. Police watched him load a number of bags into the boot of

Yona's car in the car park of the Swiss-Grand Hotel. The bags were found to contain 6.7 kilograms of ecstasy tablets.

The next day, 28 June 2004, Kauwenberghs was arrested at Sydney International Airport as he was about to board a plane (his girlfriend had left the country twelve days earlier). That afternoon police executed a search warrant on Yona's car. In the boot, they found a sports bag containing 24 large plastic packs and two smaller white bags containing 204,527 ecstasy tablets. A total of $15,000 in cash was found in Yona's hotel room.

Yona was arrested and charged. The next day, after a joint state–federal surveillance operation on the Exchange Point, the Ansari brothers were arrested and charged. With the principals rounded up, the proposed laundering of up to $3 million—the initial reason for Yona's visit—was 'nipped in the bud'.

Ten months after his arrest, Yona rolled and gave evidence against the Ansari brothers. After pleading guilty to drug supply and conspiring to commit money laundering, he was sentenced to eight years' and two years' jail respectively.

Azees and Haja Ansari were charged with more than 70 offences, but were eventually convicted on two counts of conspiring to commit a money-laundering offence and were each sentenced to a total of seven years' jail. The jury was unable to reach a verdict on a third Ansari brother, Jaleel, who lived in France and who faced the same conspiracy charges. The evidence against Jaleel was limited to intercepted telephone conversations with his brothers. His role appeared to be to facilitate the *hawala* system in Europe.

Kauwenberghs was charged in Sydney with two counts of possession of a commercial quantity of ecstasy and three counts of supplying ecstasy. He pleaded guilty to all offences.

Despite rolling over and providing information to the Dutch and Belgian authorities, Kauwenberghs was jailed for a total of fourteen years.

One of the leaders of the Dutch–Belgian syndicate to which Yona, his nephew Yossi and Kauwenberghs belonged was Yaron Abraham, the man whom Dutch authorities had wrongly suspected of being Fat Ron Haklander and whom James Kinch had misidentified as Haklander. Although Abraham and Haklander were not the same man, they had one thing in common: each was the leader of an international ecstasy syndicate.

In 2005 Abraham and six others were arrested in the Netherlands while US law enforcement authorities arrested another 30 people in the United States. Dutch court records show Abraham was suspected of making 'more than $100 million from drug sales' through a network that stretched from Europe to China, Australia and the United States. The Dutch investigation looked at 'large-scale trafficking in ecstasy tablets hidden, amongst other things, in chandeliers to be sent to Australia. The main suspect in this matter for the Dutch justice system was [Yaron] Abraham.'

The Dutch investigators thanked Australian law enforcement authorities for their assistance—in particular, the information provided by Kauwenberghs: 'Your declarations have contributed to the pool of documentary proof in order to have Y Abraham convicted for a period of eleven years of incarceration.'

CHAPTER FIFTEEN

Business partners

Released on bail three months after his arrest in March 2003, James Kinch returned to being an active player in the international drug trade. Between 2003 and 2006 the Dutch syndicate he worked for carried out nine importations of ecstasy oil and one of cocaine into Sydney. Kinch left Australia for the last time in February 2004 but continued to manage the importations. His presence was no longer necessary, since he had someone to act as his 'eyes and ears' in Sydney. That person was Mark Standen.

In November 2004 Dutch law enforcement authorities came to Australia both to brief local authorities and to be briefed by them on James Kinch and the activities of the Dutch ecstasy syndicate. One of the people they were keen to talk to was the assistant director of operations at the NSW Crime Commission, Mark Standen.

Kinch was regarded by the Dutch police as an 'active

member' of the ecstasy syndicate. This assessment was supported by an intelligence report that quoted two criminals discussing the location of a large quantity of ecstasy held in Australia: '[T]he person who would know [where the drugs are stored] would be Jimmy [Kinch] who lives in Portugal . . . Jimmy is a big mover of drugs and would know about the shipment.'

A copy of this report reached Standen but he did not act on it. He hid the report for six months before emailing the Dutch authorities in June 2005: 'I have not had much contact with H [H or Hogan was a pseudonym given to Kinch by police] lately. He is less and less interested in passing information because we are unable to get him what he wants [authority to return to Australia].'

Not for the first time, Standen's answer was a mixture of truth and lies. Kinch did want to return to Australia and Standen had been unable to persuade authorities to let him. But his claim not to have had much contact with Kinch was a lie. The pair was in regular contact and Standen could get in touch with Kinch whenever he wanted. They were in contact more than 50 times during the last ten months of 2004 and more than 110 times during 2005. In this period Kinch visited at least seven different countries: the Netherlands, the UK, Portugal, Germany, Belgium, Brazil and Thailand. Standen was well aware that Kinch had no interest in passing on information unless it directly benefited him, the syndicate and its drug network.

Kinch's arrest in March 2003 had forced the syndicate to reorganise the Australian end of its business. Three months later, Kinch's timely release on bail enabled him to make himself useful to his successor.

A Dutch national whom we will call 'Robert' arrived

in Sydney for the first time on 20 June 2003 to arrange the incorporation of a business we will call 'the front company'. Robert also organised secure storage for any importations the company might make. The parent company, which was based in Amsterdam, was described as a 'supplier of clear drop paraffin lamps'. Eighteen days after arriving in Sydney, Robert flew back to the Netherlands. Everything was now fixed for the Dutch syndicate to resume importations. Once landed and cleared, the shipments would be distributed through the old network set up by Kinch.

As the Haklander syndicate's new manager of operations in Sydney, Robert returned to Australia on 11 September to confirm arrangements for the first in a series of planned drug importations. He stayed for a week before flying home. On 22 September a shipment of lamps, together with 3350 kilograms of what was described as paraffin oil, but is believed to have been liquid ecstasy, arrived in Sydney from the parent company in Amsterdam. Robert returned to Sydney four days later, in time for the consignment to be cleared by Customs and distributed to buyers. This time he stayed for three weeks.

Over the next two and a half years six more consignments were shipped to Sydney in containers: in February 2004, August–September 2004, November–December 2004, January 2005, February–March 2005 and April 2006. Robert followed a similar pattern of travel for each importation, arriving in Sydney a week or two before the shipment was due and returning to the Netherlands a week or two after it was landed. Unidentified Dutch colleagues flew to Sydney to act as middlemen between Robert and the distribution network. Between importations, Robert visited Sydney to check on sales, security, the flow of profits to the Netherlands and preparations for the next importation.

In December 2005 Standen received his first known cash 'gift' from Kinch. It was $47,000, and Standen arranged for it to be paid into the business account of a long-time friend, Bakhos 'Bill' Jalalaty, and for Jalalaty to give him the money in a series of payments over two months to hide its source. The purpose of the 'gift', it was later claimed, was to pay for Standen to have eye surgery, estimated to cost about $5000. The balance was to pay off some of his American Express and Visa card debts.

Bill Jalalaty was born in Zgharta, a town in northern Lebanon, on 19 December 1962. He migrated to Australia with his parents when he was eight years old. Jalalaty married for the first time around 1987. The marriage lasted about three years and produced a son. Jalalaty met Dianne James in 1993, when she was working at the NCA. They married in 1998 and had two children. Dianne had joined the AFP in 1980. Four years later she moved to the Sydney office, where she became a plainclothes officer in the drug unit and later a detective. While in the drug unit Dianne began to work with Mark Standen and the pair became close friends.

After her stint at the NCA, Dianne returned to the AFP for two years. During this time Dianne introduced Jalalaty to Standen. The relationship between the three of them continued after she resigned as a detective sergeant to work with Jalalaty in his food distribution business, BJ's Fine Foods.

Standen later explained that the 'gift' from Kinch, and his request that Jalalaty disguise the source of the cash, was because Kinch 'wanted to give me something for Christmas'. According to Standen, 'I did the usual "oh no, that's fine, don't worry about it",' but Kinch insisted, 'No, I would like to do something for you for Christmas.' The pair had been speaking throughout 2005, Standen said. The subject of his laser treatment came up and Kinch had volunteered, 'How about I pay for your eyes to be done, I'd like to do that.' Standen again refused the offer but Kinch persisted and in the end Standen said, 'Okay [it's a] matter for you, that'd be really nice.'

When Kinch proposed sending him the money, Standen replied, 'How about you send it to Bill [Jalalaty]?' Standen had mentioned Jalalaty to Kinch in the context of Jalalaty's various 'business interests' and 'ran some of the ideas by him [Kinch] and he expressed an interest in anything that he might be able to do from the European end'. During their conversations Standen claimed to have told Kinch about his 'plans'. According to Standen, 'We talked about personal matters, family, what's happening—and that included my dealings with Bill and the possibility at that stage . . . of perhaps ending up in business with Bill.'

After deciding to accept the cash from Kinch, Standen rang Dianne Jalalaty and told her that he wanted to have some money sent to her husband from overseas and wondered whether Bill 'would mind if I had it sent to him'. Dianne did not think that there would be a problem and Standen rang Bill, who agreed. Standen claimed to have told Kinch the operation would cost $5000 and was surprised when Kinch sent him $47,000, but he accepted the money without demur.

Kinch's 'gift' landed in Jalalaty's account in December 2005. While the Jalalatys were laundering the cash through their business for payment to Standen, Standen told Bill, 'I've got a mate overseas that might want to invest [in your business].' Jalalaty was enthusiastic. When they discussed the matter again the next day Standen described Kinch as a 'colourful businessman' with 'plenty of money'.

About the same time, Standen told Jalalaty that he knew someone (Kinch again) who needed to get $90 million cash out of Australia. Standen asked whether the money could be secreted in the containers Jalalaty used to export goods to Dubai. There would be a commission in it for both of them—around 2 to 5 per cent of the cash sent out of Australia. The risks seemed small and even 2 per cent would give them $1.8 million. Jalalaty was interested but said he would first need to increase the volume of his legitimate trade with Dubai. This had long been Jalalaty's ambition but so far it had been thwarted by lack of money.

Much later Jalalaty told Standen, '[A]ll they've got to do is send some [legitimate] products to Dubai with his product [cash] in it and send it to Jebel Ali [a hotel in Dubai]. In Jebel Ali they don't check . . . there's people in there they don't give a shit [what] you might stuff in the container.' Jalalaty went on to describe a money-dealing operation in Dubai:

> I must have seen a hundred counting machines in this office. This is a big office. People go there and process money . . . while I was there just on the table [there was] twenty million, thirty million at least . . . All I have to do is get a container which they can deliver to me. I open it myself. I put building material in. I put, say, ten boxes of cash in the back of the container. I tape them up, you know what I mean, and I put glue and material for the panels. The panels go in the front and that weighs a tonne . . . I've got a warehouse in Dubai . . . [I] guess he needs this thing [drugs] in before he's got that [cash] to send out.

Within days of being told about Standen's 'colourful businessman', Jalalaty was on a plane to Thailand. Arriving in Bangkok on 19 January 2006, he met Kinch at the city's Sheraton Hotel. After asking 'lots of questions' about Jalalaty's business Kinch told him: 'I'll give you one [million dollars], I've got money in Australia. I'll organise it for you . . . I can earn 16 per cent in Portugal right now, so expect better than that . . . I'll give you a year to get started. It's hard to make a profit first year and then it's 20 per cent . . . Our mutual friend [Mark Standen] will be keeping an eye on my investment so don't do anything stupid.' As they parted, Kinch produced a bank note which he tore in half, giving one half to Jalalaty. 'Make sure you take this when you collect your money,' Kinch told him. 'My man will have the other half.' When Jalalaty asked how he could contact him, Kinch replied, 'Through Mark.'

Jalalaty described Kinch as a short man with several tattoos, casually dressed, carrying a black 'man bag' and wearing a gold Rolex watch. 'He carried a little bag of diamonds and he was in the company of some hookers and a few other guys.' Jalalaty recalled thinking, 'Shit, this guy looks like he's the Godfather, a crook. I knew there and then this guy should not be fucked with.'

On his return to Sydney, Jalalaty told Standen about the meeting. When he mentioned the torn banknote Standen laughed. 'That's normal procedure,' he told Jalalaty. 'You'll hear from him soon.' At the suggestion that Kinch 'doesn't look like a person to be fucked with,' Standen quipped, 'You know, people have been known to go missing who cross him.'

Within days Standen contacted Jalalaty and told him to expect a call on behalf of Kinch. The call came and Jalalaty drove to Coogee, where he called a prearranged mobile telephone number and was told to go to the Crowne Plaza Hotel. As he drove along Arden Street, a man on the footpath waved at him. Jalalaty described him as 'about six foot tall. [H]e looked like a backpacker, had surfie-looking hair and was dressed in shorts and a T-shirt. He was carrying a cheap blue vinyl sports bag and beach towel draped over it.'

Jalalaty pulled over. The man, who later identified himself as 'Stephen', came straight to the point. 'Have you got the note?' Jalalaty handed his half of the torn banknote to Stephen. The halves matched. Stephen threw the sports bag onto the back seat of Jalalaty's car, climbed into the front seat and directed Jalalaty to a nearby oval where, without a word, he got out and walked away. Jalalaty drove straight to his Maroota home on the Central Coast, 80 kilometres north of Sydney, where he counted the 'investment': $1 million cash, packed in $20,000 wads.

A jubilant Jalalaty telephoned Standen at home. 'I just met my new best mate,' he told him. 'I'm ready to . . . rock and roll . . . Your mate's invested a million dollars.'

In the coming months Jalalaty invested substantial sums in the business, but the bulk of the money—a total of $570,000, invested between February and July 2006—did not go into his own business. It was invested with clairvoyant and broker Bruce Way, who traded as CWL Investments. Jalalaty later told Standen that he had been promised an annual return of 60 per cent. (The investment scheme was traced to an unidentified Bahamas-based businessman trading in unsecured bank debts.) In September, just three months after his last deposit with Way, Jalalaty received a letter from CWL telling him that his investment account had ballooned to US$2.28 million.

A few weeks later Way warned Jalalaty that his interest payments would be delayed. A panicked Jalalaty sought help from Standen, who used his position at the Crime Commission to try to retrieve the cash and interest. Standen put Jalalaty in touch with a debt collector, but his efforts failed and the money disappeared, along with the mysterious Caribbean businessman. Amid the recriminations that followed, Way protested his innocence and claimed that he too had been ripped off.

The debt collector's name was Frank Wheeler, and Standen described him as a 'community source' who, from time to time, brought people into the commission. According to Standen, Way's debt to Jalalaty was 'typical of the types of matter that Frank Wheeler brought to the Crime Commission.' These matters 'usually involved someone investing money in something and losing the principal.' But documents written by Standen three years earlier gave a very different account of Wheeler's activities, noting that he had been 'extensively recorded on COPS [Computerised Operationals Police System] re his standover activities'. The documents were the result of several meetings with Wheeler, one of which was also attended by Wheeler's 'business associate', Michael 'No Thumbs' Pestano, concerning a complaint by Wheeler of fraud. Two million dollars had gone missing and Wheeler was attempting to recover it 'for a 50–50 split'. According to Wheeler, the fraud had been perpetrated by banks in an 'orchestrated Jewish conspiracy'. This conspiracy involved encouraging people to put a deposit on a property and sign contracts and then refusing to provide them with finance, so that they would forfeit the deposit. After his anti-semitic rant, Wheeler bizarrely declared his ambition to get a job with the Crime Commission. Standen told him 'that there was absolutely no hope of that eventuating'. Police intelligence reports led Standen to conclude that 'Any future dealings by the NSWCC [NSW Crime Commission] with Wheeler and Michael Pestano should be treated with caution. They appear to be intent on building up their organised crime contacts and underworld reputation.'

Events soon bore out Standen's prediction. On 23 July 2004—less than ten months after his meeting at the Crime Commission—Pestano and several 'colleagues' visited a small farm outside the township of Arthurville, near Wellington in inland New South Wales, armed with a gun, chainsaws and mattock handles. They threatened to rape the women in the farmhouse and murder everyone. Those in the house were 28-year-old Timothy Nam, his girlfriend and their fifteen-month old child, and Nam's elderly mother and sick father. The gang smashed windows, cut the power, drained the water supply and threatened to burn the Nams alive. The Nam family had been legal tenants on the small farm for eight years. Pestano had been hired by the owners of the property to evict the Nams by any means.

After two days of terror Nam opened fire with a .22 calibre semi-automatic rifle, killing Pestano and wounding two of his accomplices. Nam was charged with murder and wounding. In a plea deal Nam pleaded guilty to the manslaughter of Pestano and wounding of the other two. Two years later, at his sentencing in the New South Wales Supreme Court in Orange, Justice Michael Adams found the shooting was 'a direct result of unlawful violence by Pestano and Frank Wheeler employed to evict the Nams from their property'. Pestano and Wheeler had been given $9,000 by the owners to carry out the eviction. Justice Adams sentenced Nam to two years' jail, backdated to the date of his arrest, and two years and six months' parole. He was sentenced to eighteen months' jail, also backdated to the date of his arrest, for maliciously inflicting grievous bodily harm on Pestano's two wounded associates. Nam was released within days of his sentence being imposed. Justice Adams said the case was one of the most troubling he had ever heard and questioned whether Nam should have been charged at all, saying that he had 'real misgivings about whether Nam acted unreasonably'. He also said he was 'astonished' that in four visits to the farm prior to the final attack the police had not taken any action against Pestano and his gang.

■ ■ ■

While Kinch was vaguely informed of 'difficulties' associated with Jalalaty's investment, it was not until late 2007—nearly a year after the scheme began to unravel—that he was told of the 'lost' $570,000. Throughout this time Kinch continued to oversee ecstasy importations into Australia. On 26 July 2006 Robert flew to Sydney to prepare for his eighth importation. A shipment of clear drop paraffin lamps and oil arrived from Amsterdam aboard the *Wellington Express* cargo ship. On 19 August Customs covertly unpacked and began to search the consignment. Rather than staying to manage the distribution, Robert hurriedly left Australia—probably as a result of a tip-off from Kinch.

Tests were carried out on eleven of the drums, which were found to contain not paraffin oil but 1,4-butanediol oil, an industrial solvent with a variety of legal uses. Further tests were carried out but the results were negative and it was decided to release the shipment. In early September Standen telephoned Customs and told them that he had received information from a reliable source that 'the consignment contained MDMA [ecstasy]'. Standen was told that Customs was aware of the consignment, but tests had been carried out and the results had been negative. Customs added that Robert had been identified as the importer and that he was suspected of trafficking drugs. Standen told Customs that they should retest the oil. At the time 1,4-butanediol oil was a legal import (it was declared a prohibited import in 2006). When ingested, however, it changes its form and produces euphoric effects similar to those of ecstasy, hence the popular names liquid ecstasy, GHB and GBH. Retesting resulted in the twenty drums, each containing 20 litres of oil, testing positive to liquid ecstasy.

The information Standen gave Customs had been provided by Kinch a few days earlier. Documents record Kinch telling Standen that 'a European syndicate were [sic] importing MDMA oil in a container of lamps. The MDMA oil was capable of being converted into 400 kilograms of powder.' Kinch said that the shipment was in Sydney 'and was awaiting collection from a Dutch national who had also placed 100 kilograms of cocaine in secure storage in Sydney'. Standen later recalled that 'Customs had examined this shipment [the August 2006 importation of lamps and paraffin oil] and were in the process of releasing it as cleared, and he [Kinch] said to me you need to get them to retest it because it's—there's definitely MDMA in there, and I recall that I pretty much straight away rang Customs.'

Standen claimed to have rung Customs twice. On the first occasion he told them about the shipment and was told it had already been examined and cleared, and that Customs suspected Robert of being involved in drug importations. Standen relayed this information to Kinch. Having been told of Customs' suspicions, of the consignment having been searched and of suspicions that Robert was involved in drugs, Kinch took the initiative. Attempting to collect the shipment was now too risky: the drugs would have to be abandoned. Robert and the distribution network were safe and that was the priority: drugs could always be replaced. By insisting on retesting the oil Kinch was, once again, positioning himself to claim that he was still cooperating with law enforcement agencies while at the same time strengthening Standen's credibility by allowing him to take credit for the seizure.

Customs had become suspicious of Robert and his 'paraffin lamp' company as early as mid-2004, roughly a year after the company's incorporation. A profile of the business by Customs revealed many anomalies. They included: company directors who held only short-term Australian visitor visas; money for import set-up costs being sent from overseas; the absence of listed commercial premises for the company; all cargo documents going through solicitors' or accountants' offices; all cargo originating from Amsterdam; importations that did not include addresses for the company directors (only the supplier's address was given); commodities to be imported that were readily available in Australia; the value of shipments not being commercially viable; the failure of the parent company in Amsterdam to supply any other Australian importer; and the absence of documentation showing the transfer of funds to Amsterdam or anywhere else to pay for earlier shipments. Similar practices had been used by other crime syndicates to set up seemingly legitimate companies as a cover for the importation of drugs.

Once Customs had confirmed that the drums contained liquid ecstasy, they handed the case over to the AFP. Robert was long gone, but the AFP liaised with Dutch authorities who identified him before tracking him down in Amsterdam. Surveillance soon revealed that Robert had cancer and was not expected to live long. Despite the fact that no arrests had been made, Customs could feel reasonably satisfied with its part in the operation.

One hundred kilograms of cocaine said by Kinch to have been secreted in Sydney by 'a Dutch national' (Robert) was never found, although there is little doubt it existed. It is believed to have been mentioned by Kinch in order to find out whether the police knew anything about it. After it became clear they did not, the cocaine was retrieved from its hiding place and sold in Sydney and Melbourne.

In December 2005, around the time that Kinch made Standen a 'gift' of $47,000, Kinch began talking about an English drug trafficker who we will call 'Roger'. As usual, most of Kinch's information about past or current drug activity by Roger was deliberately vague, though some spectacular importations were said to be in the pipeline. According to Kinch, Roger was working with criminals in Belgium who were responsible for multiple drug shipments to Australia and other countries. The syndicate, he told Standen, had arranged for Roger to visit Sydney to receive '400 kilograms of pseudoephedrine, 600 kilograms of MDMA and 100 kilograms of cocaine' hidden in shipments of wine from Spain.

In February 2006 Kinch emailed Standen:

> Hello Mark,
>
> just a quick update. [Roger] says he is heading your way [Australia] Sat [presumably Saturday]. I no [*sic*] he has to find out something about the availability of acetone and

storage. I will make the effort to see him on his way and try and get some more details. Gotta go, busy.

Regards Jimi.

Two months later, using some of the money provided by Kinch, Jalalaty took a three-year lease on a new warehouse in Blacktown, in Sydney's outer west. The purpose of the warehouse was to increase the volume of stock 'and to create a legitimate importation profile with Australian Customs'. Before long, however, it was stacked with drums containing 1000 kilograms of acetone bought by Jalalaty at Kinch's request and with the knowledge of Standen. While acetone has many legitimate uses, it is also a precursor chemical in the production of methamphetamine, converting liquid methamphetamine into powdered methamphetamine.

After buying the acetone, Jalalaty telephoned Standen: 'B52 [Kinch] will be proud of me. I'm his go-to man. I've got $30,000 worth of acetone. I've bought $30,000 worth of acetone . . . And I bought a bladder for $8000 that has multiple taps attached to it . . . I've put the acetone in the bladder and I can then dish it out or supply it in quantities as required.' During an exchange of emails in September 2006 Jalalaty asked Standen, 'What does he [Kinch] want me to do with the drums? It's no problem to store them and keep them until they need them.'

If there was any doubt that Jalalaty knew what the acetone was for, that doubt was dispelled fourteen months later when he attempted to sell it. During an intercepted conversation with a middleman, Jalalaty was heard to say: 'When they import the drug, right, it comes in a form and then they pour the acid over it. The product cleans it and crystallises it and it uses hundreds of litres of it. That's what he told me.'

Kinch's claims about Roger's importation of ecstasy and his alleged attempts to obtain acetone were investigated but no evidence was found to support them. Jalalaty's purchase of the acetone at Kinch's request was never mentioned to investigating authorities. Nor did Standen mention the September telephone call from Jalalaty. Standen later claimed that buying the acetone was a ruse to catch Roger importing drugs into Australia—a ruse that failed because Roger 'never turned up'. If it was a ruse, neither Jalalaty nor the Crime Commission knew of it. The investigation was described as having 'died for want of information from Mr Kinch'. Jalalaty eventually sold the drums of acetone to a legitimate buyer, losing several thousand dollars on the deal.

■ ■ ■

The few years up to 2006 had been a particular busy time for the Dutch syndicate in Australia. Several successful importations had netted the syndicate millions of dollars in profits, but by mid-2006 Robert's luck had run out. Standen was now accepting bribes—the AFP received what it regarded as reliable information that Standen had been paid $200,000 for confirming to Kinch that Customs had an operational interest in Robert's container—and was hungry for more. Standen was moving from his mainly passive role as the Dutch syndicate's 'eyes and ears' in Sydney to a more active role alongside Kinch and Jalalaty in the importation of drugs into Australia.

Law enforcement, too, was starting to take a more active interest in the syndicate. In January 2006 the Dutch

National Crime Squad began an investigation into the export of pseudoephedrine by the Haklander syndicate and others to several countries, including Australia. This investigation would last for another two and a half years.

In the meantime Kinch had a final trick up his sleeve. During 2005–06 the AFP had been negotiating with Standen to take over the management of Kinch as an informant. According to Standen, the AFP 'expressed a desire to deal directly with Mr Kinch . . . because Mr Kinch was now living back in Europe, and they had liaison officers, or at least a liaison officer, in Europe.' But when Standen put the proposal to Kinch, 'not surprisingly, [he] resisted it strenuously'. Nevertheless, Standen claimed to have arranged a meeting 'for the purpose of handing [Kinch] over as an informer to the AFP'.

In August–September 2006 two AFP overseas liaison officers met Kinch in Frankfurt, Germany. The meeting satisfied no one. The AFP officers left the meeting convinced (correctly) that Kinch was again active in the international drug trade. Kinch contacted Standen and told him that he was 'dissatisfied with the way the meeting had gone' and that 'he had no confidence to deal directly with them [the AFP]'. Around the same time Standen claimed to have heard 'that some Federal police were unhappy that [Kinch] had managed to leave Australia without being prosecuted and that he continued to have dealings with me, part of which I thought was a form of professional jealousy'. The AFP was right to be suspicious of Kinch, the circumstances in which charges against him had been dropped and his ongoing relationship with Standen. The meeting had been part of an attempt by Kinch and Standen to enable Kinch to infiltrate the AFP, just as he had the Crime Commission.

The attempt failed.

CHAPTER SIXTEEN

'Hello sweetheart'

Louise Baker was 21 years old when, in September 2005, she began working at the NSW Crime Commission, monitoring telephone intercepts and listening devices targeting major crime figures. Eleven months later she began an affair with her married boss, 49-year-old Mark Standen. As the romance blossomed, Standen lavished 'the Princess', as he called her, with expensive gifts. During the first four months of their relationship he spent more than $8000 on jewellery for Baker. They dined at some of Sydney's priciest restaurants—the bills were as high as $500—and spent nights at five-star hotels 'Once a fortnight, once a month, maybe once a week—it would vary,' Baker explained. Standen also took Baker on holiday with him and paid for her accommodation on a trip she made to India in 2006.

In January 2007 Standen and Baker flew to Dubai with Bill Jalalaty. Jalalaty paid for the business class airfares and

Standen paid for his and Baker's accommodation. Baker explained that Standen had told her that 'Bill [Jalalaty] was going to try and establish citizenship there and meet a few people that he could potentially go into business with, and he wanted to introduce Mark to a few of those people and asked if I wanted to come along.' Standen, she said, was interested in leaving the commission and going into business with Jalalaty. The reason for flying to Dubai was that 'Bill used to do a lot of talking and deals didn't eventuate, so I think Mark just wanted to go over there and meet him and be a bit more active with getting the business started.' According to Baker they were to meet 'Jimmy', whom Standen described as being 'like an old friend, he used to be an informant [at the Crime Commission] and that he, yeah, he may be there as well looking for citizenship.'

Baker, Standen and Jalalaty met Jimmy Kinch one evening at the upmarket Marrakesh Restaurant. Writing in her diary, Baker noted '[Jimmy] thought I wasn't to be trusted.' She later explained that 'He was a bit strange with me. He wouldn't make eye contact. And when I questioned Mark about that later he said to Mark that he was a bit concerned because I worked for law enforcement.' Baker claimed to have asked Standen why they were meeting with 'an ex-informant and his response was that he used to be a drug importer but he wanted to become legit and invest in legitimate businesses.'

Over dinner there was discussion about Kinch 'wanting to invest in Bill's business . . . but I could barely hear him [Kinch]. He was very soft, softly spoken,' Baker recalled. At no time did Baker hear Standen, Jalalaty or Kinch discuss anything improper. According to Baker they were to have seen Kinch again on their last night in Dubai, but the meeting never happened. Unknown to Baker, however, Jalalaty did have a second meeting with Kinch, this time at the Sheraton. They discussed Jalalaty's business before Kinch turned his attention to Standen's relationship with Baker and her presence at the earlier meeting. He warned Jalalaty that 'she could compromise everything . . . If they broke up it could get ugly.'

Standen claimed not to have known they would be meeting Kinch in Dubai. '[T]he trip wasn't to see him,' Standen said, but when they did meet 'we talked about a range of business things with him.' At one point Standen spoke to Kinch 'on the side a little bit . . . largely about . . . [Darren] Leech . . . [and] his father, who's like a big crime figure in the UK, and about the fallout [of Darren's arrest and jailing in Sydney] . . . [and] about how the father was pissed off and what was happening.' It was, according to Standen, just 'catch up, chit chat'.

Kinch was not the only member of the Dutch syndicate in Dubai in January 2007. Fat Ron Haklander was in the city with his new supplier of pseudoephedrine, Loek Weerden, and three senior colleagues, Jan Plas, Thomas van den Berg and Rene Asbeek Brusse. A day or two before flying to Dubai, Haklander had met Weerden at Watergang, a rural area about twenty minutes from the centre of Amsterdam (see Chapter 18) and convinced him that there were openings in the Australian amphetamine market. Weerden agreed to accompany him to Dubai to meet Kinch.

In Dubai, Haklander introduced Kinch as his 'partner and friend', while Weerden described Kinch as 'the customer in Australia'. At the meeting Kinch outlined his plans, describing how 'both BJ's Fine Foods and Bill Jalalaty were under his control, and that he had the possibility to hold him to account'. Weerden spelt out the terms of the deal: Congolese suppliers would be paid €600 a kilogram for 500 kilograms of pseudoephedrine, and the Dutch syndicate would cover the extra costs of shipping the consignment from the Democratic Republic of the Congo to Australia. The syndicate would pay €360 a kilogram upfront and 'at delivery in Australia, Erwin [Beekelaar] and I would get paid €1 million in cash in Holland.' Eventually, the size of the shipment was reduced from 500 to 300 kilograms.

Within days of Standen returning from Dubai, the Crime Commissioner, Phillip Bradley, heard of his relationship with Louise Baker. The relationship was beginning to cause friction at the commission and plans were made to transfer Baker to the NSW Independent Commission Against Corruption. Learning that Baker was to be moved, Standen took her on a shopping trip, buying 'clothing more suitable to the new job'. The relationship continued, as did Standen's extravagant spending. A few months later he took Baker on a holiday to Barrington Tops and in August he bought her a Chanel handbag for $2980.

After Baker's removal from the Crime Commission, Standen came to resent the organisation and, in particular, its chief, Bradley. On several occasions he told Jalalaty, Baker and Kinch of his wish to 'retire from the Crime Commission and get into business with Bill'. During late 2006, increasingly frustrated at being unable to solve his financial problems and bitter at his 'separation' from the Princess, Standen told Jalalaty of his intention to resign and 'drop a big turd on his [Bradley's] desk'.

Since the late 1990s Standen had been borrowing money from friends. As one friend said, 'Standen often asked me for money and I would give him a couple of hundred on the proviso he would pay me back when he got his pay. He only sometimes paid me back. He always had more credit cards than anyone else I knew and he would often tell me they were maxed out.' Standen claimed that in December 2005, when he first accepted money from Kinch, his financial situation was 'manageable': he was making the repayments on his various loans and multiple credit cards. His financial position was, however, much worse than he would admit. Standen was living in a rented home, having sold his family home, a 52-acre property on the Central Coast, some months earlier at a significant loss. He 'got out of it almost overnight,' he said. '[I] virtually threw [it] away . . . [and lost] a shitload of money just to get out of it . . . probably lost about $80,000.' His salary was now going on rent, the repayment of bank loans (approximately $111,000) and credit card debts, which during the previous two years had almost tripled to $96,000.

Nothing better illustrated Standen's plight than his approach to a close friend around 2003 to help him with 'a serious problem'. Standen told the friend that he 'was responsible for the security of a large amount of money that had been seized during raids; that he kept the money in his safe at work but had been taking this money to help pay bills and buy food [and] that in total he had taken thousands of dollars from his safe'. The commission was going to conduct an audit of the safe's holdings 'and when they did they would find a large amount of the money was missing'. Standen admitted that he had 'lied and told the guy doing the audit that he had left his key at home' and that he was now 'under a bit of pressure to bring the key in'. Altogether, Standen is believed to have taken 'over ten thousand dollars' from the safe. The friend did not have the cash to lend Standen and it is not known how Standen managed to replace the money in time for the audit.

His financial situation continued to deteriorate. In late 2006 he bought a family house at Bateau Bay on the Central Coast for $735,700, taking out a loan for about $700,000 and borrowing $200,000 from a friend, Tony Newton, who also worked at the Crime Commission. Newton had taken out an interest-only loan with the bank, using his home as collateral. Standen was to make the repayments. However, at the time the loan was taken out Standen had only $80,000 and owed almost $100,000 on his credit cards.

Nearly a third of Newton's loan—about $60,000—was used to pay down Standen's credit card debt and most of the remainder went on everyday spending. Fifteen months after his first gift from Kinch in December 2005, Standen began to receive regular payments from Kinch through Jalalaty. Over the next eighteen months the payments are believed to have totalled more than $250,000. Yet Standen's debts continued to grow.

In March 2007 Jalalaty flew to Bangkok to meet Kinch. The pair discussed using Jalalaty's food importing business as a front to import 300 kilograms of pseudoephedrine from Pakistan hidden in a shipment of rice. As if to reassure Jalalaty, Kinch told him about a friend in Europe who built tourist buses. 'The clever thing about the tourist buses is when we build it we weld drugs into the wheel arches and we put the seats onto one of the wheel arches. The bus gets driven across Europe full of passengers and when it arrives my mate cuts it open, drugs delivered. It amazed me that the passengers couldn't smell the drugs.' Kinch then added, 'I've got customers in Australia that need product . . . Don't worry there is minimal risk. Someone will send it and someone will pick it up. You don't touch it, you don't know about it.' As an inducement, Kinch told him:

'Do this and I will wipe your debt and you might even get a bonus.'

'The whole debt?' Jalalaty asked.

'Yes.'

'What about Mark?'

'Don't worry. We go way back. He helped me out. He is my eyes and ears.'

Back in Sydney, Jalalaty discussed the plan with Standen. Both were now desperate for cash. Once again, Standen told Jalalaty to expect a call from someone on behalf of Kinch. Within days Kinch's 'Portuguese mate' called and asked to meet Jalalaty at the Luxe cafe in Bondi Junction. It was the first time Jalalaty had seen the 'Portuguese mate', whom he later described as being '5 foot 10 inches tall [178 cm], chunky build with fair skin. He had a shaved head and no facial hair. He was wearing a long-sleeved shirt and cargo pants and carried a dark-coloured "man bag".'

The man did not tell Jalalaty his name but said that he was from the Algarve in Portugal. He ate a lot and rushed his food. After a short conversation he took Jalalaty to a Westfield car park where he opened the boot of a rented green Ford sedan and took out a silver–grey cylindrical sports bag full of money. He handed the bag to Jalalaty and the two men left the car park separately. Jalalaty drove back to the city and met Standen at Platos Cafe near the Crime Commission. They walked to the nearby Wilson's car park, where Jalalaty showed Standen the sports bag containing $400,000. Jalalaty took $100,000 out of the bag and handed it to Standen, telling him, 'There is four there. I only need three. One hundred is yours.' Standen took the money, looked at it and said, 'This will solve a few problems.' After Standen had left, Jalalaty took the cash home to Maroota, where he stored it on the same shelf he had used to store the $1 million fourteen months earlier.

As members of the Dutch syndicate travelled to Pakistan to make arrangements for the 300-kilogram shipment of pseudoephedrine, Jalalaty started work on his cover story. A few weeks later he received a fax from Amsterdam introducing him to MDL Fine Food and Services India, a fictitious company created specifically for the purpose of sending the shipment. More emails and telephone conversations followed. Everything seemed to be going to plan until, three months after collecting the $400,000, an email arrived from Kinch asking Jalalaty to return 'all remaining money' to the 'Portuguese mate' at Bondi Junction. Although reluctant, both Jalalaty and Standen felt they had no choice but to do as Kinch asked. The next day Jalalaty gave back all the money that was left—a mere $145,000 of the $1.4 million they had received.

The same month, June 2007, the NSW Crime Commissioner, Phillip Bradley, and his Director of Operations Support, John Giorgiutti, were told that Mark Standen was corrupt, that he was taking bribes from James Kinch and that he, Kinch and Jalalaty were planning a major drug importation into Australia. Dutch authorities had discovered the connection during their eighteen-month investigation of the Haklander syndicate. They had already told the AFP. Speaking later to the ABC's *Four Corners* program, Commander Jan Boersma of the Dutch National Crime Squad described the discovery as 'shattering . . . He was not just an ordinary police officer but an important police officer, also in the collaboration with Europe . . . We made sure that his name did not become known anywhere, not in the investigation team either. Only the team leader, only one detective and me, were aware of the name of Mark Standen.'

By the time Bradley and Giorgiutti were told, a joint investigation was underway between the AFP and the Dutch police involving extensive physical and electronic surveillance, profiling, and the tracking of assets and money movements.

A month later Jalalaty received a fax on the letterhead of MDL Fine Food and Services India telling him that a sample shipment of 'rice, drinks, vitamins, etc.' would be sent to Sydney in a container. 'There are now three shipments to be prepared for delivery and we hope that . . . [the] . . . first will be on the way for the beginning of a long-term business cooperation . . . Mr Rashid Abdar [a name used by Loek Weerden] is available.' The fax was signed, 'Daniel Cloutier [a name used by Asbeek Brusse] General Manager Dubai Branch Office, MDL Fine Food.' Jalalaty was later advised that the first shipment—a test run—would consist of 17,000 kilograms of rice in 5 kilogram bags.

As they waited for the shipment to arrive, Standen told Jalalaty about an investigation he had worked on involving a businessman who had tried to import a container of drugs. The drugs had been detected but the businessman was not charged because the police could not prove that he knew about the drugs in the container. Standen emphasised to Jalalaty that the only thing he needed to remember was how he had got in touch with the suppliers of the rice. If the drugs were found and Jalalaty was questioned, he would need to explain that he had visited numerous countries and handed out business cards to anyone he thought would be able to help establish his food importation business. He would have to say that the people who had supplied the rice and container did not speak English. Standen told Jalalaty to keep emails and faxes between himself and the suppliers so that if things went wrong he could offer them to the authorities and pretend to be helping them find the people responsible for the drugs.

The test shipment did not arrive in Sydney until early October 2007. Disputes over paperwork and the payment of fees meant that the container sat on the wharf for several weeks. During this time Jalalaty received an angry telephone call from Weerden. Jalalaty told the Dutchman: 'I'm getting my arse kicked saying "why haven't you [I] paid the fucking money?" when it has been paid.' Weerden replied that they were dealing with 'stupid people' and that 'next time, eh, we, I will control it.'

An agitated Standen complained to Jalalaty: 'How hard is it? You'd think fucking rice would be easy . . . Geez, they can't even do rice, how could they do anything bloody valuable?' Standen promised to find out whether the container had been tampered with 'because you don't want [word indistinct] shit.'

When the shipment was finally cleared, the rice was found to have live bugs in it and needed fumigation.

It was not until 7 November, nearly a month after landing, that the rice was delivered to Jalalaty's warehouse. Jalalaty emailed Kinch: 'Out of the 851 bags, they opened about six boxes. They were checking for live bugs. They also used a Stanley knife and slashed six bags to see if [there were] any bugs inside the bags. Apart from that all other ctns [cartons] are intact.'

Kinch instructed Jalalaty to sell the rice. (It was another deal that Jalalaty would lose money on.) Two days later he emailed Kinch again: 'All is good here and I think we should get cracking on the next one'.

Within days, Jalalaty flew to Dubai to meet Kinch in an attempt to ensure that nothing went wrong with the second shipment. Kinch's 'Portuguese mate' joined them at the Al Hallab Restaurant in Dubai's Emirates Mall. According to Jalalaty, Kinch's 'mate' did not speak. 'The whole meeting was like we were to just sit there and keep our mouths shut while the boss [Kinch] talked.' Jalalaty was told that the next shipment would be 'live' and that he would be dealing directly with Weerden. The news took him by surprise—he had been expecting another trial run—but he was quick to see the benefits of an early payday. Standen, he told Kinch, was still living 'beyond his means'.

'Don't worry,' Kinch replied. 'We have a pension plan.'

Within days of returning to Sydney, Jalalaty met Standen in a cafe near the Crime Commission to discuss the trip. Standen was still bitter about the accident-prone trial run. 'So the thing they sent you [the first time] . . . was just a container of rice . . . all that mucking around . . . fucking around.' Jalalaty tried to mollify Standen, telling him that the next run would consist of about '60 bags' of pseudoephedrine (roughly 300 kilograms) secreted among the 4500 bags in the container. Jalalaty explained that the pseudoephedrine would be collected from his Blacktown warehouse by 'the baldy guy, my Portuguese mate' and shown to buyers in Sydney. Standen was not happy with the arrangement, and asked if the bags were marked with anything that could be linked to the 'rice shipment'. Jalalaty was not concerned. He said that there were some markings, but insisted that once the buyers had taken delivery of the drugs they would 'give us back the empty bags, he [the Portuguese mate] brings them back to me and I destroy them.' Standen was still not convinced. If a buyer was arrested, he might describe the rice bags to the police. This information could lead the police straight to them. 'It's not good when people know it comes in rice,' Standen told Jalalaty.

By now the second container with the pseudoephedrine was supposed to be on its way, but on 21 November 2007 Jalalaty was shocked to be told that the container had been sent to France. 'The guy from the factory [in Lahore, Pakistan], explained: "After the long wait from your side, no response, then they sent it to a buyer in France".' It was not clear whether there was pseudoephedrine inside the container or whether this had been another test run. In any case, a disappointed Jalalaty was told that a third container would soon be ready. Asked to send more money to Lahore, Jalalaty complained to Weerden that 'they [the suppliers] try to rip me off' (he had already paid around $40,000 for the first two containers). Weerden promised to ring 'the factory' and sort it out.

Despite the mystery over the missing container and his resentment at being asked for more money, Jalalaty confidently looked forward to the arrival of the real shipment. Standen, too, had high hopes, saying the shipment would wipe all their debts and enable them to pay back Kinch who, he told Jalalaty, 'was hoping to give everyone . . . a nice Christmas.'

For several days Jalalaty and Weerden haggled over costs and documents associated with the shipment. On 5 December Jalalaty's wife, Dianne, transferred $22,000 to Lahore. Three weeks later Weerden confirmed that the shipment was 'ready' and would depart in a few days.

Once again, Weerden had spoken too soon. The shipment was delayed. In Sydney, Standen was growing increasingly desperate. Facing pressure from banks and credit card companies to repay his debts, Standen spoke about needing to wipe 'the bloody slate clean' and get 'a little bit ahead of the action'. He told Jalalaty,

> [We] thought we were gonna make a squillion dollars. Last year [2006] we were talking about absolutely definitely being able to put the resignation on the boss's desk remember [and] go and drop a big turd on his desk. All that just never happened . . . I've had to buy a house . . . I can handle the house but everything else is very difficult . . . I've created this bigger mortgage . . . I've had to get the deposit off that [word indistinct] cash advance on credit cards. I've done all those things. That's the trouble, once you do that, so like I've got, like I'm running four credit cards at their maximum. I'm just doing this. I'm paying off, using it, paying off, use it, that's how I'm keeping my head above water by doing this . . . That's what I'm doing at the moment. I'm paying credit cards and so when I spoke to B52 [Kinch], well he said, ah, you know, we'll sort something. He said mate no problem, we do something . . . and that's when we got talking.

By early 2008 Standen was pleading melodramatically via email for money from Jalalaty:

> Gasp gasp gasp: Hi there CEO, What happened to our Friday catch-up or the account thing? I'm breathing through the last millimetre of the straw before drowning. Sucking in some small gasps of air....hard to breathe..... choking.....dying......AAAGGGHHHHH.......trying to hang on.......going down with the ship........tried hard.............may not last...................so close....... too young to die.

He was at it again a few weeks later: 'Has anything happened because otherwise I have a total of $22 to my name and a major expensive drama with the bank.' In another message he texted, 'CEO. Mate this is quite serious and I am genuinely desperate about it. Have had a bad stress headache all day. Can you please at least put 2 [$2,000] in to cover the immediate problem and we can discuss further next week . . . Can't live on 22 dollars.'

Jalalaty gave him money but it wasn't enough. On 29 February 2008 Standen texted: 'Hi. Three banks keep calling. Noose is tightening. In 7 days it will all turn to shit. Is any plan showing any promise or should I just drive to The Gap?'

By now Baker had begun to ask Standen where the cash was coming from. She recalled Standen telling her 'two or three times [that] he had received some money [a couple of thousand] from Bill'. The reason for this, she believed, was that 'Mark may have invested some money with him at one point'.

Baker had heard Standen on his mobile telephone talking to 'banks' about his credit cards and unpaid accounts. While admitting that he was 'hopeless with paying bills', Standen dismissed the banks' concerns, insisting that the bills had been paid or were going to be paid.

Standen's relentless demands for cash provoked regular arguments between Jalalaty and his wife. By now the Jalalatys had given Standen $70,000. Jalalaty complained to Kinch that Standen and his girlfriend would stay at the Sheraton on Sussex Street and 'she would get $300 per week facials'. With Jalalaty running out of patience, Standen had no choice but to email Kinch direct:

> I need to ask you something which is pretty bloody rude and bold considering the things that have happened with Myrtle [Jalalaty]. I won't be surprised if you fall off your chair, swearing and saying you can't believe that I'd ask. Myrtle still hasn't managed to fill all of Santa's orders from last year and it has been a constant struggle getting it in bits and pieces. She seems to be now unable to complete although she has now come close. In any event due to my little stint in hospital and visits to the specialist I find myself needing 14.5 [$14,500] soonish. It seems clear now that there is no way she can assist. I was thinking that if it was possible to do then I could add it to the bill later.

Kinch replied by email: 'I am travelling at the moment but I will arrange it. If I sent it to Myrtle [Jalalaty], are you sure she will give it to you?'

After three weeks Standen was still waiting for the cash. A series of frantic pleas from Standen to Jalalaty culminated in this text, sent on 31 March: 'AAGGHH. Panic day. Deadline day. My friend said she had expected you to have been called by now. She was going to chase it up. Any news? Tonight will become very costly if nothing happens today. Really need 5200 today. Shit I hate this.'

The next day Kinch acted. Jalalaty received a telephone call from 'Stephen', the man who had given him $1 million cash at Coogee 26 months earlier. 'I'm supposed to see you today,' Stephen told him, suggesting they meet at the entrance to the Marriott Hotel opposite Hyde Park in the city. At 10.30 a.m. Stephen handed Jalalaty a red bag containing $25,000 cash. Jalalaty went immediately to a laneway near the Crime Commission where he handed the bag to Standen.

They discussed various ways of depositing the cash without arousing suspicions at the bank—Standen needed to deposit $10,200 before the close of business—but precautions would take time, and time, for Standen, had run out. 'No one will notice,' he told Jalalaty. 'The bank won't care, but if it goes bad just say I was strapped and you, um, helped me out.' The amount was only enough to buy him 'a couple of months', but the fact that it had been sent convinced Standen that 'something must be [coming]'.

Towards the end of April 2008 the container finally arrived at Port Botany on board the *Sinotrans Shanghai*, but without the necessary clearance documents. The Pakistani agents for the drug syndicate were demanding more money before they would release the papers. The Australians had been double-crossed. Jalalaty emailed Kinch:

> I received the docs today and listen to this one. Inside the package was NO originals but a RANSOM note. This is exactly what the note says:
>
> 'Hello man
>
> I am sending the photo copy of the documents because 4 the originals B/L I must pay the money to those people who cleared the matter for me. Now I am bound to them. If you need the original then your side should pay me what I exactly must pay for these people. So please do not delay the money, so that I must pay to get the originals.
>
> Tanx
>
> NOTE; If you do not get the money quickly, I can face big problem. So take my request seriously and finish the problem as soon as possible.'

As well as informing Kinch, Jalalaty telephoned Weerden in Amsterdam 'every five minutes until he answered'. Told about the 'ransom note', Weerden was 'shocked' and 'running around trying to fix it'. Eventually the documents arrived. No more money was paid, but this would not be the last double-cross by the Pakistanis.

Kinch was in Dubai when the container arrived in Port Botany. He emailed Standen: 'Hey, just heard something. May be interesting to you? From china in bath salts. Crystal mdma. It is heading your way. Well worth a look either way!!!! If you do find it can you make the discovery date before today 8 may..// so as not to compromise me. Regards jojo.'

Standen replied, 'Hello sweetheart, Missing your funny stories, and warm cuddles. Couldn't find the clothes from China that you wanted. So much comes here it is not funny. Will keep looking in case I find the style you are after. Have you heard of "Chanel E" designs before? Take care, Love to all, Boyd xx.'

Kinch's email was not genuine intelligence about an impending importation. As on previous occasions, its purpose was twofold: to provide Standen with a cover story to justify making inquiries about Customs activity at Port Botany and to put Customs off the scent of the real importation.

Standen telephoned Customs to report the 'tip-off' which he described as coming from a source 'in Europe' who 'has a very good history with us [the Crime Commission]'. The shipment, he said, had been organised by 'a group of Dutch guys . . . [and has either] just arrived or [is] on its way'. The response from Customs was reassuring: they were not aware of any suspicious activity on the wharves.

Standen wasted no time in passing on the good news to Kinch in Dubai. Two days later he emailed Kinch again, telling him that '[a] lot of kids were saying they were expecting presents soon but they should wait patiently and not tell their friends what they're getting.' At the same time Standen kept up the cover story by asking for more information on the imaginary shipment of MDMA hidden in bath salts or crystals from China. The underlying message to Kinch was clear: the shipment was safe.

The container, however, remained stuck on the wharf and Standen was losing patience. How long would he have to wait for his money? He had played his part in the importation—he reminded Jalalaty that the container was safe and that 'they [Customs] weren't looking at it'—and was anxious to know when 'a pay cheque is coming'. For all his bluster, Standen was still worried about the rice bags. 'The only way they can catch us,' Jalalaty told him, was if Customs unloaded the whole container and checked the bags. Once the shipment was in his warehouse, they would be in the clear. The drugs would be removed from the rice bags and put in plain brown cardboard boxes to be collected by his 'Portuguese mate'. The buyers would never know that the pseudoephedrine had been imported in bags of rice. For a moment Standen appeared to suffer a pang of conscience. He 'hated doing this [importing drugs],' he told Jalalaty, 'but he believed they would look back and laugh and say how silly they were.' All he needed was $100,000 'as then I would be able to breathe.'

Although they were expecting 300 kilograms, neither Standen nor Jalalaty knew for certain how much pseudoephedrine was in the container. Weerden himself had faxed instructions to Mohammed Nawaz, his Pakistani contact, asking for '300' to be sent. Standen hoped that there was 'so much stuff in there that he [Kinch] won't want to do it again', while Jalalaty told his wife there could be as much as '600 kilograms in 40 bags out of 18 tonnes'. (This figure was consistent with plans outlined several months earlier by the Dutch syndicate.)

The original bill of landing arrived in Sydney from Pakistan on 23 May 2008. Jalalaty quickly started making arrangements for the consignment to be cleared. 'Today has been the longest day of my life,' he emailed Kinch. 'I think I will be taking some nerve settlers before bed.' A week later the consignment was delivered to Jalalaty's warehouse in Blacktown. Delighted, he emailed Kinch: 'I finally got the kids [drugs] home. They look okay but I will need to keep an eye on them for a while . . . I have aged ten years worrying about my precious kids. I will update you tomorrow on their progress.'

Kinch replied, 'Nice to hear that little Johnny and Sally are home. Tell June to put them in bed until Dr Maurice [Standen] says they are fully recovered [i.e. not to touch the drugs until they are certain there is no police surveillance or suspicion attached to the consignment].'

Emails passed back and forth between Kinch and Standen, with Kinch advising: 'Just heard Mirt [Myrtle i.e. Jalalaty] is home from the doctors. She says that the children are feeling a lot better, can you advise her to keep them off school and leave them in bed as long as possible. Better not to remove any bandages until the doctor says.'

That night Dutch authorities made their move. They had been forced into action when Dutch prosecutors reviewing an earlier case against Haklander and others for importing ecstasy into Australia sent evidence and reports, which included details of the ongoing Standen–Kinch–Dutch syndicate investigation, to defence lawyers as part of the 'new evidence' to be used to restart the earlier failed prosecution. The ongoing investigation was exposed. Over the next few days they arrested thirteen members of the Dutch syndicate (twelve men and one woman). Unaware of the arrests, Standen and Jalalaty continued to meet and talk. The pressure on Standen was beginning to tell. 'My credit rating is completely fucked,' he told Jalalaty. Standen couldn't wait to get away from the Crime Commission. 'I've just, I've got the shits with the place . . . all the stuff with the Princess [Bradley's removal of her from the commission].'

Standen and Jalalaty met several times over the next couple of days. Although impatient for the money to start flowing, they did not doubt that the importation had been a success. They knew nothing about the Dutch arrests. Then Jalalaty received an email from Kinch:

> do not like to bring bad news I just heard that ras [Rashid, i.e., Weerden] mom and father [members of the Dutch syndicate] were involved in a serious crash [police raids] a few days ago!! I am not sure who they were driving for!! they are both in their local hospital!! [locked up in the local police station] And as yet I cannot find out how serious it is?? I do not no [sic] if they had any copies of the insurance papers with them or at home but I am trying to find out so that we can see if they have cover for private health care!! Can you ask Maurice [Standen] for advice on moving the children [the shipment] I think that it would be better if they went to stay somewhere more quiet as soon as possible. Other than that everything is fine. Maurice says that it is quiet at work so has more time to relax.

On 31 May 2008 Kinch was arrested in Bangkok. Two days later, unaware of Kinch's fate and still believing the drugs were safe in Jalalaty's warehouse, Standen telephoned Jalalaty and asked for a cheque for $4674 to help him finalise the sale of a block of land he owned in Queensland. Jalalaty promised to see to it. Two hours later Standen was arrested by AFP officers at the Crime Commission and taken to their Sydney headquarters.

During an electronically recorded interview Standen denied any wrongdoing and claimed that Kinch was a friend, having originally been an informant. He said that Jalalaty had offered him money to help him out of his financial difficulties.

Less than an hour after Standen's arrest, Jalalaty was arrested at his Maroota home and taken to the Sydney office of the AFP where, like Standen, he took part in a recorded interview in which he denied any involvement in or knowledge of the importation of drugs. It was only now that Standen and Jalalaty discovered they had been the targets of a major international investigation into drug smuggling, and that the AFP had searched the container and found nothing but rice. Their Pakistani suppliers had double-crossed them again. But in doing so, they had given Standen and Jalalaty a glimmer of hope. Without the drugs, the AFP's case seemed to rest on a containerload of rice.

If the two men thought they might be released, their hopes were soon dashed. Within hours both were charged with conspiring to import pseudoephedrine. Bail was refused. Standen was also charged with conspiring to pervert the course of justice.

On 17 May 2010 Bill Jalalaty pleaded guilty to conspiring to import pseudoephedrine for the purpose of manufacturing an illicit drug. Seven months later he was sentenced to ten years' jail, the sentence to commence on 2 June 2008, the date of his arrest, with a non-parole period of six years. Jalalaty served his sentence in protective custody. The danger he faced as a result of talking to the authorities was starkly illustrated by an incident that happened soon after his arrest. While in custody Jalalaty received a card from Kinch—a none-too-subtle reminder that Kinch knew where he was and could get at him if he had to. Such a message was unlikely to have been lost on Jalalaty, who after meeting Kinch had described him as a character out of *The Godfather* and someone not to be messed with. Kinch himself had told Standen about a similar threat by the Dutch syndicate to kill Kirsty Chambers before she could give evidence against him. Although he had 'rolled', Jalalaty refused to give evidence against his co-conspirators. He was released from jail following the completion of his non-parole period.

As he waited for his court hearing, Standen maintained his innocence, claiming that, 'Although I'm in prison I don't consider myself to be a prisoner as I'm not guilty of anything.' When asked about his future, Standen replied, 'I might finish my legal studies, sit for the exam and perhaps get a job in the legal field as my law enforcement career is now over.'

While in jail Standen asked for and was given a copy of *Shantaram*, a 900-page novel by Gregory Roberts. The warders are said to have been amused by Standen's sudden interest in Roberts's story of a convicted Australian bank robber and heroin addict sentenced to nineteen years in jail who escapes from Victoria's Pentridge Prison and finds a new life in India.

There was no escape for Standen. His trial began in March 2011 and lasted five months. The Crown prosecutor,

Tim Game, SC, accused Standen of being 'motivated by greed' and of lying 'without pause' for the 25 days he was in the witness box. Standen was eventually convicted of conspiring to import pseudoephedrine to manufacture an illicit drug, conspiring to take part in the supply of the pseudoephedrine and conspiring to pervert the course of justice.

In his sentencing remarks the judge clarified the roles of Standen, Kinch and Jalalaty in the conspiracy, finding that 'Kinch was a principal' and that Kinch and Standen communicated as equals, while 'Mr Standen's position was superior to that of Jalalaty', who 'sought and accepted advice from Mr Standen and sought reassurance from him'. Jalalaty, he noted, was excluded from communications between Kinch and Standen, while Standen had access to correspondence between Kinch and Jalalaty. In an email of 24 November 2007 Kinch had told Standen, 'she [that is, Jalalaty] likes it when she can spy on us.' In other emails Kinch asked Standen to 'keep an eye' on Jalalaty. In short, neither Kinch nor Standen appeared to fully trust Jalalaty, who in return did not fully trust them. In a revealing email of 21 February 2008 Kinch described Jalalaty as 'a proper Walter Mitty. You cannot believe a word she says.' In late May 2008, when a nervous Jalalaty was thinking of withdrawing from the conspiracy, Standen had pressured him to stay, urging (or warning) him not to 'pull out of the tennis match'. In the face of this pressure, Jalalaty agreed to stay.

Standen's domestic life had not been a happy one. The judge referred to the 'long-standing alcoholism of his wife', describing Mrs Standen as 'floridly psychotic' and citing evidence given in court that Standen 'in a non-confrontational manner bore the brunt of his wife's anger, aggression and paranoia'.

During the trial a forensic psychiatrist, Dr Westmore, had suggested that the family situation and the relationship with his wife was 'more likely than not to have caused [Standen] to become distressed, maybe depressed at times'. Yet when asked by Dr Westmore whether his wife's problems had had any bearing on his crimes, Standen had replied 'I don't know'.

If there was any mitigation in Standen's family problems it was outweighed by his continued refusal to admit any wrongdoing. In sentencing Standen to 22 years' jail, the judge concluded that his motive 'was clearly financial gain for himself'.

Due to the risk of harm by other prisoners, Standen will have to serve all but the last three years of his sentence alone in a cell measuring only 4.3 metres by 3.1 metres.

At the time of his arrest Standen owed more than $1.1 million, including $115,000 on his credit cards. In addition, Standen and Jalalaty still owed Kinch $1,255,000 of the $1.4 million they had borrowed from him. While Jalalaty did not give evidence against Standen at his trial, he did explain Standen's role in the planned importations and the financial benefits that he expected to receive:

> The role of Mark Standen was extremely important. Mark was a senior law enforcement official employed at the Commission. He had an extensive network of contacts in law enforcement that he could contact to get information regarding suspect shipments that had come to the attention of law enforcement. James Kinch gave me instructions to make payments to Mark that amounted to about three hundred thousand dollars . . . Mark was also to receive about one million dollars when

> the shipment of precursor arrived. Mark . . . was Kinch's eyes and ears in Australia.

Standen's friend Tony Newton was forced to resign from the commission when he publicly supported Standen after he was charged. Newton was never repaid the $200,000 he had loaned Standen and was forced to sell his home. He had done nothing wrong, except believe Standen's claims of innocence, and he has paid a high price for that belief.

The Standen family home and a few other assets the family had were sold to partially cover Standen's debts. His family has abandoned him and his wife still requires psychiatric care.

Louise Baker now works in the financial sector and occasionally visits Standen in jail.

The Jalalatys lost their family home and business as they tried to settle their debts. Dianne Jalalaty received psychiatric care.

Within weeks of Standen's arrest in 2009, the Special Crime Unit within the Professional Standards Command (as the SCIA had been renamed in 2005), which had worked with the Crime Commission on the original Kinch arrest and prosecution, was disbanded. The command no longer had a role in the investigation of organised crime and the responsibility for providing task forces to assist the Crime Commission was transferred to the State Crime Command.

In November 2011, after 23 years at the Crime Commission—the last nineteen as its head—Phillip Bradley retired. Before joining the Crime Commission he had worked for the NCA and the Stewart Royal Commission. In September 2012 Peter Hastings QC was appointed to head the Crime Commission. Experienced in royal commissions and corruption inquiries, Hastings said his job as commissioner would be to 'restore the commission to its rightful reputation'.

■ ■ ■

After his arrest on 31 May 2008, Kinch remained in a Bangkok jail while he fought his deportation to Australia. More than four years later his extradition on seventeen drug and related charges was approved by Thai authorities and he was extradited on 26 October 2012. It was another three years before he pleaded guilty to three charges of conspiring to import drugs and one charge of laundering drug money.

■ ■ ■

In February 2016, nine years after his arrest in Bangkok at the request of the Australian government and four and a half years after his extradition to Australia, 57-year-old Kinch pleaded guilty to:

- Three charges of conspiring to import a commercial quantity of ecstasy; the total weight of the drug being in excess of 1.1 metric tonnes, about five million pills, with a street value of about $200 million.
- One charge of money laundering of more than $3.55 million (the exact amount is not known) through corrupt money-exchange operations in Sydney and Melbourne.
- One charge of conspiring to import a commercial quantity of pseudoephedrine (more than 300 kilograms) valued at $12 million, intended for use in the manufacture of methamphetamine. The pseudoephedrine

> could have yielded between 141 and 228 kilograms of methamphetamine with a wholesale value of between $22 million and $41 million.

Kinch was sentenced to a total of 22 and a half years in prison, six months more than his Sydney-based partner in crime, Mark Standen, who described Kinch as a 'friend'. Kinch will be eligible for release on parole on 10 February 2024.

CHAPTER SEVENTEEN

Radoslav Spadina and Adam Watt

In mid-2007 Mark Standen telephoned the AFP to ask whether they were 'working on' 42-year-old Radoslav 'Ray' Spadina, a dual Australian–Croatian citizen with a history of involvement in the drug trade. It was, to say the least, a curious inquiry, since at the time Standen's employer, the NSW Crime Commission, had no official interest in either Spadina or his partner in the drug trade, 39-year-old Adam Keith Watt. The most likely explanation is that Standen was corruptly calling on behalf of James Kinch in an attempt to discover the security of an importation being planned by Kinch's Dutch colleague, Jan Plas, in association with Spadina, a frequent overseas traveller, and Watt. What neither Standen nor Kinch knew (and Standen was not told when he inquired) was that Spadina had been under close observation by the Dutch police for nearly two years.

While Watt was a relative newcomer to the drug trade, Spadina had a long history of trafficking drugs in Sydney, beginning around the early 1980s when Spadina was in his twenties. Within a decade he was supplying large quantities of precursors used in the manufacture of amphetamines. In mid-1993 Spadina met 42-year-old Richard Simpson, a New Zealander who had moved to Brisbane in 1975 to work as a musician. Following their meeting Simpson moved to Sydney's north shore. He was already using amphetamines but once in Sydney he spent much of his time at the Mitchell library researching methods of manufacturing the drug, focusing particularly on chemicals that could be easily bought at hardware stores. Simpson began 'cooking' and quickly gained a reputation for the quality of the drugs he produced. The Nomads outlaw motorcycle gang became one of Simpson's biggest clients and in turn provided him with large quantities of precursor chemicals. Simpson's reputation continued to grow and his services were increasingly sought after by major drug traffickers.

By the mid-1980s Simpson's clients included several outlaw motorcycle gangs, major eastern suburbs trafficker Craig Haeusler and Robert 'Aussie Bob' Trimbole's former associate Reginald 'Mick' O'Brien. (O'Brien delivered drug money to Trimbole several times while he was on the run overseas. In 1992 he was shot dead through the screen door of the granny flat where he was living at Granville in Sydney's western suburbs. The murder is still unsolved but there was, in the coroner's words, 'an abundance of suspects'.)

Simpson was arrested in 1991 for operating a clandestine laboratory, but beat the charges. Two years later Spadina introduced him to a friend we will call 'George', who owned a chemical company on Sydney's north shore and another in

Queensland. They discussed the chemicals Simpson required for an ecstasy cook. In August, September and October 1993 George delivered drums, each containing 20 litres of sassafras oil, to Spadina, who passed them to Simpson.

In 1994 Simpson was arrested and charged with operating a clandestine drug laboratory in Botany. The following year, while under remand, he took on corrupt police Bill Duff and Bill El Azzi as apprentice cooks. Simpson was still cooking as his trial began in February 1996. He was eventually convicted of manufacturing and supplying amphetamines and sentenced to eighteen months' prison. On his release, Simpson immediately resumed his drug activities.

In November 1997 Duff was imprisoned for three years over a 1994 heroin supply charge. He was released from prison and was still on parole when, in June 1999, he was arrested over an amphetamine cook, but the charges were eventually dropped.

El Azzi was charged in 1999 with conspiring to manufacture amphetamines. He was convicted and sentenced to seven years' imprisonment. The main witness against El Azzi was Simpson, who had discovered that El Azzi was having an affair with his wife. The same year, Simpson pleaded guilty to manufacturing amphetamines and was sentenced to four years' imprisonment.

Simpson's legal problems and the fact that he had rolled over to police in the El Azzi case did not deter Spadina, who continued both supplying precursors for the manufacture of amphetamines and selling the finished product. By the late 1990s he had been the subject of several police investigations, each time avoiding arrest. Spadina did have a 1994 conviction in the District Court for aiding and abetting the manufacture of ecstasy, for which he was placed on a bond and fined $3000, but his record consisted mostly of traffic offences. As one law enforcement officer who worked on Spadina said, 'He was well connected with corrupt police and was able to stay one step ahead of us all the time'.

In 1998 Spadina began working as a front man for a financial services company with offices in Adelaide and on Sydney's north shore. One of the founders of the company was Vaso (also known as Vasa) Ulic, a major player in the Balkan-centred drug network to which Spadina was also linked (see Chapter 7). Funds for the financial services company were provided by a number of outlaw motorcycle gangs; they were the proceeds of crimes and of fraudulent borrowings from banks and finance companies. The company laundered money and made short-term loans at exorbitant interest rates to finance drug deals, property frauds and other criminal activities, as well as property investments. Journalists Nick McKenzie and Cameron Houston, writing in *The Age*, revealed that in the 2003–04 financial year the Adelaide office of the company loaned $3 million to the family of Antonios Sajih 'Tony' Mokbel, the mastermind behind the Melbourne amphetamine trade and suspected killer of several of those murdered during the 1998–2010 Victorian gang war. In 2012 Mokbel was convicted of three drug charges relating to a sophisticated drug cartel known as 'The Company' and sentenced to 30 years' prison.

Three years after he began working as a front man for Ulic's company, Spadina opened a nightclub in Manly. By now Spadina and Watt had known one another casually for several years. Both were well known on the northern beaches. Each had a reputation—Spadina as a major drug supplier and Watt as a four-time world super cruiserweight kickboxing champion who was teaching and promoting kickboxing, running a gym and promoting sporting goods. Watt met Jan Plas through the latter's role as a kickboxing trainer and tournament organiser. It was after Watt started coming to the nightclub that he and Spadina began talking about the drug trade.

In late 2003 the Australian Crime Commission established Task Force Schumacher to investigate major criminal groups active in several states, some of whom were linked to the finance companies set up by Ulic in Adelaide and Sydney. Scrutiny from Task Force Schumacher, together with pressure from bad loans, caused the collapse of Ulic's finance companies and hastened the end of his dealings with Spadina. This was the spur for Spadina and Watt to start planning drug importations with Plas and the Dutch syndicate that already had Mark Standen on its payroll.

Spadina needed money for his failing nightclub. During his frequent trips overseas he had been involved in numerous attempted business deals for commodities including 'iron ore from Asia, diamonds from the United Arab Emirates, oil from the Middle East' and even 'herbal sexual stimulants from China'. He also had an extensive range of business and personal contacts in Malta, the United Arab Emirates, China and the Netherlands, as well as in his native Croatia. But Spadina was perpetually short of cash.

On 8 December 2005 an associate of Spadina and Watt, whom we will call 'Bill', deposited $110,000 into an ANZ bank account in the name of Mendika Liquor, which traded as Chinatown Cellars. Bill rang Spadina and told him that the 'grog' he had ordered ('grog' was code for a down-payment on the pseudoephedrine importation) would be delivered 'tomorrow'. The same day an international funds transfer of $108,000 was sent by Chinatown Cellars to Weerden's business, J & L Continental Investments Co. in Amsterdam. Later that day Spadina met Watt in Manly. Over the next few months there were numerous telephone calls and emails between Watt, Spadina, Plas, Weerden and Michael Clemm von Hohenberg about a trip to Dubai to 'sign the contract'.

The conspiracy almost came undone when, on 22 April 2006, Watt was arrested and charged with resisting arrest, intimidation and two counts of trespass. As journalist Kate McClymont wrote in her *Sydney Morning Herald* article 'Mother Tells of Shock at Finding Boxer in a Frock', Watt had been found by the owner of a flat in Dee Why lying on her couch muttering incoherently, wearing a long white dress and having rearranged the pictures on her wall. The owner did not know Watt and had been woken by the noise. She screamed for him to leave and said that she was going to call the police, to which Watt replied, 'If you call the police I will come back and then you will be in real trouble.' When the Dee Why police arrived they found Watt on the couch, still rambling. As they took him away, a scuffle broke out.

Seven months later the charges against Watt were dismissed at court. Watt lived in the flat directly above the one in which he had been found on the couch. He told the court that he had drunk two bottles of wine with a female friend and had taken two Stilnox sleeping tablets because he could not sleep. 'I can't remember anything after that,' he said. His only explanation for wearing the dress was that it came from Dubai. In dismissing the charges, the magistrate said that she could not be satisfied beyond reasonable doubt that Watt had meant to intimidate the occupants of the flat nor that he had knowingly resisted arrest. The two charges of trespass were dropped because police had brought the charges under the wrong section of the Inclosed Lands Protection Act.

On 30 April, eight days after Watt's arrest, Asbeek Brusse flew at Weerden's request to the Congo, where he met two other members of the Dutch syndicate. One was responsible for organising the transport of the consignments in and out of that country while the other arranged for previously confiscated consignments to be released by Congolese officials bribed by Weerden. It was Weerden who directed that the 'Jerry' shipment be prepared and on 4 May he was told, 'Jerry is in order' and was 'all ready now'.

The Dutch syndicate members referred to each other and to Watt and Spadina in coded language. The code for Watt was 'Jerry', 'the tall one' or 'the long one' while Spadina was referred to as 'Jerry's boss' or 'Ray'. The pseudoephedrine importation bound for Australia was referred to as the 'Jerry' or the '210' shipment.

On 15 May Watt flew to Dubai to finalise and confirm plans with Plas and other members of the syndicate. Coded communications continued between the Australian buyers and Dutch suppliers. On 15 June Weerden sent an SMS message to Clemm von Hohenberg: 'Jerry on the weekend on the way. Jan is visiting him.' Plas arrived in Sydney the same day, but the pallets containing the pseudoephedrine had not left the Congo.

Asbeek Brusse flew to the Congo and was driven to a house near Kinshasa where the shipment had been stored. Arrangements were made for the drugs to be sent by air freight to Botany, in Sydney's south-eastern suburbs, via Brussels. A self-employed truck driver known to Spadina was to be told as soon as the consignment arrived. Still in Sydney, Plas met regularly with Watt and Spadina and was in frequent contact with Weerden in the Netherlands. In one of his conversations with Weerden, Plas stated that 'everybody is very happy now' and they would 'like it very much and very fast'. On 21 June, having confirmed with Weerden that the shipment was on its way, Plas left Sydney, advising Watt from Singapore to 'stay tuned'. But once again the shipment did not arrive.

In mid-July Weerden told Plas that there was something 'not right' because the shipment should have been delivered four weeks earlier, but the 'supplier has hung onto it; he never sent it'. A few days later the Dutch syndicate was told that the shipment had been seized by Customs in the Congo and was being held pending the payment of a bribe. Around 31 July Weerden sent around $10,000 to the syndicate member in the Congo to secure the release of the shipment.

On 1 August 2006 Plas met Watt in Munich, Germany, and they spoke over several days. Watt also spoke with Weerden on the phone. Having once again been assured that everything was okay, on 7 August Watt returned to Australia and waited, but the shipment never arrived. The Dutch syndicate believed they had been ripped off by middlemen in Pakistan.

Between January 2006 and 25 September 2008 Spadina undertook at least fifteen overseas trips. On one occasion he was out of Australia for 120 days. Given his history and his constant need for money, there can be little doubt that the majority of trips—perhaps all of them—involved drugs.

On 25 September 2008, two months after Mark Standen's arrest, Watt and Spadina were charged by the AFP with conspiring to import 210 kilograms of pseudoephedrine from the Congo between 2006 and 2007. They were also charged with aiding and abetting the supply of a commercial quantity of pseudoephedrine. The drug was to be hidden in tins of coconut milk and used to manufacture a quantity of the drug ice with a street value of more than $52 million. At the time of the arrest, the AFP told the court that the pseudoephedrine was destined for a 'well-organised drug ring based in the Manly area', but that a civil disturbance in the Congo and an international investigation led by the Dutch police, supported by the AFP, had stopped the shipment from reaching Australia.

Nine months after their arrest, the prosecution served them with the brief of evidence, consisting of around 50 volumes of statements and annexures and 79 discs of electronic material. Of the discs, 41 contained Australian telephone intercept records and ten contained telephone intercept records from the Netherlands. About 250,000 telecommunication connections had been intercepted by the AFP during its investigation of Watt and Spadina, about 1500 of which were included in the brief of evidence.

The committal proceedings opened on 25 September 2009. Six days later, while on remand in Parklea Prison, Watt was bashed with a 7-kilogram metal sandwich maker in a pillowcase. The assault was caught on prison CCTV. Knocked unconscious, he fell to the ground and was struck on the head again. Part of his ear was torn off and he suffered a deep laceration to his right temple. After regaining consciousness Watt was taken by ambulance to Westmead Hospital. He was returned to jail that night but four weeks later was transferred to Auburn Hospital for further treatment, which continued for several months. During this time Watt refused to cooperate with police.

His assailant was 34-year-old Django Womack O'Hara, with whom Watt had recently argued. O'Hara was serving a total sentence of nearly seventeen years for murder. In March 1995, at the age of nineteen, he had shot and killed a security guard during an attempted robbery at a house in Roseville on Sydney's upper north shore. In prison O'Hara made a career of assaulting prison inmates and guards. He threatened to have prison officers followed and vowed to attack them after his release and to kill their families. Forty-two disciplinary orders were taken out against him and he spent almost five of his first seven years in prison in segregation. In 2006 O'Hara appealed unsuccessfully against his sentences for murder and attempted robbery, arguing that he was being held in harsh conditions, but prison authorities stated that the conditions in which he was being held were the result of his conduct while in prison, not of the crimes that had put him behind bars.

Five months after the attack on Watt, O'Hara was released from prison. Although police were still investigating the assault, they were not in a position to lay charges. In August 2010 O'Hara was arrested for speeding in a school zone and driving without a licence in the inner-Sydney suburb of Summer Hill. Granted bail, he 'disappeared'. Two months later police issued a warrant for his arrest for the attack on Watt. In November O'Hara was admitted to Royal Prince Alfred Hospital in Camperdown with five stab wounds to his back and hands. About the same time, another man had gone to nearby St Vincent's Hospital in Darlinghurst for treatment for stab wounds to his arms and stomach. Police were notified but both men refused to cooperate. O'Hara was arrested and charged with causing grievous bodily harm with intent to murder Watt.

In January 2011 O'Hara was granted bail at the Parramatta Local Court. The magistrate, Janet Wahlquist, found there were 'exceptional circumstances' why bail should be granted. 'The primary factor really is the delay in charging [him]', the magistrate said. She also noted that O'Hara had 'made a life for himself' since leaving prison; was needed by his father who was suffering a terminal illness; had committed no major offences since his release, and would have restricted access in prison to facilities he would need to prepare his case.

On bail, O'Hara committed a string of robberies across Sydney. In November 2011 he was charged with stabbing the man who, a year earlier, had attended St Vincent's Hospital with knife wounds, and with stealing more than $70,000 worth of cash and jewellery. This time bail was refused. In October 2012 O'Hara was convicted of, among other things, recklessly wounding, stealing, entering a building with intent to commit an indictable offence and aggravated break and enter. The various sentences saw him jailed for seven years.

While O'Hara was on the rampage outside prison, the prosecution of Watt and Spadina on drug charges continued in the courts. In August 2010 Watt was granted bail, largely as a result of the serious injuries O'Hara had inflicted during the jail bashing. Four months later Spadina was released on bail of $1.75 million and ordered to report daily to Manly police. Three people lodged $500,000 each and another person lodged $250,000, all of which would be forfeit if Spadina failed to meet his bail conditions.

The Watt and Spadina committal was a lengthy and complex process. The Netherlands National Police Agency (NPA) investigation involved 35 suspected Dutch-based syndicate members. It was not confined to suspected Australian buyers but dealt with the supply of pseudoephedrine to customers around the world. Members of the syndicate with Australian connections were: Louis 'Loek' Weerden; Michael Clemm von Hohenberg; Jan Plas; Asbeek Brusse and Thomas Van Den Berg.

In late December 2011, fifteen months after the start of their committal hearing, the pair were sent for trial. Spadina applied to the New South Wales Supreme Court to have the trial date vacated due to the fact that much data from electronic intercepts was missing from material supplied to the defence. However, transcripts and summaries of the missing material were available through the Netherlands National Police Agency system and His Honour, Justice Price, found that these could be used by Spadina to assist his defence. A temporary stay was granted. The trial was expected to last five months. More than 200 witnesses were to be called, including 50 from overseas.

Watt, meanwhile, raised questions in the Supreme Court as to his fitness to be tried. Since his bashing he had continued to receive medical treatment for disabilities that included 'sudden loss of consciousness, double vision, slurring of speech and poor concentration" Assessments by at least thirteen doctors, professors, psychiatrists, psychologists and consultants, together with hospital notes, were provided to the court. On 16 December 2013 Justice Price found that 'on the balance of probabilities' Watt was unfit to stand trial. He ordered that Watt be released from custody for no more than three years 'to attend the brain injury outpatient clinic at the Royal Rehabilitation Centre Sydney and to take part in its community-based outpatient program and such other programs as may be directed'.

On 19 July 2013 in the Sydney District Court O'Hara was convicted and sentenced to nine years' jail for causing grievous bodily harm to Watt.

Spadina had led a charmed life but his luck finally ran out in March 2015 when, after a month-long trial in the New South Wales Supreme Court, he was convicted and sentenced to ten years and six months' imprisonment for conspiring to import 210 kilograms of pseudoephedrine from the Congo.

In 2014 Watt claimed to have 'got a .22 for 5000 [dollars]' for a hit man to carry out a job for a drug gang, but was told, 'That's not big enough, I need something with more calibre.' Apparently unable to obtain a higher calibre weapon, Watt dropped out of the conspiracy, but was still charged by police. On 19 August 2016 the firearms charge and the charge of being an accessory before the fact to the murder were dropped.

Watt's three-year release on the conspiracy to import drugs charge to enable him to seek medical treatment expired on 15 December 2016. At the same time, however, Watt has launched a civil action against the government, reputedly seeking more than $750,000 compensation for injuries suffered as a result of the attack by O'Hara. Watt claimed that Corrective Service officers ignored a tip-off from the AFP that another inmate was planning to kill him; failed to isolate him; and allowed an inmate to return a weapon to O'Hara after an earlier unsuccessful attempt to kill him.

CHAPTER EIGHTEEN

The Dutch syndicates

The Netherlands has long been a transit country for drugs and a base for syndicates exporting drugs to the US, Canada, Australia and the rest of Europe. Lawrie McLean used the Netherlands as a trans-shipment point for his cannabis importations into Australia during the 1980s, while McLean's former partner, Joe Matthews, ran a drugs business in Amsterdam for nearly a decade and a half before his murder in 1992. During the 1990s Dutch-based syndicates led by Fat Ron Haklander and Loek Weerden dominated Australia's ecstasy market.

Haklander was born in Amsterdam in 1961. An intelligence report described him as living in a 'luxurious and expensive house in Amsterdam . . . Ron and his colleagues own houses all around the world including yachts and houses in Spain . . . Fat Ron has about ten Harley Davidson motorcycles and ships them to Italy to attend rallies. Fat Ron also owns various cover companies including a number of video stores in the Netherlands.'

Haklander and his Dutch colleagues were trafficking drugs long before they met James Kinch, who entered the drug trade in the mid-1990s through a Birmingham-based heroin syndicate that sold ecstasy for Haklander in the UK. Kinch himself soon began working for Haklander. As a senior syndicate member in the late 1990s, Kinch was responsible for maintaining the Australian connection.

From the mid-1990s the Haklander syndicate had access to seemingly limitless quantities of what was described as 'the Rolls-Royce' of ecstasy tablets. But around 2003 the flow of ecstasy tablets was disrupted and the syndicate started dealing in liquid ecstasy. Four years later there was another switch. The Haklander group formed a partnership with another Dutch group headed by Louis Aloysius Cornelius 'Loek' Weerden.

Loek Weerden was born in 1965 in Amsterdam. His company, Normi Land Systems B.V., based in the Dutch city of Almere, sold military equipment. In 2011 the company's website described it as 'one of the leading suppliers and exporters of spare parts, equipment and complete assemblies of military battle tanks and military armed vehicles'. It claimed that it undertook deliveries 'according to international law and regulations for the export of military and strategic spare parts for military armed vehicles'.

The company claimed to have a long history as an arms supplier, to be 'a regular partner of NATO' and to have had dealings with countries such as Yemen, Pakistan, Israel and Egypt. In 2002 Weerden was involved with another company in a deal to supply new parts from Israel for South Korean tanks; instead, he supplied used parts from the US. In the subsequent fallout, Weerden turned to the international drug trade. His connections in the Congo gave him access to large quantities of pseudoephedrine destined for legitimate markets in the Congo, India and Pakistan. Ostensibly intended for medical use and humanitarian aid, the pseudoephedrine was corruptly diverted to Europe for export to the US and Mexico, where it was used in the manufacture of amphetamines. Weerden was described by one syndicate member, Asbeek Brusse, as being 'the supplier of the stuff [pseudoephedrine] from Congo'.

Michael Clemm von Hohenberg, a dentist from Freilassing in Bavaria, was, according to Weerden, his 'business partner . . . friend and confidant'. The pair had 'done lots of [drug] projects together'. In intercepted telephone conversations von Hohenberg frequently referred to 'we' and 'us' and to 'our shipment'. He described how he created false documents and acted as an intermediary between the 'transporter' (the person or group responsible for handling the exportation and obtaining a receipt at the other end) and clients. Weerden mentioned regular trips to Dubai where he and von Hohenberg met their criminal associates.

Even more important than von Hohenberg was Jan Plas, a man described by Weerden as 'a friend, a confidant and a travel partner'. Born in 1945, Plas was considered to be one of the fathers of kickboxing in the Netherlands. He studied the sport in Japan and was instrumental in the formation of the Dutch Kickboxing Association (NKBB) in 1976. Two years later he established the Mejiro Gym in Amsterdam, training many world-class fighters.

Plas began his career in organised crime in the 1970s as a bodyguard to Klaas Bruinsma, a drug boss whose distribution network extended throughout western Europe and

Scandinavia. In the mid-1980s Plas was involved in the kidnapping of Gijs van Dam Jnr, the son of a major cannabis dealer, Gijs van Dam Snr. After demanding a ransom—the equivalent of about €4 million—the kidnappers freed their hostage without any money being paid. In 2002 van Dam Jnr was left disabled after a gangland shooting. Two years later, aged 37, he was shot in the head and killed while sitting in his car with his five-year-old son.

Around the same time as the van Dam kidnapping, Plas was involved in the murder of one of Bruinsma's bodyguards, André Brilleman, for allegedly faking the killing of a rival and accepting payment for the hit. Plas and a number of other thugs working for Bruinsma beat Brilleman with baseball bats before shooting him. His mutilated body was encased in concrete and dumped in the Waal River.

By the end of the 1980s Bruinsma was regarded as one of Europe's most powerful drug bosses, but his time at the top didn't last. In 1991 he was murdered by Martin Hoogland, a corrupt former Dutch police officer and cocaine user. A member of the so-called 'Yugoslav Mafia', Hoogland shot Bruinsma four times during an argument in which Bruinsma had threatened to kill Hoogland's wife and children. Two years later Hoogland was jailed for 20 years for the murder of Bruinsma and another drug trafficker. In 2004, while serving his sentence in an open jail, Hoogland himself was shot dead while riding his bicycle to town to do some shopping; he was 47.

After Bruinsma's murder Plas remained active in organised crime as a heavy with useful contacts. By the early 1990s he was working with Haklander; a decade later he was supplying contacts and customers to Loek Weerden while maintaining his high-profile role as a kickboxing trainer.

Asbeek Brusse was born in Amsterdam in 1973. He lived in Zaandam, near Amsterdam, and worked as a carpenter in the building industry. In the mid-1990s Asbeek Brusse met and became friends with Plas. Through Plas, Asbeek Brusse was introduced to Weerden in 2006. Soon Asbeek Brusse was working for the syndicate. According to Weerden, 'Rene did the execution, checked the goods and travelled'. Asbeek Brusse described Plas as having 'acquaintances with benefits . . . Jan Plas's role was, Loek told me literally, in Italian, that he was his *consigliere* . . . Loek needed Jan for his knowledge and contacts . . . He is also definitely someone that Loek sees as protection.'

Weerden was glowing in his praise of Asbeek Brusse, telling Hohenberg that 'Rene has done good work to contact people direct [in the Congo]' and that he 'makes a lot of money for them [the syndicate]'. In turn Asbeek Brusse described Weerden as 'the boss, the manager . . . the top of the pyramid', who supplied instructions in writing: 'We [Asbeek Brusse and Plas] would receive notes . . . describing the things we had to do.'

Two other men were central to Weerden's drug operations: Thomas van den Berg, who provided protection, met buyers and collected payments, and Erwin Michel Beekelaar, whose role was to find customers outside Europe—notably in Mexico and Australia—who were interested in buying pseudoephedrine. It was Beekelaar who, in January 2007, introduced Weerden to Haklander and Kinch, who were looking for new opportunities. Within days of their first meeting, Weerden and Haklander flew to Dubai to see Kinch. Standen and Jalalaty were there for the same reason. Over the following eighteen months Weerden and Beekelaar regularly discussed the possibility of importing drugs into Australia from Pakistan.

On 9 April 2006 Asbeek Brusse drove to McDonald's in Sloten, a village near Amsterdam, and collected two boxes of Congolese pseudoephedrine from a middleman. His instructions were to deliver the drugs to Beekelaar, Plas and Weerden at a warehouse in Amsterdam. This was Asbeek Brusse's first known involvement in the drug trade. Having successfully carried out the mission, he was sent to the Congo in search of further deals.

During May several meetings took place in Amsterdam between Weerden, Asbeek Brusse, Plas, Beekelaar and their Congolese suppliers. The outcome was an agreement by the Dutch to buy one consignment of 126 kilograms of pseudoephedrine. On 31 May a Belgian police surveillance team in Antwerp saw Asbeek Brusse meet 'an African man' and drive off with him. The two men later split up and drove in two cars to Deurne, in the municipality of Antwerp, where they were seen exchanging bags. The police moved in for the arrest and Asbeek Brusse was found to be carrying €55,000. He had received the money from Weerden earlier that day. Digital scales and bags containing 'a white powdery substance' were found in the boot of Asbeek Brusse's car, together with documents referring to a shipment of 126 kilograms of 'cassava flour' from the Congolese capital of Kinshasa. Two similar bags were found in the car driven by the African man. Pseudoephedrine was found hidden in sealed bags inside the four larger bags of flour. Both men were arrested and held by police, but later released without being charged. Plas had played the role of minder. Keeping out of sight and communicating with his colleagues by walkie-talkie, he had escaped arrest.

Asbeek Brusse visited the Congo on Weerden's behalf several times during 2006 to 'keep track of activities'. During these visits he was directly involved in at least three exportations of pseudoephedrine, one of several hundred kilograms to Mexico and another of a similar size to Australia.

After a promising start Weerden's Congolese operation faltered. Supplies of Congolese pseudoephedrine began to dry up. Watching their profits collapse, Weerden's syndicate started searching for a new supplier. On 25 April 2007 a small-time drug dealer, Hendrik Baars, introduced Weerden and van den Berg to an elderly Pakistani named Abdul 'Appie' Razzaq. Although 'sick and partially blind', Razzaq impressed van den Berg with his boast of having 'lots of contacts in Pakistan'. Later, van den Berg was heard telling von Hohenberg that the old man 'has arranged everything . . . it's amazing . . . you think he can't do anything—everything arranged—prices, delivery, everything . . . he said I have the supplier, I have everything available.' Weerden was also impressed. Later he explained that he had been

> looking for a direct delivery option from India for a few months and we encountered a few problems . . . I had asked Abdul if he could arrange through his contacts in Pakistan a delivery from India to Pakistan . . . [Abdul said] that he had arranged everything over the phone with his contacts in Pakistan. Abdul was able to get the ephedrine to Pakistan [Karachi] from the factory in India, without need for a permit, for an amount of 600 euros a kilo. Payment was 300 euro before and 300 euro on delivery of the bill of lading. Abdul would also arrange for all the companies for export and for cargo description. I myself passed the customer client details onto him, and the

> money, and . . . which product the customers required for the cargo description.

On 22 June Asbeek Brusse arrived in Pakistan. He was picked up at the airport by an associate of Razzaq's identified only as Mubashir (Asbeek Brusse nicknamed him Manuel 'because he was the spitting image of Manuel from *Fawlty Towers*') and taken to a hotel to meet Razzaq, who had flown to Pakistan from Holland. A few days later Razzaq returned to the hotel with a sample of 'white powder' in a clear plastic bag and told Asbeek Brusse there was '300 kilograms of this white powder sitting in a factory in Pakistan'. On another occasion Asbeek Brusse was told he could buy 500 kilograms if he wanted it.

At subsequent meetings Mubashir suggested various goods that could be legitimately exported to Australia as a cover for illegal drugs. They included 'rice, lemonade, ceramic pots and white pepper'. Asbeek Brusse dutifully relayed this information back to Weerden in Amsterdam, either by telephone or email. The two men never referred to each other by their real names. According to Asbeek Brusse, 'Loek [Weerden] was really into nicknames.' Asbeek Brusse also flew to the Netherlands to brief Weerden in person. As the syndicate's representative in Pakistan, Asbeek Brusse set up bank accounts to facilitate the planned drug shipment.

Between May and July 2007 Weerden received payments from would-be customers—including Bill Jalalaty in Sydney—totalling at least €230,000. He gave Razzaq €50,000 cash when Razzaq was in Amsterdam and sent him €180,000 in a series of payments made through a laundromat in Javastraat, Amsterdam, using the 'underground banking system'—a system Razzaq had used before.

Meanwhile, in Amsterdam, van den Berg, Plas and Asbeek Brusse met regularly in 'roadside diners'. At one of these meetings—in La Place, Almere—they discovered police listening devices. The men left the restaurant, taking the listening devices with them (they were later destroyed by van den Berg). Surprisingly, the discovery failed to make the plotters more cautious. The fact that 'it was done so clumsily' convinced them that they could not be under surveillance. It was a lucky break for the Dutch authorities because arrests were still a long way off.

Two days after the discovery of the listening devices, Asbeek Brusse returned to Pakistan 'to purchase goods, such as rice'. According to Asbeek Brusse, it was during a meeting in Razzaq's hotel room that he saw a fax headed 'pseudoephedrine hydrochloride quality control laboratory' and 'certificate of analysis'. He took the fax, thinking that Razzaq would not notice its absence 'because he was blind'. After Googling the name of the substance, Asbeek Brusse realised that 'it could be . . . used to manufacture drugs'. Until that moment Asbeek Brusse had been under the impression—or so he later claimed—that the powder he was buying in Pakistan would be used to make weight loss pills.

Insisting that Weerden had deceived him, Asbeek Brusse flew back to Amsterdam. Meanwhile, the syndicate wanted questions answered. During meetings with Weerden, Plas and others, Asbeek Brusse was asked why the first delivery, concealed in a shipment of rice, had not yet left Pakistan. It was from these meetings, Asbeek Brusse said, that he learnt the destination of the shipment: Bill Jalalaty's Sydney-based company, BJ's Fine Food. Was Asbeek Brusse in or out? According to Asbeek Brusse, another conversation with Weerden about the fax he had found in Razzaq's hotel room convinced him to have nothing more to do with the enterprise: 'I said, "Thanks but no thanks".'

Weerden was already having second thoughts about Asbeek Brusse's ability to get the deal done. He complained to Plas:

> I say [to Asbeek Brusse], are you totally fucked, you bastard, I say I am taking all the risks, it's my money that I'm investing, I'm taking all the risks for the money and then you're telling me that I am talking about something I don't know, I say it's because of me that you are involved at all . . . if I tell you that you have to sit in your hotel room for two weeks and play your Nintendo, then you are going to do that and if you don't want to do it, I will send someone else who will.

Later in the same telephone conversation Weerden told Plas: '[H]e doesn't understand, he thinks he's in charge there, no I'm in charge and he executes it because I have 100 per cent information and he has 30 per cent information and I am twice as clever or ten times as clever as him . . . he should just do what I tell him to do.' Plas's reply: 'Yes I understand you are in control, you don't have to tell me'—left no doubt about who was the boss.

In another conversation Weerden told Plas that Asbeek Brusse had 'started to think too much for himself . . . He feels he is important again over there [in Pakistan] . . . but what is he doing over there with his big head, just causing trouble.'

Asbeek Brusse's actions were not those of a man who had decided to quit. He returned to Pakistan in mid-September 2007 to organise the shipment of 'rice' that was to be sent to Australia. 'I had to try and source rice from a different source,' he said, 'as Mubashir had not been successful.'

Weerden told Asbeek Brusse to book himself into a particular guest house and wait for instructions. A few days later Razzaq introduced him to Shahid Ali, 'the man from the mountains'. Ali spoke little English and Razzaq translated for him as they spoke about 'hashish and other substances' that Ali claimed to have access to. As usual, details of the conversation were conveyed to Weerden.

Twelve days after arriving in Pakistan, Asbeek Brusse travelled to Dubai to see Weerden, von Hohenberg and Ali. Returning to Amsterdam, he sent a package to Weerden containing his prepaid SIM card, details of the bank account and blank cheques for his Karachi-based company, Global Bizz, and a farewell note. 'At that stage I broke off all contact with him,' Asbeek Brusse claimed.

With Asbeek Brusse apparently out of the picture, Weerden was losing patience with Razzaq and Baars. By September 2007 there had been too many broken promises and too many excuses. The failures in Pakistan were costing Weerden and his syndicate money and customers. Towards the end of October Razzaq died. Mubashir took over the role of middleman but Weerden no longer trusted him. This was Ali's chance to grab a bigger slice of the deal by proposing one of his associates, Mohammed Nawaz, as the new middleman to replace Mubashir. In conversations with Weerden, Nawaz talked up his contacts in Pakistan, promising to deliver 'better stuff' than Mubashir could obtain, and suggesting they use a different supplier.

In January 2008, with Mubashir unaware of Ali's betrayal, Weerden and Plas flew to Pakistan to meet Nawaz. Weerden was impressed, telling van den Berg by telephone that 'The contact here is top class . . . A good agent for all the business . . . We've already talked to the supplier . . .

Samples were no problem. Everything is arranged . . . We have a new line, we've found a new supplier, also a new factory, so everything should run smoothly.'

But in Pakistan nothing ever ran smoothly. Within weeks Ali was demanding more money. Weerden argued with Haklander and Kinch about who should pay. In the end the extra money was sent but by then Ali wanted more. He then proposed adding an extra 300 kilograms of pseudoephedrine to the shipment on credit because 'the profit would be more interesting'. While the Dutch and Australian conspirators argued over money, the shipment was redirected to France. Around the middle of December 2007 the long-awaited Australian shipment began its journey, arriving at Sydney's Port Botany in late April. On top of their demand for yet more money, the Pakistanis pulled off their final double-cross: the shipment that would send Jalalaty and Standen to jail consisted of nothing but rice.

In late May 2008 Weerden and Haklander and several members of their syndicates were arrested in the Netherlands and charged with drug trafficking, money laundering, firearms and other offences. Weerden cooperated with authorities and was jailed for eight years. On appealing his sentence, he was granted bail and immediately resumed his activities in the international sale of military arms and equipment.

Haklander was jailed for two and a half years.

Sixty-three-year-old Plas was charged with fraud, drug dealing and money laundering. He was convicted and sentenced to four years' jail. On 1 September 2010 he committed suicide in his cell.

Asbeek Brusse was arrested and charged with conspiring to export pseudoephedrine. He still had the document headed 'Pseudoephedrine hydrochloride quality control laboratory' and 'certificate of analysis', a copy of which was also found on Weerden's home computer. Asbeek Brusse could not explain his reason for having the document. Nor could he explain the cash and pseudoephedrine he was carrying when arrested two years earlier in Belgium. After pleading guilty and rolling to Dutch prosecutors, Asbeek Brusse was sentenced to three and a half years' jail.

Other members of the syndicate were convicted and given sentences of between two and five years' jail.

A series of arrests in Australia aroused suspicions of a traitor either inside the syndicates or among their English and Australian co-conspirators. Two people were mentioned as possible rollovers, but the fact that both came from influential English crime families gave them some protection.

Significantly, James Kinch was never suspected by the Haklander syndicate of rolling over, in either Australia or Miami.

■ ■ ■

What were the reasons for the downfall of the Haklander and Weerden syndicates? For many years the Haklander syndicate had been known for its ability to deliver large quantities of high-quality ecstasy tablets. This changed after 2003 when Haklander and several other members of the syndicate were charged over the importation of ecstasy tablets into Australia the previous year. The charge was based on the evidence of a rollover who had been involved in the importation, but whose evidence was not supported by electronic or physical surveillance. The charges were dismissed at trial but the Dutch prosecutors were unwilling to give up and soon began searching for new evidence that might allow them to appeal the court result and restart the case. Haklander was free, but in the aftermath of the arrests the syndicate lost its access to a ready supply of drugs.

Joining forces in 2006, the Haklander and Weerden syndicates appeared to have found a solution to the supply problem: pseudoephedrine from the Congo. But when civil war disrupted the flow, the syndicates had to look further afield. In the search for a new supplier the once-cautious Haklander allowed himself to be led by Weerden who, driven by ego and greed, became further and further taken in by Pakistani promises. The more Weerden was deceived, the more desperate he became. As Jan Boersma, head of investigations with the Dutch National Crime Squad, explained to the ABC's *Four Corners*: 'Information came in from different angles. An ecstasy lab blew up in the Netherlands . . . There were some observations regarding a delivery of a big batch of acetone in Amsterdam and there was a bomb attack in the Netherlands, and in all these situations a group came forward that kept themselves busy with the transport and sale of chemicals intended for the production of synthetic drugs.'

In his headlong rush into the arms of Pakistani conmen, Weerden put his and Haklander's syndicates on a course that, within two years, would land both leaders in jail.

The multiple arrests in Australia and the Netherlands in 2008 did not spell the end of the Dutch connection. Of the many members of the Haklander syndicate sent to Sydney since the late 1990s to supervise drug importations, at least ten are thought to have escaped arrest. As many as a dozen members of the syndicate or its broader network settled in Sydney and still live there, and at least six involved in laundering drug money back to the bosses in Amsterdam remain free and active.

Several of the syndicate's Australian distributors are still in business and have found new suppliers.

Afterword

Organised crime is addicted to the illicit drug trade, so its interest in Australia is hardly surprising. According to the *World Drug Report 2014*, published by the United Nations Office on Drugs and Crime, Australia has the highest proportion of recreational drug users in the world. Australia comes first in the use of ecstasy, third in methamphetamines (particularly ice, also known as 'crystal meth') and fourth in cocaine. More than 10 per cent of the working-age population regularly uses cannabis. Australia ranks second in addiction to prescribed or black market opioids such as codeine and morphine. Despite having some of the world's highest prices, Australian drug use—especially of ice—has continued to rise. New drugs are regularly introduced. Patterns of use vary significantly with age, gender, location and social class.

The Australian Criminal Intelligence Commission's *Illicit Drug Data Report 2014–15* reveals that the number of drug arrests increased by 19.5 per cent from the year before, while the number of drug seizures increased by 13.7 per cent (from 93,086 to 105,862). Significantly, however, the weight of drugs seized decreased by 13.9 per cent (from 27.3 tonnes to 23.5 tonnes). Detections of clandestine laboratories also fell. Only 667 clandestine laboratories were detected in 2014–15, the lowest number since 2008–09.

Operation Gordian, which was led by the Australian Crime Commission with help from state, territory and federal law enforcement agencies, ran for eighteen months from early 2005 and identified the transfer of $300 million in drug money from Australia to Asia, resulting in 73 prosecutions. Gordian also seized drugs with a street value of around $30 million. In 2007 the Australian Crime Commission launched Operation Dayu. During its four-year operation more than $10 million in suspected drug money was authorised to be sent overseas in an attempt to flush out international drug bosses. According to Nick McKenzie's book, *The Sting: Australia's plot to crack a global drug empire*, Dayu seized drugs with a street value of nearly $800 million and identified a triad-led international gang, known as the 'grandfather syndicate', responsible for importing drugs worth more than $1.2 billion into Australia every year. The syndicate is still active today.

More than three decades ago the Costigan Commission revealed the extent of crime and corruption on the nation's wharves. Members of the Federated Ship Painters and Dockers Union were implicated in fifteen murders during the 1970s and were involved in corruption, smuggling, standovers and large-scale theft from the wharves. Describing the crimes as endemic, Costigan noted that only a small fraction of the crimes were reported to the police. He went on:

> The criminal activities of the members of the union were not restricted to any particular sphere of crime. In my reports, I referred to crimes of violence, theft, extortion, intimidation, fraud, illegal gambling and trafficking in

> drugs. There was evidence of wide-scale racketeering, loan sharking and active participation in organised prostitution. I doubt whether there were any forms of criminal activity in which there was not some active participation.

Although the union was deregistered in 1993, several prominent members played a significant rôle in organised crime and corruption, particularly in Victoria, for decades to come.

The Costigan Commission did not put a stop to crime and corruption on Australian wharves. In July 2010 Task Force Polaris was established by the federal government and AFP to investigate organised crime on Sydney's waterfront. It was heralded as the first multi-agency task force to combat organised crime on the wharves in New South Wales.

After two years the task force, comprising officers from the AFP, Customs, the Australian Crime Commission, the NSW Police and the NSW Crime Commission, had made sixteen arrests resulting in 77 charges. It had seized more than 12 tonnes of illicit substances and precursor chemicals, 114.8 tonnes of loose leaf tobacco and 92.7 million individual cigarettes. The task force had investigated more than twenty allegations of corruption involving government officials, including Customs employees and licensed customs brokers. Drug and tobacco traffickers were alleged to have been tipped off before containers were searched and top-secret information was alleged to have been leaked to criminal syndicates. Fifteen Customs officers and officials had been suspended or sacked over allegations of misconduct or corruption, including one officer with close ties to a Middle Eastern crime family in Sydney.

In May 2012 the then federal Home Affairs Minister, Jason Clare, announced 'a major crackdown on organised crime and a major overhaul of security of the waterfront and the entire supply chain'. As part of the crackdown an individual could be banned from working on the wharves if there was compelling evidence that he or she was involved in organised crime. As well as boosting visible and covert patrols of the waterfront by Customs, an increased focus was to be given to figures in the private sector supply chain, such as freight forwarders, customs brokers and cargo handlers. Taskforce Trident was established in Melbourne in July 2012 and the following year Taskforce Jericho was established in Brisbane. A task force similar to Polaris had previously been established in Perth.

Citing evidence that Mexican and Colombian drug cartels were already targeting Australia, the then AFP Commissioner Tony Negus said, 'These reforms will harden the borders . . . and make sure that these particular overseas crime groups aren't looking at us to get their narcotics through to make lots of money based on the misery of the young people in this country.'

In 2014 the Perth waterfront operation was closed down because of a lack of results. The following year, for the same reason, Brisbane's Task Force Jericho merged with the AFP's Joint Organised Crime Task Force.

In July 2014 Stuart Ayres, the New South Wales Minister for Police and Emergency Services, and Michael Keenan, the federal Minister for Justice, jointly praised Operation Polaris, commenting that it was:

> vital in the Coalition Government's ongoing commitment to detect and disrupt and undermine the business models of organised criminal syndicates . . . Protecting the

> Australian waterfront is fundamental to the security of our nation, and the involvement of NSW Police in the Operation Polaris Taskforce is critical to the ongoing success of the Taskforce . . . The Polaris Taskforce has been successful in identifying significant vulnerabilities in the criminal supply chain and has achieved major seizures of drugs, guns and other contraband resulting in numerous arrests and the disruption of organised crime syndicates ... The Polaris Taskforce represents a united effort by Commonwealth and NSW law enforcement to combat the threat of serious and organised crime activity on Sydney's waterfront.

Mr Ayres added, 'The NSW police force has had a significant role in this multi-agency taskforce, which has proven highly successful both in terms of operational results and equally important, the identification of maritime vulnerabilities in the public and private sector and of prevention strategies to combat serious and organised crime.'

By the end of 2015 a total of 128 arrests had been made and 529 charges preferred; funds were being restrained and confiscated, illicit drugs and precursor chemicals were being seized along with loose leaf tobacco and individual cigarettes. Of 32 separate investigations, the overwhelming majority uncovered extensive corruption on the waterfront and along the supply chain.

In the original agreement between the state and federal governments, the federal government was to meet all the costs incurred by the NSW Police in Polaris, including police salaries. This funding was to be treated as an advance payment on future asset seizures and was to be withdrawn from the federal confiscated assets account. Over six years until mid-2016 that 'advanced payment' ranged from around $2.7 million to around $3.5 million a year in 2015–16. By 2015, the federal government was so impressed with the results of Polaris that it considered it to be 'a mature operation' whose law enforcement value was so significant that it should be transformed into 'an ongoing operation' with each party meeting its own costs. In May 2016 the NSW Police Commissioner, Andrew Scipione, refused to pay the cost of participation and Polaris closed down in June 2016. The NSW Police Minister, Troy Grant, supported the decision. There was no public announcement of the decision by either the police or the state government.

The decision by New South Wales not to pay its share (about $3.5 million per year) is said to have been based on the view that the work of Polaris—disrupting the importation of drugs, protecting our borders and so on—was a federal government responsibility. Technically, this was true. But the criminals targeted by the operation knew no boundaries and committed both federal and state crimes. While the importation of drugs is a federal offence, once the drugs are landed they lead to countless state crimes including using, street level selling and trafficking drugs, shootings, robberies, thefts and assaults. The decision to withdraw from the operation abetted the spread of corruption and made a mockery of claims about the value of federal–state collaboration in the fight against organised crime.

Taskforce Trident, which was established in Melbourne in July 2012, is still achieving impressive results. As at February 2016, Trident had resulted in 39 arrests and 90 charges, the seizure of 32.5 kilograms of ice with a street value of $86 million, 71.7 tonnes of tobacco leaf, more than 69 million individual cigarettes, a machine gun and four pistols. More than $243,000 in cash had been seized and almost $20 million in property had been restrained.

In a joint media release, Michael Keenan, the federal Minister for Justice, and Martin Pakula, the Attorney-General of Victoria and Minister for Racing, announced a $4 million boost over two years 'for phase two of the operation to expand the focus of Trident beyond the waterfront, including at an international level, to stop the importation of illicit goods and substances at the source rather than waiting until they reach the Australian waterfront'. Echoing comments made about Polaris, Keenan said, 'Trident is vital in the Commonwealth Government's ongoing commitment to detect and disrupt and undermine the business models of organised criminal syndicates. Protecting the Australian waterfront is fundamental to the security of our nation, and Trident is critical to these efforts.' Pakula commented, 'Criminals don't care about borders and Taskforce Trident will help police stop drugs and guns from getting past our ports. It is vital that our state and federal agencies work together to keep drugs off our streets.'

A foothold in any state gives organised crime access to all. Australian law enforcement agencies have had some success in cracking crime syndicates, arresting and jailing syndicate members, intercepting and seizing drugs, weapons and other contraband, and confiscating the proceeds of crime. But there have been major setbacks, especially in New South Wales. The decision to save $3.5 million a year by opting out of Operation Polaris is likely to generate many times that amount in profits for organised crime, and result in increased harm to the community.

One person who knows better than most how criminals exploit lax law enforcement is Mark Standen. While in jail,

Standen has been studying to become a lawyer, but perhaps unsurprisingly he failed the 'ethics' component of the course. He has since retaken the subject and passed. Although Standen has now completed the course, he is yet to acquire a practising certificate. It remains to be seen whether Standen will be judged to be 'a fit and proper person to be admitted to the Australian legal profession'.

As Standen serves out his sentence he will have plenty of time to reflect on the growth of organised crime in Australia, which the NSW Crime Commission now concedes is effectively out of control. According to the commission's 2015–16 annual report, overseas-based drug bosses have been left largely untouched, leaving only low-level 'foot soldiers' at risk of arrest in Australia. Encrypted communications between criminals have made detection increasingly difficult. Seizures have had little or no effect on the price or availability of narcotics. As a corrupt law enforcement officer who enabled international drug syndicates to penetrate to the heart of the Crime Commission, Standen would have understood why the fight is being lost.

Bibliography

Much of the information used in writing this book was obtained first-hand in the course of police investigations, from court records and from personal interviews conducted by the authors. Some sources have been cited in the text; others, for obvious reasons, must remain anonymous. The authors are grateful to all the people they have spoken to, named or unnamed. Without their courageous cooperation this book could not have been written.

Books and major articles

Bottom, B., *Bugged: Legal police telephone taps expose the Mr Bigs of Australia's drug trade*, Sun Books, Melbourne, 1989

Chugg, M., with Shedden, I., *Hey, You in the Black T-shirt: The real story of touring the world's biggest acts*, Macmillan, Sydney, 2011

'Dutchman supplied weapons to Egypt', *NIS News Bulletin*, 21 May 2011, www.nisnews.nl/public/210511_2.htm

Kamper, A. and Miranda, C., *My Brother's Keeper: The story of a powerful surf brotherhood and the chilling and bloody killing of a brutal underworld figure*, Allen & Unwin, Sydney, 2006

'Lord of War: Loek Weerden', *Camilleri*, 20 May 2011, www.camilleri.nl/2011/05/lord-of-war-loek-weerden [15 October 2011]

McClymont, K., 'Mother Tells of Shock at Finding Boxer in a Frock', *The Sydney Morning Herald*, 23 November 2006

Marks, H., *Mr Nice: An autobiography*, Vintage, London, 1998

McKenzie, N., *The Sting: Australia's plot to crack a global drug empire*, Victory Books, Melbourne, 2012

Miranda, C., *Deception: The true story of the international drug plot that brought down Australia's top law enforcer Mark Standen*, Allen & Unwin, Sydney, 2012

Moffitt, A., *A Quarter to Midnight: The Australian crisis—Organised crime and the decline of the institutions of state*, Angus & Robertson, North Ryde, 1985

Morton, J. and Lobez, S., *Gangland Melbourne*, Victory Books, Melbourne, 2011

Neighbour, S., 'Good Cop, Bad Cop', *Four Corners*, transcript, 27 October 2008, Australian Broadcasting Corporation www.abc.net.au/4corners/content/2008/s2402675.htm [10 June 2011]

Shand, A., *The Skull: Informers, hit men and Australia's toughest cop*, Black Inc., Melbourne, 2009

——*King of Thieves: The adventures of Arthur Delaney and the Kangaroo Gang*, Allen & Unwin, Sydney, 2010

Shepherd, J., *Mr Asia: Last man standing*, Macmillan, Sydney, 2010

Small, C. and Gilling, T., *Smack Express: How organised crime got hooked on drugs*, Allen & Unwin, Sydney, 2009

——*Betrayed: The shocking story of two undercover cops*, Allen & Unwin, Sydney, 2010

Australian government publications, official reports and court cases

Anderson v R [2010] NSWCCA 130 (23 June 2010)

Australian Crime Commission, *Australian Crime Commission Annual Report 2003–04*, Report, December 2004, www.crimecommission.gov.au/sites/default/files/files/annual_reports/0304/annual_report_0304_complete.pdf

——*Organised Crime in Australia*, Report, 2008, www.crimecommission.gov.au/sites/default/files/files/annual_reports/0708/annual_report_0708_complete.pdf

——*Organised Crime in Australia*, Report, 2009, www.crimecommission.gov.au/sites/default/files/files/annual_reports/0809/ACC_AR_0809%20COMPLETE.pdf

——*Organised Crime in Australia*, Report, 2010, www.crimecommission.gov.au/sites/default/files/files/annual_reports/0910/ACC_AR_2009-10.pdf

——*Organised Crime in Australia 2011*, Report, 2011, www.crimecommission.gov.au/publications/organised-crime-australia/organised-crimeaustralia-2011-report.pdf

——*Organised Crime in Australia 2013*, Report, 2013, www.crimecommission.gov.au/sites/default/files/ACC%20OCA%202013-1.pdf

——*Illicit Drug Data Report 2010–11*, Report, 2012, www.crimecommission.gov.au/sites/default/files/files/IDDR/2010-11/iddr-2010-11-complete.pdf

——*2012–2013 Illicit Drug Data Report*, Report, 2014, www.crimecommission.gov.au/publications/intelligence-products/illicit-drug-data-report/illicit-drug-data-report-2012-13

——*2014–2015 Illicit Drug Data Report*, Report, 2015, www.acic.gov.au/sites/g/files/net1491/f/2016/08/acic-iddr-2014-15.pdf?v=1470178813

Australian Federal Police, *Platypus Magazine*, Edition 96, September 2007

Australian Industrial Relations Commission, 'G.F. Fletcher and Commonwealth of Australia (Australian Federal Police), Termination of Employment, (C2006/3102)', Sydney, 26 March 2007, http://netk.net.au/Standen/Fletcher.pdf

——'G.F. Fletcher (C2007/2658) and Commonwealth of Australia (Australian Federal Police) (C2007/328), s.170 application for relief re termination of employment (C2006/3102)', Melbourne, 6 June 2007, http://netk.net.au/Standen/Fletcher.pdf

Australian Institute of Criminology, 'Other transnational and organised crimes', www.aic.gov.au/crime_types/transnational/other.html

Bradley, P., Chairman, New South Wales Crime Commission, *Crime Commissions: Organised crime investigations and police corruption investigations*, paper delivered to Joint Standing Committee on the Anti-Corruption Commission, National Conference of Parliamentary Oversight Committees of Anti-Corruption/Crime Bodies, 2003, *Report No.* 7, 36th Parliament of Western Australia, 2003, Appendix 12, www.parliament.wa.gov.au/Parliament/Commit.nsf/(Report+Lookup+by+Com+ID)B1C5509E6E0BF05648257831003E95CF/$file/NationalConferenceParliamentaryOversightCommittees03.pdf

Commonwealth–New South Wales Joint Task Force on Drug Trafficking, *Investigation of Harry Wainwright, Nugan Hand Limited and its associated companies and the affairs of Murray Stewart Riley and his associates as recommended by the Further Report of the Royal Commission into Drug Trafficking, May 1980*, vol. 1,

January 1982; vol. 2, June 1982; vol. 3, October 1982; and vol. 4, March 1983, Australian Government Publishing Service, Canberra

Costigan, F., *Royal Commission on the Activities of the Federated Ship Painters and Dockers Union: Drug trade*, Final Report, vol. 5, Australian Government Publishing Service, Canberra, 1984

——*Royal Commission on the Activities of the Federated Ship Painters and Dockers Union: The union*, Final Report, vol. 3, Australian Government Publishing Service, Canberra, 1984

Department of the Prime Minister and Cabinet, *Strong and Secure: A strategy for Australia's national security*, Report, 2013, http://apo.org.au/files/Resource/dpmc_nationalsecuritystrategy_jan2013.pdf

Forbes, C., NSW Deputy State Coroner, Inquest into the Disappearance of Ante Yelavich, 19 March 2012

Forbes, C., NSW Deputy State Coroner, Inquest into the Death of Andrea Wharton, 21 September 2012

Lawler, J., '2011 Anti-money laundering and counter-terrorism financing conference', Keynote address, 7 November 2011, www.crimecommission.gov.au/media/keynote-address-2011-anti-money-laundering-and-counter-terrorism-financing-conference

Lee, J.A., The Hon Mr Justice, Royal Commission, *Report of the Royal Commission of Inquiry into the arrest, charging and withdrawal of charges against Harold James Blackburn and matters associated therewith*, June 1990

McClelland, R., '2009 Anti-money laundering and counter-terrorism financing conference', Opening address, 1 April 2009, http://lawisanass-wingate.blogspot.com.au/2009/09/attorney-general-robert-mcclelland.html

Mitchell, S., Magistrate, NSW Deputy State Coroner, Inquest into the Death of Trudie Adams, 1 April 2011

National Crime Authority, *Organised Crime in Australia: NCA Commentary 2001*, 2001

New South Wales Crime Commission, *Annual Report 2015–16*, www.crimecommission.nsw.gov.au/files/Annual_Report_2015-2016.pdf

New South Wales Independent Commission Against Corruption, *Investigation into the Department of Corrective Services—Fifth report—Two escapes*, Report, The Commission, Sydney, 2000

Patten, D., Report of the Special Commission of Inquiry into the New South Wales Crime Commission, 30 November 2011, www.dpc.nsw.gov.au/__data/assets/pdf_file/0008/133748/SCOI_into_NSW_Crime_Commission_-_PUBLIC_REPORT_December.pdf

R v Bakhos Jalalaty [2010] NSWSC 1561 (20 December 2010)

R v Kinch [2016] NSWSC 63 (12 February 2016)

R v Mark William Standen [2009] NSWSC 1499 (17 December 2009)

R v Mark William Standen [2010] NSWSC 1157 (1 September 2010)

R v Mark William Standen [2011] NSWSC 1038 (17 February 2011)

R v Standen [2011] NSWSC 1422 (8 December 2011)

R (Commonwealth) v Mark William Standen [2011] NSWSC 1040 (21 March 2011)

R (Commonwealth) v Mark William Standen [2011] NSWSC 1043 (10 May 2011)

R (Commonwealth) v Mark William Standen [2011] NSWSC 1044 (26 May 2011)

R (Commonwealth) v Mark William Standen [2011] NSWSC 1045 (2 June 2011)

R (Commonwealth) v Mark William Standen [2011] NSWSC 1046 (9 June 2011)

R (Commonwealth) v Mark William Standen [2011] NSWSC 1047 (23 June 2011)

R v Tween [1965] VR 687 (6 August 1965)

Standen v Commonwealth Director of Public Prosecutions [2011] NSWCCA 187 (4 March 2011)

Standen v Regina [2015] NSWCCA 211 (13 August 2015)

Stewart, D., *Royal Commission of Inquiry into Drug Trafficking*, Report, Australian Government Publishing Service, Canberra, February 1983

——*Royal Commission of Inquiry into the Activities of the Nugan Hand Group*, Report, Australian Government Publishing Service, Canberra, 1985

Woodward, P., Royal Commissioner, *Report of the Royal Commission into Drug Trafficking*, Report, vols 1–3, October 1979

Foreign government reports, official publications and court cases

Court of Haarlem, Criminal Division, Judgment on Louis Aloysius Cornelius Weerden, File Number: 15/751637-06 (9 July 2010)

Office of National Drug Control Policy, *US–Mexico Counterdrug Cooperation*, Report to Congress, September 1997, www.whitehousedrugpolicy.gov/publications/enforce/rpttocong/report.pdf

United Nations Office on Drugs and Crime, *World Drug Report 2014*, Report, www.unodc.org/wdr2014/

Newspapers and periodicals

The Age
The Australian
Courier–Mail
Daily News (Los Angeles)
Daily Telegraph
The Guardian (UK)
Herald Sun
The Independent (UK)
Irish Times
Los Angeles Times
The Mirror Online (UK)
NBC World News
New Zealand Herald
Sun-Herald
Sunday Age
Sunday Telegraph
Sydney Morning Herald
The Telegraph (UK)
The Times (UK)
West Australian

Index

INDEX

INDEX